W9-BIO-838

The Paternal Romance

Reading God-the-Father in Early Western Culture

Robert Con Davis

University of Illinois Press
Urbana and Chicago

Frontispiece: "Pious Aeneas" and family. From John Ogilby, *The Works of P. Virgilius Maro. Translated, Adorned with Sculpture, and Illustrated with Annotations.* London, 1654.

1 2 3 4 5 C P 5 4 3 2 1

This book is printed on acid-free paper.

Library of Congress Cataloging-in-Publication Data

Davis, Robert Con, 1948–
     The paternal romance: reading God-the-father in early western
culture / Robert Con Davis.
        p. cm.
     Includes bibliographical references and index.
     ISBN 0-252-01949-0 (cloth).—ISBN 0-252-06265-5 (pbk.)
     1. Classical literature—History and criticism.   2. Mythology,
Classical, in literature.   3. Father and child in literature.
4. Literature and society—Greece.   5. Literature and society—Rome.
6. Fatherhood in literature.   7. Patriarchy in literature.
8. Fathers in literature.   9. God in literature.   10. God
Fatherhood.   I. Title.
PA3015.R4D38 1993
880.9'001—dc20   92–11433
                                                                      CIP

For Julie

The new age begins with the return to the Greeks.
—Friedrich Engels

In the wonderment of this taxonomy, the thing we apprehend in one great leap, the thing that, by means of the fable, is demonstrated as the exotic charm of another system of thought, is the limitation of our own, the stark impossibility of thinking *that*.

But what is it impossible to think, and what kind of impossibility are we faced with here?
—Michel Foucault

and dream of masculine
filiation, dream of God the father
emerging from himself
in his son,—and
no mother then.
—Hélène Cixous

What is man that the itinerary of his desire creates such a text?
—Gayatri Chakravorty Spivak

Contents

Preface

This book explores a single, complex topic—the fusion of Western reason with images and various cultural constructions of paternity. I try to narrow this huge inquiry by focusing on a few ancient Greek and early Christian texts and by isolating in them two modes of understanding. Following Plato, the first mode can be called "poetic" and encompasses prose in its essayistic and fictional forms— the modern sense of what we call "narrative" understanding. This is the tradition of particularizing knowledge of the world by acknowledging the moment of knowing as historically unique and then finding value in the significance of specific decipherment and engagement. Countering this tradition is a different mode of reflection and analysis found in the focus on formal logic, science, and assumptions about absolute "objectivity." This is the tradition of Western reason and rigor associated with Greek philosophy and modern science. I recently explored modern aspects of the first tradition in a book (written with Ronald Schleifer) about the deployment of "critique" in modern literary and cultural criticism—*Criticism and Culture: The Role of Critique in Modern Literary Theory.* More recently, Schleifer, Nancy Mergler, and I discussed the less evident and sometimes hidden narrative dimensions of scientific rigor and objectivity in *Culture and Cognition: The Boundaries of Literary and Scientific Inquiry.* In *The Paternal Romance* I now attempt to trace the early interrelation of both traditions. I identify ancient Greek approaches to scientific analysis as "paternal" and show that, from the same perspective, narrative understanding in various forms is usually denigrated as "maternal." I address how the Western *father* becomes, in effect, a *scientist*, the very model of the authoritative knower.

This book examines these traditions through its definition and description of the *paternal romance*, and through its attempt to turn the power of critique back on the "father" as a specific and highly repressive cultural institution. I sometimes use the term "romance" to designate the Western love affair with the father, Western idealized configurations of paternal authority in texts. But I also use the term to describe the mechanisms for advancing paternal power. In other words, I discuss relatively simple depictions of paternity, and I investigate the paternal romance as a complex set of protocols intended to advance paternity as the inevitable and natural embodiment of ultimate coherence and truth. These mechanisms, usually interpretive strategies, are comparable to Freud's ideas about ideologically motivated obfuscation in his version of the "family romance." In the latter part of the book, I follow the modern decline of the paternal romance and examine contemporary strategies for dismantling it further.

Many people have helped me to think about the paternal romance. For critical engagement and patient listening, I thank Andrea Gale Hammer and the Faculty Discussion Group at St. Mary's College, the Faculty Workshop at Oklahoma, the English departments at the University of Arizona, Northern Illinois University, the University of New Orleans, Kansas State University, and the University of Kansas, and Gita Rajan and the Louisiana Endowment for the Humanities. Patrick O'Donnell, Sherill L. Spaar, and Isaiah Smithson gave timely support. I also discussed the book in broad terms with Thomas A. Hanzo, Ronald Schleifer, and Gayatri Chakravorty Spivak. At Oklahoma, I received valuable suggestions from John Catlin (on Greek language and culture), Lisa Jan Clark, George D. Economou (on Greek language and culture), Susan Green, David S. Gross, Michael Morrison, Paul Ruggiers, and Alan R. Velie. Dale M. Bauer, Ann Lowry, Patrick McGee, and Thaïs Morgan repeatedly challenged me to make the book clearer. Jonathan Scott Lee (in many ways my ideal reader) gave the manuscript a thorough critique, making many valuable suggestions. Finally, Paula Stacy and Melanie Wright helped with the manuscript, and the Office of Research Administration and the College of Arts and Sciences at Oklahoma provided support for the book's completion. I am deeply grateful to all of these friends for their assistance.

Paternity Suite

[A paternity suit is an action against the father] to determine
whether alleged father is in fact father of illegitimate child and
as such responsible for support.
—BLACK'S LAW DICTIONARY

Who has known his own engendering?
—HOMER, ODYSSEY

Modern literary and philosophical texts routinely push contemporary readers back to classical works and the very textual and
cultural considerations this book addresses. If the modern era "begins
with the return to the Greeks," in Friedrich Engels's words (218), then
modern and postmodern readers frequently revisit that beginning in
the re- and de-Hellenizing critiques so common to cultural theory,
as Michel Foucault shows in the *History of Sexuality* and as Jacques
Derrida demonstrates all through his work on the history of philosophy. The self-conscious beginnings of modern cultural theory can
be traced back to the work of Friedrich and Wilhelm Schlegel and
to their attempts to "reconstruct" the sensibilities of Greek poetry in
post-Enlightenment contexts. They believed the viability of modern
institutions of art and culture would depend upon the success of a
critique of Greek art and thought. This tradition of fascination with,
reinvolvement with, and idealization of the Greeks gathers momentum again at the turn of the twentieth century in the work of Friedrich
Nietzsche, Matthew Arnold, and Irving Babbitt, among modernist
thinkers, and continues (with diminishing idealization) through the
present in the work of Luce Irigaray, Sarah Kofman, Jacques Derrida,
the Frankfurt School, and others.

I easily remember my own strong attraction to the romance
of paternal authority when, as a twenty-year-old student, I first

encountered the *Odyssey* and James Joyce's *Ulysses*. I remember reading the Proteus chapter of *Ulysses* and following Stephen Dedalus as he walked on a beach in Ireland, watched a dog sniffing at a dead dog on the beach, and mused about his own dead mother, about his own coldness when she died, and his subsequent guilt. His mind then wandered to the nature of God and transcendent truths, but also to the divided nature of fatherhood: "From before the ages He willed me and now may not will me away or ever. A *lex eterna* stays about him. Is that then the divine substance wherein Father and Son are consubstantial" (38). In the context of this major modern work, the idea of a paternal *lex eterna* struck me, as it could any undergraduate, as extremely daunting. Even cut with irony, in other words, there is still an extraordinary amount of idealism and romanticism about fatherhood in Joyce, as in so much modern literature. What I could not then see, although no secret generally, is the degree to which Stephen Dedalus's ruminations reflect a pervasive view of the underpinnings and development of cultural authority, the Western view that culture is founded on the family and that the family is structured by paternal prerogatives and power.

Later, as a graduate student, I was simply too naive about these claims for paternity when I edited *The Fictional Father: Lacanian Readings of the Text* (1981). In my own contributions to that volume, for example, I intended to situate a critique of paternal authority in Jacques Lacan's work, particularly in relation to narrative practice. Years later, I saw that I was safeguarding the idealization of paternity by my unwillingness ever to turn Lacan's critique back on itself, especially by my reluctance to question Lacan's own assumptions about the inevitable paternal cast of culture. Now, after teaching for a decade in the aftermath of deconstruction, Marxist feminism, and cultural studies, I find this romanticized view of the father both quaint and dangerous. While recent historians and cultural theorists from Roland Barthes to Julia Kristeva consistently draw on the paternal metaphor, the male "gaze," and the name-of-the-father, they rarely reflect on the development of Western culture *as paternal*. As often as not, these assumptions—committed as they are to what I will call the paternal romance—go unchallenged and even unnoticed. In other words, I agree with Beth Kowaleski-Wallace and Patricia Yaeger when they say that "the problem . . . is not simply to change our focus from father-as-center to mother-as-center but to reinvent the discourse of the father altogether, to move outside an oedipal dialectic that insists upon revealing the father as law, as the gaze, as bodiliness, or as the symbolic, and to develop a new dialectic that refuses to describe the father function as if it were univocal and ahistorical" (*Refiguring* xi).

I have written in other places about paternal authority in classical and modern texts and have tried to raise the issue of the "father" in culture so as to avoid assumptions about monolithic patterns and monologic texts. I have tried to critique the notion of culture conceived as an expression of paternity, the frequent notion being that "culture" somehow owes its origin, its validity or legality, even its coherence, to some deep structure or principle identified as *the* father. I have identified such gestures in order to demystify culturally sanctioned notions of a superior male ideal and to align myself with attempts to work across literary and cultural boundaries. I have wanted to critique values associated with paternity that remain persistent in Western culture and ideology.

In *The Paternal Romance*, however, I am less interested in the cautionary mode of such criticism. I do not intend in any simple way merely to avoid the mystifications of paternity. On the contrary, here I am focusing *on* that very mystification: that is, on the idealization of paternity in ancient Greek and early Christian texts. In working closely with a variety of texts across disciplines and cultures, I want to deconstruct the deployment of paternal authority by reading it as a textual practice.

This book is about paternity's being configured and projected in Western texts as an origin of culture and world order and as a guarantor of cultural law and justice, what the Greeks called *nomos* (law) and *dikē* (justice). My strategy for reading early Western texts involves resituating them *as texts*, as cultural artifacts, and comparing what they *show* about paternity as textual constructions with what they *say* about the father when they make claims about paternity's supposed origin and power. I am interested, in short, in the *saying* and the *performing* of paternal authority. The points of contradiction separating the claims for paternity and the construction of paternal authority *in* those texts contribute to the history of the "father" from the Greeks through the formulation of Christian trinitarian doctrine. Reading those texts against their own claims—discovering what they say as opposed to what they show—I am examining the engagement of these texts with Western values and the development of subsequent works on which those texts have had such impact.

As a male academic in the late twentieth century, I recognize the need of men (and women) to reconfigure cultural understandings in relation to the crumbling monuments of specifically "male" authority. Committed to feminist goals and values in my own life and work,

I do not care to be taken as an innocent bystander in these developments. This book is one expression of my commitment to take the measure of paternal authority in texts that have been most influential. By examining classical texts, I am attempting to lay bare and dismantle the appeal of the paternal "tradition" that still haunts contemporary texts and culture.

My strategy involves examining thematic, textual, and ideological dimensions of paternal narrative, or "the paternal romance." Paternity is projected as an idealization *in* narrative, for example, when male subjects such as Zeus and Jehovah are promoted as either creating or governing the world or are said to be ultimately responsible for its maintenance. This is the romantic theme of the father projected as a perfect and transcendent origin, usually of the entire world and the institutions of culture—the father, finally, as the world's ultimate author or maker. By contrast, the textual dimension of paternal authority constantly counters the ideal by exposing paternity as a local construct, an effect *of* narrative—that is, paternity not as an ideal but as a social and wholly constructed version of cultural authority within narrative; a fiction. This is "the" father as the production of an effect or operation in narrative, an effect symptomatic and always highly revealing for the culture that produced it.

The third dimension, of ideology, consists in locating strategic points of contradiction separating the first two. What are the exact junctures at which the idealized claims about the father in narrative diverge from the significations of paternal authority as an operation in narrative? Where are the points either at which the father is not mystified, or at which the symbolic force of that mystification has lapsed or somehow has failed? This third dimension also critiques the narrative strategies to dismiss, hide, and "forget"—by formal and institutional means—the implications of the fundamental cultural disjunction between what is *said* and narratively *demonstrated* about paternal authority.

Here I am using the term "ideology" not just in the sense "of beliefs characteristic of a particular class" or as "a system of illusory beliefs" (Williams 1977, 55) but in a much broader sense of whole systems of representation. I am taking values to be signified through textual function, in the deployment of codes and in the development of characters, motifs, and plot that make up a text. These functions in texts are rendered intelligible to us when we read them against a specific and encompassing cultural frame of reference, a set of assumptions and associations that always takes the form of other texts. Cultural values and the system of ideology to which they belong are articulated most fully in the whole system of textual operations that includes the deployment of narrative codes and particular textual effects of genre and even theme, what is usually characterized in critical terms by "representation."

My argument here, putting it most boldly, is that representation and ideology are nearly identical concepts. They both involve a textual transmission of values. This association of representation and ideology is the basis of Raymond Williams's notion of ideology in *Marxism and Literature*, "the production of meaning through signs" (70). Williams paraphrases Vološinov to say that "ideology" should be "taken as the dimension of social experience in which meanings and values are produced" (70) and then goes on to acknowledge the difficulty of making the concept of ideology carry so much freight as always a mode of representation. I shall promote this definition as unavoidable and usually productive, despite the difficulty. Jean Baudrillard expresses the same idea of "ideology" as the "very form that traverses both the production of signs and material production." Moreover, "ideology," he argues, "[lies] . . . in the internal logic of the sign" (144) and is a dimension of semiosis. *The Paternal Romance*, too, argues for this relationship between ideology and representation. I shall return to this point often, for it is crucial to my case for analyzing the reciprocal relationship of ideology and representation in "paternal" narratives.

The "romance," or idealized view, of the father as I will discuss it runs through Greek culture from approximately the late ninth and early eighth centuries B.C. through the rise of Christianity. In Christian texts and patristic theology the paternal romance evolves into tenets about God's fathering of the world. Jehovah incorporates and strategically alters the attributes of Zeus to become a more thoroughly idealized version of the "father of men." This process can be followed through the doctrine of the Trinity and the development of the Catholic mass, both of which are strongly tied to pre-Christian patriarchal traditions in ritual sacrifice. Surveying some forms of Western paternal authority from Zeus's placement in the pantheon through the advent of Jehovah, I suggest an account of paternity in the West, a sense of how Zeus and Jehovah ascend (or appear to ascend) to positions where they have authority that theoretically encompasses the operation of the entire world.

In *Dissemination* Jacques Derrida discusses many mystifications, or idealizations, of paternal authority when he considers the ancient Greek inclination to take the father as embodying "the good (*agathon*), *the* chief, *the* capital, *the* good(s)"—"everything" connected

with and highly valued as Western civilization and culture, sum-
marizing that "*patēr* in Greek means all that at once" (83). Because
of a fusion between the father as a figure and Western values—and
also because of Western institutions of understanding—"to speak
[about him] simply or directly" is impossible. It is "no more possible,"
Derrida adds, "to look [the father] in the face than to stare at the
sun" (82), because the act of looking and the thing looked at are to
a great extent grounded in the same assumptions about coherence,
logic, and legitimacy. I will show in chapter 4, for example, that
Aristotle's idea of logic—supposedly disinterested, objective, and self-
verifying—is in fact already implicit in his assumptions about gender
and reproduction. He promotes an ideal of male "form" (*eídos*) in
the reproductive texts and then silently institutes that notion of form
in his canons of logic, all the while suppressing what he takes to be
the model of the malformed female body. Hence the nature of being
male and the male ability to father are employed as assumptions in
the Western foundation of reasoning, and even in the advent of scien-
tificity. This is an instance *in flagrante delicto* of the fusion of paternal
authority and one of the principal tenets of Western culture.

Derrida concludes that if *patēr* means *this* much all at once, "it
is extremely difficult, we must recognize, to respect this play in a
translation, and the fact can at least be explained in that no one has
ever raised the question" (83). That is, from a certain angle the father
may seem too powerfully an aspect of what culture is and has been,
including the tools used to examine it; too much a part of how Western
culture sees the world; too much of what we unconsciously and
consciously assume about the world's order.

The concept of "culture" is enormously complex, and the consideration of questions about representation in texts introduces
another set of difficulties. (See *Criticism and Culture*, where Ronald
Schleifer and I discuss many of these concepts at length.) Raymond
Williams writes in *Keywords*, for example, that "culture" is "one of
the two or three most complicated words in the English language"
(76)—defined by social and historical referents yet serving as the
representation of those very referents, a word at once essential to
any discussion of life in the West yet problematic in almost every
instance of its use. The word "father," which Derrida connects to
Greek cultural values, is problematic in similar ways for the entirety
of Western culture. Even limiting *patēr* to more or less formal considerations having to do with some aspects of communal and state
authority, we will find that the word still defies manageability, partly

because it carries with it ideas about the origin of "culture" and the economies of justice that in the West have been thought to govern the world. I am speaking about ideas concerning what it is to be rational, objective, persuasive, superior, and significant— assumptions traditional with paternal authority.

Thus the larger, daunting figure of the Western Father cannot in any simple way be seen through, moved around, or defined. The "father" and the ideological apparatus he symbolizes can appear to be at once elusive and inescapable, as modern feminist and ideological critiques continually rediscover and regret. There indeed may be limits to what can be understood about him—or any ideological manifestation—at any particular moment. It may be literally impossible to move completely outside certain ideological relationships, regarding the economies of Western reasoning and the protocols of cause-and-effect relations, to examine what the father represents and, in a conventional sense, *is*.

I shall not try to theorize the Western father in some global or comprehensive way or to perform a thorough critique of paternal authority in early Western culture. I do not know enough, and I doubt that a full critique of paternal authority is what is needed now anyway. If, as Shakespeare has Theseus say in *A Midsummer Night's Dream*, the natural superiority of the father is to be the "form" structuring and guiding female "matter," "as a form in wax / By him imprinted and within his power / To leave the figure or disfigure it" (I,i,49–51), then the romantic and exclusive attribution of such power for "imprinting" and "disfiguring" to the father will spur the most pressing questions about paternity in early Western culture. Recognizing and critiquing the textual granting of authority to the father may be as close as we can (or need to) get to understanding the father's "essence." My investigation is of the "paternal romance" as both the advancing of certain procreative functions in narrative and a mode of reading that positions those attributions to be taken as "natural" and inevitable. I am not undertaking a full critique of Western paternal authority but am attempting to position paternity so as to account for the effect of its symbolic manifestations. My aim is to determine what happens in early Western texts to make paternal authority *seem* central and important—the "father" as an effect "in" a text, and also an interpretation "of" narratives. How far can such an enterprise move toward a "critique" of paternal authority? That is precisely the question I am trying to answer in writing this book.

The Father and the Family

We can gain a useful perspective on the issue of paternal authority
in early Western culture by looking briefly at a scene in Latin epic
poetry, a "late" text in relation to the other texts discussed in this
book. Virgil's *Aeneid* displays a prominent vision of paternal authority and the family and evidence concerning a moment of cultural
transition when Aeneas flees the destruction of Troy. In the drama
of this scene, there also appears to be an instant of hesitation, a
moment of deliberate decisionmaking, where Aeneas becomes "pious
Aeneas" and where two conflicting cultural codes are compared and
ranked.

In Book Two of the *Aeneid*, Aeneas stands with his family
before the burning rubble of Troy and prepares to flee to Carthage.[1]
From there he and his family will go to Sicily, and later to Italy,
afterward laying the historical foundations for what will become the
Roman Empire. He is "pious" in that, surrounded by son, wife, and
father, he acts to recommit his family to the values of civilization at
a moment when civilization itself seems to be in jeopardy. He stands
at a point where the values of one world intersect with another, and
the classical familial ties reflecting social ideals are on the verge of
moving into the main currents of the Western tradition.

The scene is further complicated in that it is now encumbered
by many classical, Renaissance, and even subsequent framings.[2] For
example, this scene is demonstrably important to the family conceived
as a cultural institution in the West, in that it represents a threatened
family who struggles but "triumphs." The scene itself suggests no
explicit action in epic terms; rather, it portrays adversity in the manner
of a domestic trial. Family members persevere in order to reinstitute
certain of their values.

From the standpoint of the fleeing family, however, there is also
something alien in the scene, a shadowy representation of an interior
and not fully acknowledged complication, a moment of familial alli-
ance interrupted by a betrayal. Anchises, Aeneas's elderly father, sits
atop his son's shoulders and holds the household gods (sacred statues)
saved from the fires of Troy. Anchises looks straight ahead, figuratively fixated on the future. Aeneas, weighed down by his father,
goes forward somewhat staggering. He holds the hand of Iulus, his
own son, who looks up at his father with an apparent trusting gaze.

Aeneas's wife, Creusa, stands oddly apart from the men. She
clutches her breast, her face drawn and downcast. She walks behind

and seems not to be acknowledged by the men, and she is positioned as if at odds with the momentum of what propels them forward. Walking ahead of her as if separated by some actual barrier, the men even appear to huddle and luxuriate in a common bond, forming a kind of male "family" in its own right.

As all of this happens, Creusa continues to lag. In the narrative's next moment, she will fall behind and die, marking an apparent thematic connection with the general destruction the men leave behind in Troy. There is, in other words, a strict division in the scene that groups the men together on one side while isolating her on the other. The men seem to guard themselves in a circle positioned away from her, *against her*, as if to break free of everything associated with Troy *and* with her—as if reacting against a taboo. Given the incendiary events of the scene and Creusa's death, an appropriate legend for the picture of this scene could be: "the woman who stands in darkness on behalf of the men, walking behind them alone, lost to the community of men as if to enfranchise yet not disrupt their ties to each other." Her placement in the picture replicates the Homeric iconography (as Norman Austin describes it in *Archery at the Dark of the Moon*) of life positioned figuratively *in front* and death *behind* a person or a community (90). When she dies, she merges into the realm of death and thereafter bears and transmits dark secrets about the future, especially concerning isolation and suffering. These will be brought to light as prophecy when Creusa's shadow informs Aeneas of her death and of his fortunes to come in the founding of Rome.

This scene is a puzzle. From one perspective it shows horizontal connections with a promise of unity, continuity, and stability—a family of great affections and loyalties facing tremendous external threats. At the same time, men are posing together in a plane separate from and against a background of destruction and death. Because that world contains a female, it conjures the spectre of men in flight from her. Appearing self-sufficient and contented, the men separate themselves from a woman and from the dangers of fire, pain, and death that the scene's composition associates with her.

The bond between the men is further indicated in the way each looks to the other for a re-evocation of specific values and ideals. Anchises clasps the statues (*patrios Penates*, 2.717) that represent the gods of the past and looks forward to the resituating of those gods in Italy. Iulus looks up at his father and, in Aeneas, finds the agency of a promise about the future. As the bridge between past and future, destruction and regeneration, Aeneas carries, literally *carries*, the values and bonds of the past while he looks ahead to new tasks and difficulties. He and his father and son will reiterate certain values about culture and the men who inhabit it; they will do so, ultimately, in the replication and reinstitution of those values in Roman civilization and even eventually (though this is not part of the story) in the rise of Christianity. Creusa stands alone, expendable, and will not be seen again except as a shadow in Hades. She is not a part of what is dominant in this picture or, by extension, in the transition from early classical to Roman culture. She is not formally *in* the scene.

Virgil is the most "Christian" of pre-Christian writers, the poet of the holy family, the great apologist for the life lived in harmony with nature *and* the state. Later, of course, he will be figured as Dante's stable guide and common reference point through the cultural disharmonies of the Inferno. As a poet of the Roman Empire, Virgil wrote during the decline of Greek philosophy and religion in the century leading into Christianity. He is the Latin poet who most successfully elevated nature to the status of an ideal moral vision and virtually defined cultural life in the setting of a complexly civilized but ultimately "natural" world. In his articulation of pastoral values in the *Eclogues*, for example, he helped invent the mode of poetic devotion to nature—"pastoralism"—and the wisdom of living in accord with nature's own systematization and precepts, the cycles of bud and bloom and seasonal renewal and decay in an economy shaped by the Divine Maker.

Poised as a poet situated almost perfectly between the idealized Kosmos invented by the Greeks—the many-tiered formulations of the Greek Pantheon and First Philosophy—and then the advent of the Kingdom of God-the-Father in the Christianized Roman empire, Virgil is the great champion of communal stability and the family, the poet of high Western sophistication and sensibility. He championed not only the idealized inner life in accord with nature but the all-important coordination and potential harmony, the "oneness," of the familial, social, state, and religious orders.

Virgil's rendering of "pious Aeneas," then, suggests fairly explicitly an idealized narrative, or romance, constructed around men, patriarchal, and familial values. This scene articulates a narrative about the institution of power in particular forms of inclusion defined by male interests and fortunes. By reading the scene as a "romance" about men, I am accentuating the ritual of male inclusion and female exclusion to underline the idealization of male relations in Virgil's text. Here a paternal romance signifies both this text's seeming promotion of male cultural references as explicitly identified with the privileged positions of a decisive Western narrative, as well as the tendency to read texts in a way that "forgets" this promotion *as an activity of narrative* and then takes the effect of emphasizing male dominance as "natural," "inevitable," and essentially "true." Paternity in such moments is taken to be even the efficient cause of world order, as if the authority of the father *were* somehow the essence, the underlying matrix, of the concept of order itself. Whereas the repetition of male figures in the "pious Aeneas" scene points to the privileging of certain values concerning rational order and the law in community, there is also a "romance" of inducement and seduction—whether "in" the text or "in" a textual interpretation—to take paternal and male configurations as absolutely and inherently given and unassailable. This effect of idealization, a deft and persuasive gesture of textual emphasis, is the most telling characteristic of this scene's construction of the paternal romance.

The Family Romance

My defining "the paternal romance" as the practice of constructing narratives to reflect these commitments to paternal authority echoes, of course, Freud's "family romance" and his reading of another classical text, *Oedipus the King*. Freud's initial theory about the family romance was limited, having to do with the way children and neurotics continually monumentalize their parents. Both the young and the unstable project their parents and certain authority figures in a grandiose "fantasy [that] is no more than the expression of a regret that those happy days [of prior childhood] have gone" ("Family Romances" 241). In Freud's formulation of the family romance, as Jean Laplanche and J.-B. Pontalis comment, "the subject [actually] invents a new family for himself and in so doing works out a sort of romance" (160). In its first phase, "the child imagines that he was not born of his real parents, but rather of noble ones" (160). In the "later stage in the development of the neurotic's estrangement from his parents" (238), as Freud says, the child appears to doubt only his paternal origin and the nature of, the extent and legitimacy of, paternal authority. Freud described these fantasies largely in relation to the conflicts of the Oedipal crisis and as a stage of personal development. It is then quite easy to extrapolate this phase into a structural dimension of Western civilization, a predictable phase of culture itself.

Freud's connection of the family romance to the Oedipal crisis suggests a recurrent experience of culture itself and a pattern continually repeated in the situating of Western families. Conveniently made explicit by Sophocles in fifth-century Athens, and thereafter traceable in Western culture, it appears in countless incarnations of a primal Oedipal scene. This is the perspective that Jean-Joseph Goux (to take a fairly recent example) encourages, in a global view showing how the personal psyche and historical/cultural texts interact in important ways.

Such a connection is evident, for example, in Book IX of *The Republic*, where Plato discusses (571c–d) the fascinating psychology of the transformation of a democratic person into a tyrant. The account makes much of love and dreams (see especially 574d–575a) and a young tyrant's relationship with his parents. Plato describes how the "rational and tamed" part of the soul normally keep the appetites under the control of reason, but when it slumbers "the wild animal part . . . becomes rampant" and "does not shrink from attempting in fancy unholy intercourse with a mother" or "hesitate to commit the foulest murder." Here Plato's virtual gasp at "unholy intercourse" signals a recognition of deep ambiguity in the family's constitution, revealing both personal psychological investment and a pattern of social construction in fifth- and fourth-century Athens. Apparently scandalized by his own ability to imagine maternal incest and patricide, the negative sublime of the family romance, Plato is also establishing the frame of a historical period when the competition of male and female versions of authority was at a particular moment of crisis. Goux discerns an "unconscious" struggle between the sexes, a scandal of contested gender authority and the conflation between personal, historic, and erotic economies in an early "mode of primitive production" for classical culture and the family (*Freud, Marx* 258).

In a post-Freudian era, however, the conflicts of the family romance are less obviously taken as a generalized, phylogenetic "fact." Rather, they may be posited more as a historically specific response in psychoanalysis's own participation in the Western conception of male authority, a subjective and historical ideological configuration. This is the suggestion of recent critical theory of the family as discussed by Mark Poster (1978) and others. We can see traces, for example, of Freud's ideal of the family romance along side and layered in with the paternal romance in Wenceslaus Hollar's Renaissance engraving of the "pious Aeneas" scene.[3] This picture (see frontispiece) depicts a moment in the *Aeneid* and classical culture in relation to Renaissance concerns with the import of "pious Aeneas." The engraving foregrounds two perspectives on the scene reflecting the family romance and the paternal romance. If we focus on Creusa, there is an ideal pattern given structure: a father and mother are bonded together and are the objects of a child's projections and investments. This is Plato's view (and more or less Freud's) of the family romance as an ideal and seamless form of graduated human experience. On the other hand, the picture exposes the paternal romance—the privileging of father figures and males as manifestations of authority and value, men grouped together against women and what women are identified with. This subversive vision exposes the paternal romance beneath (or inside) the family romance, setting forth the Realpolitik of familial relations that must be viewed from an oblique angle.

Still, the scene, in one important sense, is perfectly innocent. Aeneas's family—like any other, like the "happy" ones Tolstoy describes in nineteenth-century novels—strains against adversity. It encounters a crisis, sustains a loss, and then survives as best it can. In this way, all families look alike, in that they represent and inscribe a fixed set of positions that constitutes the family romance. But we also know that, in the next moment in Virgil's text, the "family" will shatter when Creusa is lost. Insofar as this picture is a mythical representation of a historical development, it exposes the family's reliance on the ideological matrix of the paternal romance. Rather than being innocent or serene, the scene reveals a hidden ideological commitment and a potential force for oppression. That is, this picture-text articulates a "paternal" order that invades and displaces the family.

The ambiguity about the connections of the family and paternal authority, about the apparent superiority and supposed "naturalness" of the paternal bond, is a strategic feature of this double romance. The men virtually force their male circle around the multiplicity of possible values that are minimally signified by Creusa's "accidental," dismissible position in the composition. The graphic text of the engraving also highlights the family as a pattern of fragmented, metonymic relations. Visually Creusa is merely an appendage to the group of men, readily broken away from them. She is singular, dispensable in other words, and easily lost in time, suggesting the family's nature as fragile and ephemeral. However, the relations of parent and child at the center of the picture suggest metaphoric, totalized relations, relations foregrounded as coherent and permanent. Concealed behind the façade of the family, behind the semblance of sameness and coherence—behind a family as well formed as any other—are a patriarchal order and the power of violent metaphors and hierarchies to advance that order.

I am trying to highlight the paternal romance not as a theme in a picture or a static motif in narrative, but as an ongoing cultural operation and a specific engagement of cultural values. Precisely in reading such texts as the "pious Aeneas" scene against themselves can textual values be reframed and exposed, shown to be included in strategies to as accomplishing cultural work. Texts do this by constructing a cultural paradigm, or, rather, by constructing culture itself, in relation to certain ends. That cultural paradigm, once in place, creates lines of force and probabilities for certain kinds of institutions: those of subjectivity, communal order, kinship relations, religion, statecraft, and so on. Here cultural work is power in the broadest sense, the construction and imposition of a matrix that will enable and shape the products of culture. In the case of the paternal romance, that matrix specifies monologic meanings, the ascension of metaphoric substitution over metonymic associations, and the association of males with rectilinear, noncontradictory models of logic, objectivity, and persuasivness. The ideal, textual, and ideological aspects of paternal authority are situated in an economy of cultural relations, the dynamic transactions of which allow lines of intention to move in certain directions. Throughout the rest of this book I shall foreground and explore this dimension of textual economy and representation.

Reading God-the-Father

Remember that my focus in the "pious Aeneas" scene is not on the global significance of "fathers" in Western culture, and certainly not on the whole system of male privilege and oppression, but on the interrogation of a particular text—ultimately, Western texts from ancient Greece and early Christianity. I am investigating what constitutes the "law" (nomos), the "good" (agathon), the "just" (dikē), and "truth" (alētheia): in a word, "god" (theos) in paternal authority. This is a study of specific strategies that establish paternal authority as decisively influential among Western discourses. Such discourse is generally "unconscious," not positioned on the surface and in the themes of texts, but transmitted through discursive patterns and rhetorical structures whose power works to realize particular political and social ends. I am ultimately arguing that the father, the "king," as Hamlet said, is not a "thing" and not a reified essence of power. He is not an absolute source of authority, or even an identifiable principle of procreation, except as he is a manifestation of power and an ideological orientation in particular texts. The "father," in other words, is an effect of textual and narrative practices and strategies for the management of power within texts. (I intend "practices" here in the sense of a culture's, and not an individual person's, intention.)

Broadly, the "father" is an ideological configuration that has existed and developed at least since the time of Greek epic narratives and continues up through the present in various forms. The traditional "procreative" function of the father as both seed carrier and philosophical prime mover, or unmoved mover, is defined explicitly in early Greek and Christian narratives. The father is said to participate in a kind of ontological and epistemological "origin," an absolute point of initiation for everything imaginable throughout the Kosmos. In this classical view, all modes of personal experience, communal order, law, economy, and justice (that is, "justice," or *dikē*) derive from a beginning marked by paternal reference, a locus in a hierarchy of associations articulating origin and order. In this regard the "paternal romance" indicates, in the classical tradition, the transcendent authority for cultural references, a set of ideals that are depicted as further enfranchising the institutions of culture.

As I read texts such as the "pious Aeneas" scene, Hesiod's *Theogony*, Homer's *Odyssey*, Aristotle's *Organon*, and Augustine's *De Trinitate*, among others, I discern that the texts that make the case for the "father" as epistemologically unique and original are also the very ones that most persuasively undo that case. Indeed, they demonstrate that the father is *not* an absolute and inevitable cultural orientation, but a particular effect of power within the textual relations of Greek and early Christian culture, a textual achievement with ideological implications for the interaction of various social, political, and sexual "texts" of early Western culture. The farther back we go into Greek culture (the more distant we become from the present and its ideological commitments), the easier it may be to disentangle and dissociate the father from assumptions about cosmological order and "truth," and then to examine him in the context of the cultural and textual mechanisms that produced him. It becomes easier to see him, in other words, as an artifact *produced by* (and not the "creator" or even the absolute first reference of) Western culture. I maintain that the paternal romance in early Western culture puts the father in the position of seeming to be the origin of "everything," even the narrative practice that produced him.

Focusing on what I am calling the mystifications of the paternal romance, I am exploring the paternal theory of narration, identifying the operations that make it seem "natural," or necessary, to think about narration and various forms of cultural authority as functioning

in a manner fundamentally "paternal." What happens in early Greek
and Christian narrative forms tells much about the Western logic of
representation, including classical mimesis and the functioning of
narration as a representation of "truth." Pertinent here are texts by
Homer, Hesiod, Aristotle, Hippocrates, Plato, and Augustine that
localize specific issues that appear to structure Western narrative
practices, particularly concerning how the father underwrites the
"positions" of narrative (as in "father," "mother," "child," "hero," "heroine," "opponent") that underscore discourse and are essential much
later to the advent of the novel and romantic narratives, as well as
histories. I am referring to the broad discourse of social and cultural
narratives, the representation and articulation of values, that organizes culture in terms of paternal investments.

     I am examining narrative constructions of paternal authority in
their dimensions (1) as an ideal projection, (2) as a textual construction, and (3) as an ideological articulation in order to locate key
cultural shifts in which Zeus-the-character is situated as the father
of men. I shall then follow Christianity's altering of paternal authority
as Zeus becomes Yahweh and the law of the world, also examining
how Yahweh "becomes" Jehovah. These shifts isolate textual moments
important to Western culture, epochs in which the positioning of the
signifier shifts in decisive ways. As Jacques Lacan demonstrates
throughout his work, such signifying shifts reconstitute the knowing
"subject" and what a subject should know in relation to authorizations
of significance and value. These changes suggest dramatic textual
shifts in paternal authority in ways that continue through today,
posing a challenge to the father's legitimacy as a cultural referent.

     In chapter 1, I map Zeus's specific place in the Pantheon, study-
ing how Zeus came to be, what he controls and what controls him,
how he administers justice (dikē), and what Greek justice is. I also
discuss the Greek view of paternal authority, what Homer in an
epithet calls "patēr esthlos" (Odyssey 1:115), a formulaic term that
meant little more to the Greeks than the designation of "noble" as
opposed to "common," and that Robert Fitzgerald and others render
as "great father" (p. 5 in Fitzgerald). Homer's words literally mean
the "good" or "noble" father; but here, by drawing on the figuration
of a "great father," I intend to focus on the construction of cultural
priorities conceived largely in paternal terms, that is, the grand paternal romance as it is advanced in Greek epic culture. Then, in the
Theogony, in addition to powerful male gods, there is a complex
relationship with hugely significant female deities. There are traces
in the Theogony even of anti- and non-paternal orders of culture and

nature, gaps in paternal authority, especially the feminine forces that Zeus cannot completely assimilate into the Olympian regime—that is, signs of specific ways in which Zeus does not control the Kosmos, is not the *patēr esthlos*.

In chapter 2, I discuss the "great father" as a constructed representation of authority in Homer's *Odyssey*. As a narrative, the *Odyssey* is immensely more complex and informative than the *Theogony*, and it permits discussion of gender and political issues raised only tangentially in the *Theogony*. The *Odyssey* is in some ways "the" father text of Western culture, the text that gives the strongest formulation of the paternal romance. Yet even it offers no unproblematic advocacy of paternal values or ideology, no undivided or non-textual presentation of paternal authority. In fact, it already critically situates and implicitly critiques the paternal romance and the great father as I am defining those terms.

Chapter 3 discusses the gendered subject in the West. By this I mean the Greek system of gender relations, what it is to be a male or female as coordinated with Greek notions of logic and reasonable and scientific thought—what it means to be "contrary," "contradictory," "coherent," and "true" in relation to being male or female. Aristotelian canons of reason and scientific thought advance assumptions about the "logical" ordering of gender as part of the structure of making sense and reflecting the Kosmos's true order, *phusis*. These same assumptions are evident in Greek medical texts on gynecology, especially in the place of authority created for the male doctor in relation to the woman's body and her own knowledge, and lack of knowledge, about her body. The same ideological orientation governs canons of logic, gender identity, and health in Aristotelian and Greek thought. Specific ideological structures shape Hippocratic texts with protocols of logic as articulated in Aristotle's *Organon* (*Categories*, *On Interpretation*, and the *Analytics*).

In chapter 4, I compare Zeus as a character and a sign of particular cultural functions with the God of the early Christian Church. Zeus is a precursor of and model for Yahweh (and Jehovah) in that Zeus's authority resides in his utility, as a character, to represent and negotiate material and ideological conflicts in the justification of cultural institutions. God, on the other hand, while he draws structural features from Zeus, does not technically represent anything—according to Christian doctrine, cannot represent anything. In this way he signals a drastic departure from the versions of paternal authority as Greek culture constructs them. A crucial dimension of Jehovah's construction is that he does not *represent* cultural law or divine providence, precisely because he embodies the act of representation as well as what is represented. It follows, in Christian theology, that God does not represent goodness but *is* the good, does not represent power but *is* power, and so on. He stands as the very embodiment and essence of cultural and natural priorities. This dramatic elevation from the master manager's position held by Zeus situates the Christian God in an entirely different dimension and dramatically recasts the cultural references significant for the paternal romance.

While from one viewpoint God is still the product of narrative, an actual construction in narration of character, the claims made for his perfect authority are sharply at odds with anything that may be said in an analytical frame about narrative. God is in no sense "made," a character signified and interpretable in the environment of a narrative. This dilemma, in fact—in the narrative production of the supposedly trans- or extra-narrational reference—institutes a number of important and highly problematic developments in theology and cultural theory, to which the history of Christian theology is largely a response. I shall explore this crisis in the constitution of the signifier and paternal authority as I consider God, Satan, women, and the "remaindered" nature of the world in Christianity.

I draw further from the Aristotelian theory of signs and propositions and argue that the Christian construction of God necessitates an "excess," or point of resistance, to a realm apart from and "beyond" the systematic expression of paternal authority. That realm can be identified with Satan as the opposition to Trinitarian structure. I discuss the paternal romance in Christian culture in relation to the politics of "textual authority"—touching on an ideological dimension of paternity that brings urgency to the study of the paternal romance in relation to contemporary cultural concerns. Such concerns are, in fact, still tied to the fortunes of Zeus, Jehovah, and Satan as male signifiers of cultural priority. The hegemonic tendencies of Greek religion and early Christianity remain evident in the monologic tendencies of thought and cultural practice usually referred to as patriarchalism in Western culture up through the present.

In chapter 5, I discuss responses to the paternal romance since the rise of Christianity, especially the allegorization of the paternal romance in the construction of a Great Chain of Being. This discussion progresses up through modern and postmodern rebellions against and critiques of paternal authority. In discussing critiques of the paternal romance by Hélène Cixous, Gayatri Chakravorty Spivak, and several other feminist theorists, I suggest how twentieth-century discourse about the father often attempts to work through the impasses of the paternal romance and to "forget"—that is, to deconstruct and discard—the specific terms of the paternal romance as a hegemonic cultural force. I fully agree with Arthur and Marilouise Kroker in *The Hysterical Male: New Feminist Theory* (1991), where they argue that what I am calling the paternal romance—"the specular coherence of unitary male subjectivity" (xiv)—is now in the process of shattering. I argue that what remains of the paternal romance in the twentieth century will not be so much destroyed in fantasies of "acting out" against the father, brought down with a single blow, as "worked through," assimilated as a dimension of our cultural past that need not oppress us in the future. That "working through" encompasses cultural critique and all manner of situating paternal authority within cultural contexts that hitherto have been repressed, occluded, or marginalized.

Notes

1. "Then come, dear father. Arms around my neck:
I'll take you on my shoulders, no great weight.
Whatever happens, both will face one danger,
Find one safety. Iulus will come with me,
My wife at a good interval behind.
Servants, give your attention to what I say.
At the gate inland there's a funeral mound
And an old shrine of Ceres the Bereft;
Near it an ancient cypress, kept alive
For many years by our fathers' piety.
By various routes we'll come to that one place.
Father, carry our hearthgods, our Penates.
It would be wrong for me to handle them—
Just come from such hard fighting, bloody work—
Until I wash myself in running water."

When I had said this, over my breadth of shoulder
And bent neck, I spread out a lion skin
For tawny cloak and stooped to take his weight.
Then little Iulus put his hand in mine
And came with shorter steps beside his father.
My wife fell in behind. Through shadowed places
On we went, and I, lately unmoved
By any spears thrown, any squads of Greeks,
Felt terror now at every eddy of wind,
Alarm at every sound, alert and worried

Alike for my companion and my burden.
I had got near the gate, and now I thought
We had made it all the way, when suddenly
A noise of running feet came near at hand,
And peering through the gloom ahead, my father
Cried out:
                    "Run, boy; here they come: I see
Flame light on shields, bronze shining."

                                                    I took fright,
And some unfriendly power, I know not what,
Stole all my added wits—for as I turned
Aside from the known way, entering a maze
Of pathless places on the run—

                                        Alas,
Creusa, taken from us by grim fate, did she
Linger, or stray, or sink in weariness?
There is no telling. Never would she be
Restored to us. Never did I look back
Or think to look for her, lost as she was,
Until we reached the funeral mound and shrine
Of venerable Ceres. Here at last
All came together, but she was not there;
She alone failed her friends, her child, her husband.
Out of my mind, whom did I not accuse,
What man or god? What crueller loss had I
Beheld, that night the city fell? Ascanius,
My father, and the Teucrian Penates,
I left in my friends' charge, and hid them well
In a hollow valley.

                    I turned back alone
Into the city, cinching my bright harness.
Nothing for it but to run the risks
Again, go back again, comb all of Troy,
And put my life in danger as before:
. . . .
Then to my vision her sad wraith appeared—
Creusa's ghost, larger than life, before me.
Chilled to the marrow, I could feel the hair
On my head rise, the voice clot in my throat;
But she spoke out to ease me of my fear:

"What's to be gained by giving way to grief

So madly, my sweet husband? Nothing here
Has come to pass except as heaven willed.
You may not take Creusa with you now;
It was not so ordained, nor does the lord
Of high Olympus give you leave. For you
Long exile waits, and long sea miles to plough.
You shall make landfall on Hesperia
Where Lydian Tiber flows, with gentle pace,
Between rich farmlands, and the years will bear
Glad peace, a kingdom, and a queen for you.
Dismiss these tears for your beloved Creusa.
I shall not see the proud homelands of Myrmidons
Or of Dolopians, or go to serve
Greek ladies, Dardan lady that I am
And daughter-in-law of Venus the divine.
No: the great mother of the gods detains me
Here on these shores. Farewell now; cherish still
Your son and mine." (Virgil, *The Aeneid*, lines 711–800)

2. For a discussion of this tradition of commentary, see Winfried
Schleiner's excellent "Aeneas' Flight from Troy."

3. See John Ogilby's Renaissance edition of *The Works of P. Virgilius
Maro. Translated, Adorned with Sculpture, and Illustrated with Annotations*
(London, 1654). This work is discussed in Schleiner.

CHAPTER ONE

The *Theogony* and the Paternal Romance

SOCRATES: And if he touches a thing, he touches something, and if something, then a thing that is.
THEAETETUS: That also is true.
SOCRATES: And if he thinks, he thinks something, doesn't he?
THEAETETUS: Necessarily.
SOCRATES: And when he thinks something, he thinks a thing that is?
THEAETETUS: Clearly.
SOCRATES: But surely to think nothing is the same as not to think at all.
THEAETETUS: That seems so.
SOCRATES: If so, it is impossible to think what is not, either about anything that is, or absolutely.
THEAETETUS: Evidently.

—PLATO, THEAETETUS

The famous Olympian court scene from the *Iliad*'s Book Eight contains perhaps the most extravagant claim for paternal authority in all of classical literature. Zeus, angry that other gods are interfering with the Trojan War, calls all together on Mount Olympos to discuss who among them is legitimately in charge—who will decide the war's outcome. He delivers a final, stern warning: "Let no one, god or goddess, contravene / my present edict... / [not] to assist the Danaans or the Trojans." Anyone who disobeys "will be flung... / into the murk of Tartaros that lies / deep down in [the] underworld." His point made, he goes on with a threat that seems to elevate his power even further:

                              Or prove it this way:
    out of the zenith hang a golden line

and put your weight on it, all gods and goddesses.
You will not budge me earthward out of heaven,
cannot budge the all-highest, mighty Zeus,
no matter how you try.
                    But let my hand
once close to pull that cable—up you come,
and with you earth itself comes, and the sea.
By one end tied around Olympos' top [*rhiōn Oulumpoio*]
I could let all the world swing in mid-heaven!
That is how far I overwhelm you all,
both gods and men. (8:18–29)

In the face of this threat, the other gods are "awed and silent" (8:29), but Athena finally responds for all by saying, "highest and mightiest father of us all, / we are aware of your omnipotence" (8:32–33).

Zeus's claim is not simply that Greek gods can be flung "deep down in [the] underworld," but that his power is absolute, to the point of "omnipotence" over "earth itself . . . and the sea." He specifically vows to "let all the world swing in mid-heaven!" locating Olympos as the absolute ground (*rhiōn Oulumpoio*), the underpinning, of the rest of the world, gods included. Everyone but Zeus must live in a contingent relation to that firm ground. Zeus's ownership and control of Olympos's immovable terrain suggests that he sits atop the entire *scala naturae*. Also, Zeus's reference to a golden cable suggests a technology of power reflecting the authority of *procreation* coupled with destruction; that is, the patriarchal control of circumstances so as to orchestrate beginnings and endings for others. By possessing the world's cable and the place to anchor it, Zeus directs the entire Kosmos and himself serves as the place to which all things living and inanimate are ultimately fixed. Finally, Zeus can even abandon the world altogether if he so wishes, leaving it behind him in chaos.

Many other textual moments of classical literature offer quite different and contradictory views of Zeus. The *Theogony* and the *Odyssey* show both the genesis and cultural situating of the "great father"; Zeus appears as one among many powerful upstart Olympians, and he manages barely to gain the upper hand over his father, Kronos, and the other Titans. In this view Zeus is not, in fact, the embodiment of all power but the signifier, as the *Theogony* shows, of a relative position in a hierarchy. Even in the *Iliad*, where Zeus *claims* absolute ownership of the Kosmos, and where he seems not averse to a Trojan victory, they lose. The *Odyssey* also shows Zeus's continuing to struggle with the other gods, repeating the cosmic perspective of the *Theogony*, where Zeus is but one significant divinity and one agent of the Pantheon as a social and political economy. The composite view of the great father in action that emerges from these texts is decidedly more political and less "divine." Certainly Zeus here does not transcend the Kosmos, does not possess the elevated status that he claims for himself in Book Eight of the *Iliad*. All of these texts imply that Zeus is, rather, a Machiavellian figure who organizes a regime and takes power by outmaneuvering the competition.

So while Zeus is a prized and sacred object, he is also an actor in motion, not so much an object of worship but a subject initiating strategies and plans. Both Zeus the ideal and Zeus the "actor" are prominent in Hesiod's and Homer's texts, but these versions of him tend to be kept separate and to resist easy reconciliation. The elevated version of Zeus is predicated on perfect potential and idealism; the other is predicated on the conflict and limitations of dramatic situations. In other words, Hesiod's and Homer's texts suppress the omnipotent great father when they show Zeus to be acting on the world and vying with the other gods. When Zeus is projected ideally, especially in epithets, aphorisms, and other conventional formulas, he is again the omnipotent "great father" (*patēr esthlos*), an epithet that is a synecdoche for the abundance of epithets whose accumulation suggests the stature of a "great father" in Homer's texts.

The two Zeuses can, of course, be accounted for in part by the poetic techniques of the oral tradition, where "passages" in a poem were composed at quite separate times. Zeus is "father of Hours," the "father of gods and men," the human "savior" and "Liberator," "defender" of supplicants, guardian of the foundations of society, and so on—62 pages of such epithets about Zeus are listed in the two main indexes, 22 in *Epitheta Deorum* and 40 in *Ausfurhliches Lexikon der griechischen und romischen Mythologie*. But when Zeus-as-"great father" acts to establish or protect his power, he again becomes the imperfect and fallible figure of heroic, rather than divine, stature. The epithets about him give fixed and static views of paternal authority as projected in a narrative romance, whereas the narrative action sequences in these epic poems tell how the great father actually functions as an agent of the law in the Greek world.

Formidable difficulties arise when reading these texts. One must understand the extent to which the two dimensions of Zeus should be kept separate, and one must also discern each text's implicit rationale for maintaining or bridging that separation. Northrop Frye, a usually astute reader of classical texts, claims in *The Anatomy of*

Criticism (1957) that the façade of Zeus in the Pantheon masks a
fundamental monotheism in the Greek world: "Zeus remarks, at the
beginning of the eighth book of the Iliad, that he can pull the whole
chain of being up into himself whenever he likes, [and] we can see
that for Homer there was some conception of a double perspective
in Olympos, where a group of squabbling deities may at any time
suddenly compose into the form of a single divine will" (142). Frye's
figure of a Zeus who can pull the world into himself is a rich image
and highly provocative. In addition to monotheism, it suggests Zeus's
ambiguous gender and a maternalized patriarch who stands at the
world's origin, as much a "great mother" as a great father. However,
in point of fact Homer's Zeus claims only that he can pull the world
loose with his cable (8:19–29), and that the cable is anchored to the
"*rhiōn Oulumpoio*" (8:26), a "promontory" or "horn" at Mount
Olympos. This line is rendered literally in Fitzgerald's translation as

> But let my hand
> once close to pull that cable—up you come,
> and with you earth itself comes, and the sea.
> By one end tied around Olympos' top [*rhiōn Oulumpoio*]
> I could let all the world swing in mid-heaven! (8:24–28)

No major English translation renders the line as Frye does or shows
Zeus to be the maternalized patriarch pulling "the whole chain of
being up into himself." Nowhere in the *Iliad* or any other Greek text
is Zeus able to perform such a feat. Hugh Lloyd-Jones, in *The Justice
of Zeus* (1983), does discuss the same passage and generally grants
to Zeus the idealized omnipotence Zeus claims for himself; but even
he does not construe the passage as Frye takes it (Lloyd-Jones 4, 82).

The point is not Frye's misremembering of a passage, but the
rationale for misreading this important scene. What, in Frye's perspective, would encourage a view of Zeus entailing such large con-
sequences? The answer, I believe, has to do with an apparent and
surely unconscious Christianizing of a classical text and a classical
figure. Frye focuses on the two versions of Zeus, the transcendent
ideal and the local agent, and conflates them. This conflation amounts
to a resolution of Zeus's divine and social (contingent) selves into
one ideal form. Frye's reading of Zeus as one who can absorb the
world into himself, as if the world could at any moment return to
the womb or omphalos of its creation, contradicts Greek cosmology
as it is projected in the *Theogony*. Instead, it virtually advances an
original creation of the Kosmos *ex nihilo*, a view more properly
applied to the Christian genesis of the world and a truly omnipotent

Jehovah. The version of Zeus as encompassing the Kosmos amounts, then, to a radical and false "Christianizing" of Zeus. Like Yahweh eight centuries later, this Zeus situates the creation as emanating from himself. Frye's Zeus mediates and reconciles omnipotence in both name and epithet with action in the world, with the potential effectively to merge the (sacred) one with the (worldly and profane) many.

In this fascinating gesture, a virtual melding of Machiavelli and Savior, Zeus's two sides collapse into one, and the tension between Zeus and the Kosmos and the cosmic laws that govern Greek culture dissolves. This gesture amounts to what Jacques Lacan calls a "forclusion" in discourse, or the way Aristotle uses *apophora* to mean "removal" in the *Metaphysics* (1046b.14). It strategically suppresses the Homeric, inherently bifurcated conception of Zeus and occludes the Greek great father as an ideal alongside the performative, action-oriented challenge to that ideal. This way of reading the *Iliad* passage enacts a fundamental aspect of the paternal romance, in that for the moment of reading Frye we would seem to forget the textual nature of paternal authority and, subsequently, take Zeus-as-father to be an idealized totality. He would become "everything," a transcendent version of perfect fatherhood (*patridos*).

The two versions of Zeus in Homer's text designate power as knowledge *and* as action, knowing and doing. This tension within paternal authority foregrounds the cultural struggle to understand and to represent Zeus in both epic and philosophical narratives. ("Knowing and doing," *logôi te Kai ergôi*, is, in fact, one of the credos of Homer's heroes—the call to an ideal to succeed in word and deed.) This is the Zeus that Arthur O. Lovejoy describes as at once "an apotheosis of unity, self-sufficiency, and quietude" yet also the deity depicted in Plato's *Timaeus*, who is characterized by "diversity, self-transcendence, and fecundity" (Lovejoy 82–83).

The *Theogony*

This two-dimensional portrait of Zeus comes into focus dramatically in relation to other issues of gender identity and power in Hesiod's *Theogony*. The *Theogony* is one of several antique texts indispensable for depictions of the world's grand scheme, its outline and details. It tries to explain how the Kosmos could come out of Chaos as an ordered world and is comparable to the *Enuma Elish* (the Akkadian-Babylonian creation story) and other theogonies within the Greek tradition by Pherecydes, Epimenides, Aristophanes, and the "Orphic" writers. I am focusing here on accounts by Hesiod and (in the next chapter) Homer, which differ on the details of the world's beginning. In Hesiod, the world begins with Chaos, Gaia, Tartaros, and Eros, while in Homer it begins with Okeanos and Tethys. (It is not clear whether Okeanos and Tethys are connected with the origin of the world or only with the origin of the gods—see *Odyssey* 14.201.) Otherwise these two accounts generally agree in their presentation of the cosmic schema and in treatment of other religious material. Critical opinion about which poem is older changes frequently. Against claims for the priority of the *Odyssey*, for example, M. L. West (1966) argues that the "*Theogony* . . . [is] the oldest Greek poem we have" (46). Martin Bernal in *Black Athena* (1987) more recently places the *Theogony* in the tenth century B.C. and puts the *Odyssey* at the turn of the ninth century (88). Pietro Pucci in *Odysseus Polutropos* (1987) argues that, for now, the exact date of either one or "the question of the 'first one' in the epic tradition is hopelessly unresolvable" (234).

These two works not only narrate the cosmic genesis and organization of a society among the gods, but also advance the principles (and ideology) of that world's operation as "natural" and inevitable. Those principles are purportedly derived from the laws of "nature" (*phusis*) itself. In Hesiod's *Theogony* this aim is fulfilled in the tracing of the Kosmos from its "natural" origins in Chaos, with Gaia and Uranus, through the advancement of civil society and political statecraft culminating with Zeus's rise to power. More than the *Odyssey*, the *Theogony* concerns Zeus's role as a politician in the Greek Pantheon, especially regarding the implications of situating paternal authority within a thoroughly politicized, rather than a "natural," context. The *Theogony* also demonstrates a huge ethical separation between the interests of the gods and those of humans. Zeus in the *Theogony*, unlike even Zeus in Hesiod's *Works and Days*, is not evidently the champion and guardian of justice (*dikē*) as a cultural mandate.

Even so, the formulations of Hesiod's grand scheme for the Pantheon and the Kosmos foreshadow the enormous Greek "new start" in philosophy and secular values. In the sixth and fifth centuries, the actual beginnings of Greek philosophy appear with Heraclitus, Anaximander, Parmenides, Socrates, Plato, Aristotle, and initial Greek attempts (especially by Anaximander) to reframe the world in an order of thought. This new order substitutes abstractions for narrative, replaces mythology's mythic densities with the new mathematical and logical relationships that will be prevalent in Aristotle's *Organon*. Hesiod's world of Titanic combat and Olympian "society" does not in any simple or direct way suggest a mathematical formulation wherein images and narration are replaced by abstractions; however, it does begin to structure society, including the gods' society, as a systematic formulation of natural and rule-governed activities, rather than mystic forces. "The cosmic order [even for Hesiod]," as Jean-Pierre Vernant argues, "was already [at this time becoming] dissociated from the royal office, freed of any link with ritual" (1982, 117). "*Monarchia*," he goes on, "was replaced . . . by a rule of *isonomia*," or balance (122). In other words, even as early as the eighth century, during the time of formulaic oral narratives and the great theogonies, Greek culture was becoming less a "natural" and more an established or "made" place in a hierarchy of human and divine organization. So, while not "mathematical" or highly abstract in its scheme—it is not yet "philosophy" in the sense of Plato's credo over the door of his academy: "Let no one enter here who is not a geometer" (quoted in Vernant 128)—the *Theogony* nonetheless focuses on the schematic *structure* of a social and political economy. It assumes the "logic" of Zeus's rule within a system functioning according to cosmic laws, even when those laws are not always immediately and rationally ascertainable by humans.

If there is only a burgeoning sense of systematized knowledge and structured culture in Hesiod's time, the *Theogony* nevertheless manifests a new economy of the world in its basically rational presentation of the Kosmos. The Kosmos is viewed as a system of predictable implications and exclusions, and is projected by Hesiod as a *system* for the management of power. In Hesiod's account, the systematic view of the Kosmos begins with Gaia (Earth)—along with Chaos, Eros, and Ouranos, part of an elemental quaternarium—and ends with Zeus as the world's monarch. Hesiod's narrative thus articulates a discourse of gender, moving from female to male and from divine solitude to a semblance of human community. (The same transferral of authority from female to male occurs at the beginning of Aeschylus' *Eumenides*.) The intervening lines show the genesis and development of the divine, material, and human worlds, all of which work to explain the Kosmos's emergence from Chaos, the triumph of *themis* and *nomos* (law and convention) over *phusis* (nature). This rise is marked by four important events, each of which decisively moves the world in a different direction and sets up a subsequent event, as follows:

1. Gaia moves out of Chaos to begin producing the "world," first through parthogenesis and then through sex.
2. Kronos castrates and overthrows Ouranos, thus creating a fundamental pattern of paternal strife.

3. Zeus rebels against Kronos and, in so doing, challenges the prior, strife-ridden order of the Titans.

4. Finally, Zeus and the Olympians defeat the Titans and effect the consolidation of state and civilized rule after the war. Social complexity and political organization increase in the Kosmos; that is, a complex social economy appears and develops.

The details of these four events are important for what they reveal about the ideological dimension of the Greek Kosmos. Because the *Theogony* is not read as often as other Greek narratives, I will first go over them in some detail.

1. For example, Hesiod says that the beginning of the world was Chaos, in that Chaos was the first being. Hesiod says little of this shadowy entity but goes on to say that after it came Gaia ("Earth"—whether from Chaos is unclear) and then Eros. From Chaos comes "Darkness" and "black Night." Out of their union comes "Light and Day." Gaia next makes "tall mountains," "barren waters," and then a husband in Ouranos—"all without the passion of love" (Brown's translation 56). Gaia next mates with Ouranos and creates "the violent Cyclopes—Thunderer, Lightner, and bold Flash" and the three "Hundred-Hands" figures: Cottus, Biareus, and Gyes.

2. The first husband, Ouranos, rejects his powerful children and forces each to stay inside Gaia even as he engenders more. Full of children, Gaia eventually offers her assistance to one of the unborn to overthrow Ouranos. When Kronos volunteers, she provides him with a plan and with a "sickle with jagged teeth" as a weapon. Kronos follows the plan by castrating Ouranos, who afterward puts a curse on the "Titans" who have defeated him and proclaims that "they [will] have to pay in time to come" (59).

3. Gaia and Ouranos then inform Kronos that one of his own children will usurp his power, so Kronos, too, must battle his own offspring to keep from being deposed. As Hesiod says, "he kept a sleepless watch and waited for his own children to be born and then swallowed them" (66). When he has swallowed six children, Kronos's wife, Rhea, appeals to Gaia and Ouranos to save the unborn. Gaia then secretes the child Zeus into hiding in Crete, while Rhea fools Kronos by giving him a stone wrapped in blankets to swallow. As a result of Gaia's plan, Kronos disgorges the other five children, and Zeus intervenes immediately to liberate and organize his siblings. In gratitude, the other children reward Zeus with "thunder and the lightning-bolt and flash" (67) as weapons for use in the fight against Kronos.

4. The war between the "new" Olympians and the "old" Titans goes on for ten years. When Gaia enters the fray again, she foretells "all the future to [the Olympians], prophesying that with the aid of the Hundred-Hands they will win the glorious triumph which they prayed for" (71). Zeus then makes the strategic decision to free the three Hundred-Hands monsters from Kronos's prison, enlisting their loyalty before the final battle begins. The combination of Zeus's "lightning-bolt and flash" and the awesome rock-throwing power of the three Hundred-Hands is too much for the Titans. After their fall they are imprisoned in underground caverns with bronze doors, guarded by the three Hundred-Hands figures. With the war over, Zeus wisely pays all of his political debts, giving "rights and privileges" to those who supported him (78). He has created political stability in the Olympian community, and his authority, as the poem ends, goes unchallenged.

This summary of events in the *Theogony* points up the strategic process of Zeus's ascension to power, the political alignments and strategic choices. The poem's first few lines deal not at all with Zeus, however; rather, they describe the physical setting on earth and heaven. After attending to mountains, rivers, and so on, the poem enumerates the natural forces as distant reflections of what will be primal human traits. Then, Night gives "birth to hateful / Destruction and the black Specter and Death"—also "Retribution to plague men . . . and stubborn Strife" (59). Night, in other words, is part of the world that Zeus must inhabit. Any conflict between them, as Vernant says, would be unwise for Zeus, for it would show him "backing down before the ancient Nux, Night, seized with reverential and religious awe" (Vernant 1980, 102). Such an encounter, in fact, is described in the *Iliad* (Book 8), where it is clear that Zeus has not created and cannot destroy the elemental materiality of the natural world.

Much of the "given" Kosmos that Zeus cannot control (e.g., Night and her destructive progeny) is feminine. This suggests that Zeus's authority is at odds with female forces in the world, yet he is dependent on the cooperation of the feminine forces over which he reigns. Gaia is part of the feminine matter of the world to which Zeus gives patriarchal form through his manner of rule. At the same time, she herself originates "everything" in the world (except Chaos and Desire) and specifically creates Ouranos, who will oppress Kronos, and then spurs Kronos to overcome Ouranos—all the while threatening Kronos with the knowledge that even he will be overthrown. She next plans Zeus's attack on Kronos and supplies information about the Hundred-Hands' potentially decisive role in defeating the Titans. She also gives assurance of victory if the Olympians follow her counsel.

Zeus, in fact, receives considerable support from several females: Rhea's assistance against her husband, Kronos, the help of Styx, Ocean's daughter, and that of various major and minor goddesses in waging his war. And while Zeus's political power comes through his own military and political victories (with Gaia's and other "maternal" aid), his ability to rule intelligently comes from the goddess Metis, who embodies intelligence and craft. He impregnates Metis and then, fearing usurpation by her child, actually swallows the goddess, thus acquiring her mental power. He later gives birth to Athena through his own head, making her forever "of" him, instead of the daughter of her mother, Metis. Zeus is thus dependent on, yet at the same time in opposition to, the females he subdues and shapes according to his own paternal design.

His relationship with Gaia, though, *is* ultimately formative beyond all others in the *Theogony*. In one sense, Gaia is a malleable female ready to serve males in the Greek world, the earthly material out of which Zeus fashions the world order. At the same time, her political agency underpins and makes possible his rule. She does not shape the world herself; Zeus does. Yet his authority clearly derives from her, in that she set in motion the process that will bring him to power. It would also seem that the force for the poem's transition from female to male power is, in an important sense, first located in Gaia's impulse to action.

Yet Gaia's paradoxical power over patriarchs is drastically modified by her own double exclusion from culture. On the one hand, as Hesiod shows, Gaia precedes "culture" and herself brings culture out of Chaos. On the other, when human culture is created, she has no direct influence on its administration and is part of what Zeus shapes according to his own design. Then again, while she does not rule, she does not allow any male *to be* fully a patriarch, either. Each subsequent "father" occupies the position temporarily, only to be pushed aside later, in a seemingly endless cycle of male displacement.

Each patriarch, furthermore, is a *castrato*, technically powerful but clearly limited in what he can effect as a father. When Ouranos is castrated, he curses those who will follow him similarly as *Titans*. (*Titainontas* refers literally to those who tighten the noose on and destroy themselves; see Brown, *Hesiod's Theogony* 21). Accordingly, all subsequent patriarchs will possess the same qualified power to *procreate*, to set in motion a process of engendering. But theirs is a "succession," as Robert Lamberton says, defined strategically "by castration" (41), forever denied the power actually to originate anything. They cannot give birth to children or really create anything, either sire children in any direct sense or bring a new world into being.

Let us again take the example of Kronos. While he can procreate, doing so is not fruitful, and he even tries to undo the effects of procreation before they occur, in effect canceling his own efficacy. Zeus, by contrast, does procreate in such a way as to be specifically productive for cultural development. Zeus is certainly in the same line of "succession by castration" and hears the same prophecy that he will be usurped by one of his progeny. But when Zeus swallows Metis, he does not actually resist the prophecy; rather, he maneuvers to align himself with it politically, henceforth becoming the prophecy's avatar and agent. He comes to *represent* the "law" as expressed in the prophecy and will be the signifier of the law to others. All who live in the Kosmos after Ouranos are indeed "castrated" in that their freedom is circumscribed by an injunction that says no one can possess or "originate" communal prerogatives in any absolute way. Zeus becomes the vehicle for transmitting this injunction, and even he is subject to it. As the *Odyssey* and *Works and Days* show more clearly than does the *Theogony*, Zeus himself is bound to a principle of order, a hierarchy of communal function, which he reiterates and articulates in his own manner of rule. He, too, is "castrated," "bound" by the structuring power of this law; the difference is that (in both Hesiod's and Homer's texts) he is the signifier of that law, a signifier in the manner of what the Greeks called, in a late word, *Diosemia*, a "Zeus" or "God" sign. Other texts indicate the "God sign" as *echesamia* (another "late" word), a "stop-sign," explicitly paternal interdiction. Being bound to the law means being circumscribed and limited,[1] symbolically "castrated," as the line of Ouranos and Kronos indicates.

After Gaia, the Erinyes are the major female "otherness" in the Kosmos for Zeus. The *Theogony* explains that when Kronos castrated Ouranos, "the drops of blood that spurted [forth] were all taken in by Mother Earth [Gaia], and in the course of the revolving years she gave birth to the powerful Erinyes" (58). Under the aegis of Fate (Moira) the Erinyes avenge wrongs, especially blood crimes, perpetrated particularly against mothers. They are not enraged when Oedipus kills his father, but when Jokaste commits suicide they actively pursue Oedipus for possibly causing her death. Swift with punishment for actual matricide, they hear no appeals and intend to spare no one.

While supreme in her power, Moira is *not* a goddess who could, for example, dictate to Zeus. She is, rather, a name for the universal "portion" or "lot" that everyone in the Kosmos must abide by, a recognition that since something "has happened, evidently," as E. R. Dodds says, "'it had to be'" (6). Heidegger describes Moira as the "presencing of what is present" and the dispensing of "the destiny of Being" as that which necessarily "comes to pass" (97).

Zeus cannot rule Moira, the Erinyes, or any version of Fate. Even when his own son Sarpedon is dying in the Trojan War, he can do nothing (*Iliad*, Book 16). Hera points out that *anomie* would result if Zeus saved his son, and all the other gods would then want the same power to deflect fate. The Erinyes, in other words, also represent the "law" according to which the Kosmos functions, for Zeus as for all others.

The earthly origin of the Erinyes, born from Ouranos's blood spilled on the earth, suggests not only chthonic deities but possibly indigenous gods, whereas Zeus is a "sky" god not native to Hesiod's Boeotia. If the Erinyes "are a product of the older, chthonic religion," matriarchal in impulse but included in "a later patriarchal amalgamation" (67), as Philip Slater notes, they are, in effect, products of Gaia's (Earth's) womb and a special instance of female power actually governing the world. Their revenge function tends to come into play on special occasions when the administration of justice has otherwise failed, or when Zeus as patriarch has already had his say. The Erinyes can intervene on behalf of justice at any time, and they will always act—as Gaia's representative, as a female *Diosemia*—as a supplement or a correction to Zeus. The Erinyes can always *add* something to authority, even as they mirror the order of the law that the father belongs to and himself obeys. They are a sign of a certain fundamental authority positioned marginally. Just as Gaia's position as a supplement to Zeus's authority constitutes exclusion from the direct administration of culture, so the Erinyes are also prime signifiers of a system of justice (*dikē*) characterized most immediately by the male/female opposition of which the father's authority is a part.

Gaia represents the channels through which the patriarchy can move and develop. She peoples the Kosmos with castrati, males with a highly qualified "procreative" function. Culture in the Kosmos, evidently, is wagered on a binarity and on the "impossibility" of patriarchy—that is, on instituted male authority *and* the simultaneous fact of its inherent and imminent failure. A castrato at the "origin" of the world, or as a replacement for Gaia at its origin, institutes a rule of succession assuring that all regimes will be displaced via a cosmic principle of dynamic substitution, signification, and repression. Male death structures culture and the Kosmos, and Gaia's existence marks a trace of the primary system which is both the "origin" and provides the functioning rule of the world, a mechanism that of necessity destroys and reconstitutes itself by dispersing patriarchs and male/female "origins" across the Kosmos as it operates. (The divinity who originally was supposed to supplant Zeus is the androgynous Dionysus, perhaps suggesting a gender synthesis that would have put an end to history.)

The interplay between males and females in the whole economy of the *Theogony* suggests the institution of a "law" of difference in Greek culture, the establishing of a hierarchy of function and the positioning of culturally sanctioned roles and relations. Gaia and Zeus, in particular, continue to appear throughout the *Theogony* as well as other texts so as to articulate aspects of this discourse. The gendered discourse they articulate tends to be a major aspect of the world's structure based on a law of priority and the encompassing structure of the Kosmos represented as justice (*dikē*). Each figure signifies the operation of a dynamic mechanism in a specifically gendered discourse. In the *Theogony* this operation can be easily obscured by the poem's relentless foregrounding of "male" concerns and his evident misogyny. Paternal authority and male privilege are strongly advanced in this poem, and fathers are unrelentingly elevated; this patriarchalism can overshadow and obscure other implications in the poem's construction of gender. (In the works of later authors, by the way, Gaia as mother of the Giants becomes more of an opponent to Zeus.)

As in *Works and Days*, the *Theogony*'s relations of gender foreshadow logical relations that will show up in Aristotle's work in the fourth century B.C. In the *Physics*, for example, Aristotle proposes four kinds of relationships that can occur between propositions conceived as minimal pairs—that is, minimal binary couplings that manifest an inherent ordering for actual relationships in the world (224b.35–225a.12). Aristotle's claim is professedly *not* to advance a logic of real-world relations, but to focus on the logic inherent to descriptions of such relationships. To this end, Aristotle postulated descriptive relations in a hierarchy of increasing complexity ranging from simple affirmative statements to complex relations of change encompassing affirmation and negation. He posited a series with its own principle of progression in which later propositions are logically dependent on the prior relationships.

Aristotle's thinking about scientific thought constitutes a paradigm defining coherence and reason. First in this paradigm is the "contrary" relationship of an affirmative proposition A to an affirmative proposition B, as in the relationship of difference called "equipolence"—the difference, for example, between male and female. A person cannot be described as "male" and "female" at the same time; even so, "male" and "female" can exist separately and simultaneously. Propositions A and B could also be distinguished by the exclusionary relationship called "privation," that is, the principle of difference based on the presence or absence of a quality, of "opposite" qualities such as whiteness and the lack of whiteness, or blackness. Regardless of whether A and B are equipolent or privative in the contrary relationship, they are both "affirmative" propositions capable of existing simultaneously within the same logical frame. While the principal subject indicated in these propositions cannot be both A and B at the same time, the existence of A and B and their relations can be said to institute a particular frame of reference (A:B).

Aristotle describes the "contrary" relationship as formally logical, but his distinction cannot be reduced to simple deductive or syllogistic operations, as in the mere addition or subtraction of integers. Aristotle sees an ethical dimension to the contrary relationship when he says that the relationship of A:B establishes a range of possibilities for characterizing the underlying subject assumed in the operation of propositional logic. The contrary relationship is a kind of axis for representing the varieties of human experience as imagined in Greek culture. The contrary axis will signify a *substantial* orientation (relating to *ousía*, or substance) that specifically affects a subject. The contrary relationship should be seen, then, as an axis marked by what John Peter Anton calls the *"termini,"* or reference points, of "distributive being" (25). "Distributive being" here means the structural nature, the initial staging of the subject that Aristotle is describing in the sequence of his logic. Proposition A participates in this relationship as a subject addressing an object in B, with the structure of this relationship situating A within a context of possibility represented along the axis of the particular contrary relationship with term B.

Second in Aristotle's sequence is the "contradiction" expressed as A and the negation of A. Zeus, for example, cannot be both ascending and descending in the Pantheon, at least not simultaneously. To use Aristotle's own example, saying "all men are white" directly contradicts and excludes the possibility that "not all men are white." This contradiction could take the form of a universal proposition, a broad generality, in relation to a particular reference. The subject or focus of investigation, in any case, could not be both A and not-A, there being no mediate or third position for the relationship of contradiction.

The point of the A:-A contradictory relationship is to express change in a subject (*metabolē*), such as form/privation or generation/destruction. Through the trope of "contradiction" and the contradictory extremes it represents, the broadest and most definitive limits are expressed about a subject as a focus of critical inquiry. Whereas the contrary relationship situates the subject in particular terms along an axis consisting of (1) *substance* (what the subject is in relation to an *other* case, a *heteron*), (2) *quality* (the subject's attributes), and (3) *quantity* (the completeness or incompleteness of those attributes), the contradictory relationship expresses the furthest limits of substantial change, such as generation/destruction, virtually the scope of a subject as a whole and independent entity.

The fourth possibility is the relationship of not-A to not-B, as when one proposes that something is neither just nor unjust (-A:-B), neither white nor not-white, neither degeneration nor growth. Aristotle poses this possibility as logically necessary but is little interested in it, because the double negative cannot refer to anything that exists in the world. He further reasons that in the linear logic of contrary relations "there is no opposition between two negative terms," as Anton explains, no "logical" determinacy at work (50). Why think about possibilities that do not exist and are not "logical"? This is a revealing judgment on Aristotle's part. That is, he sees this fourth formulation as a wild card in that the -A:-B possibility would not be derivable in a linear fashion from the A/B terms of the other propositions. Rather, -A:-B would express an oppositional option other than, *anything* other than, that of A/B and their derivatives. This -A:-B formulation, in sum, poses a potentially complete and radical departure from the other propositions of the series and represents an irrational violation of the specific terms of the preceding propositions. -A:-B would be possibly intelligible but not categorically significant within a rectilinear model.

In that the fourth proposition potentially represents rational discontinuity and change, it is understandable that Aristotle would want to bracket -A:-B as a conceptually necessary statement of limits, but not a logically productive formulation, as lacking the specific, rational discourse of relations established by the prior terms. Aristotle, therfore, advances no extended argument about -A:-B as an impossibility in relation to the other terms of the sequence; he simply objects to and marginalizes in importance the radical unpredictability of -A:-B and the irrelevance of things that do not really exist. He also focuses on the fact that this instance of contingency and change cannot be known or predicted in advance, precisely because it is the possibility of change unconnected to the prior terms. (I shall return to Aristotle's logic in relation to a scientific "subject" of inquiry in chapter 3.)

The Logic of the *Theogony*

I am arguing that Aristotle's sequence of logical possibilities can be used to model the gender relations of the *Theogony*. The poem's precarious situating of Gaia-as-Mother actually foreshadows that logic. As I have discussed, Gaia has what can be called "originary" power as the agent for the world's beginning, although in the operating Kosmos she is not the locus of power and is not "in power" in any practical sense. One could take Gaia as the "spirit" or transcendental presence always nurturing the patriarchal order. Such a gesture, however, idealizes Gaia out of the poem altogether and potentially only legitimates the poem's patriarchal order. The point should not be to mystify Gaia as the special case of female power that must be brought to, but is not *already* inherent as, a figure positioned in the poem's value order.

The same can be said about certain historical explanations of the gender relationships reflected in the poem. If historical claims about matriarchy are brought to the poem without also accounting for Gaia's narrative positioning, little has been addressed. The relationship of Gaia and Zeus is little explained by merely importing a chronological priority of matriarchy, and then patriarchy, to argue that Gaia represents an indigenous matriarchal culture colonized by an invading patriarchal one. Certainly the question of the historical priority of matriarchy over patriarchy is a complex and much-debated issue.[2] Of more immediate concern is Gaia's positioning on the margin of the narrative's action and as a peripheral dimension of Hesiod's patriarchal discourse. Gaia is not positioned as a matriarchal power in her own right, and she is not directly an agent of patriarchy. She is caught in a double exclusion that needs to be situated as part of narrative structure.

The paradox of Gaia's situation can be described in the logic of Aristotle's oppositional relationships. She carries the signifier of power, yet she is powerful neither as a matriarch nor as a patriarchal agent. Lacking an evident position in either discourse, she is in the nonposition of double exclusion. An attractive option is simply to affirm the terms of Gaia's paradox. She possessed pertinence to the institution of power in the distant past, and she is signified but excluded from the exercise of power in the present. What is known about Gaia is what, in being excluded from two relationships, she is not. She is characterized, in other words, by the equivalent of the proposition -A:-B. The sequence of propositions that could logically generate the terms of her placement involves prior assumptions about patriarchal authority that coincide with the developments of the *Theogony*. The male dominance, misogyny, and male/female relations generally present in the poem can be positioned within the economy of these logical propositions. The relationship of Gaia and Zeus, in short, foreshadows the logic of Aristotle's interpretive algorithm— that is, if the relationships before -A:-B begin with the assumption about value (not chronology) of male priority in relation to a female.

In Figure 1, "male" and "female" occur in a "contrary" relationship: both are positive terms, capable of existing at the same time. Zeus, representating the law and marking the extreme changes that a "male" may go through, stands in a "contradictory" relationship to the first position. He is categorically not human, yet as a god he signifies the limitations of generation/destruction, form/privation. He embodies the Father as interdiction and accommodation, as *echesamía*, the negation, or death, as well as life of a subject of inquiry. Exactly where that line of negation is drawn defines the Male as a subject *and* as a subject-in-process in its relation to the Female and the Kosmos.

Gaia, it follows, occupies the position of agency *other than* male subjectivity as figured in the first position of Aristotle's square. She is neither simply a Female as an abstract correlate to a Male, nor is

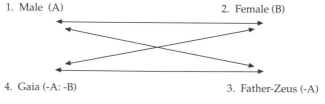

1. Male (A)   2. Female (B)

4. Gaia (-A: -B)   3. Father-Zeus (-A)

Figure 1.

she the paternal agent representating the law according to which the Male is known as a subject. Her precarious position in the patriarchal order, situated-as-suppressed, is so extreme as to suggest that she may be part of an order *other than* the one signified by the prior propositions in this gender economy.

In this analysis the primary term in the sequence of oppositions is the "subject" of discourse to which all the other pairings relate. For Aristotle, the "subject" or *hupokeimenon* (which I will discuss further in chapter 3) refers to the whole system of substantial relations, that is, the substratum of relations manifested in all the phases of contrariety that define a subject of discourse. (*Hupokeimenon* can also designate the single speaking subject as a grammatical subject of enunciation, which would be the first position of oppositional relations as it institutes the whole sequence.)

"Gaia," then, can be seen as an alienated figure in representing a complex otherness quite separate from the paternal order Zeus represents. Following Aristotle's conclusion, however, she would be insignificant in the *Theogony*, merely an instance of logical and notional necessity, an abstraction that proves the ontological impossibility of something existing outside the boundaries of patriarchal order. In the fourth position she is suppressed in the discourse she is part of, placed logically at its margin. At the same time, her defaced and undefined ideological potential sets her up to emerge at some indeterminate and yet-to-occur moment as a substitute "subject" in a new set of oppositional relations. In this way, she could be a revolutionary subject able to further break from and supersede the paternal order. Aristotle, however, prefers to say that this possibility for the fourth proposition is neither interesting nor logically significant.

Philip Slater and many others see Gaia as coming "before" Zeus historically and representing a once ascendant matriarchal order. This explanation does not account for Gaia's position in the narrative, although it tries to suggest an external circumstance explaining how the narrative came to be. But Gaia's presence as an oppositional figure *in* the *Theogony*, as an evident counter-order to patriarchalism, makes sense only when Zeus is situated as speaking subject. I am situating the *Theogony*'s fundamentally patriarchal and misogynistic orientation structurally. We see this positioning as we gain a clearer view of Gaia's relations in the poem.

The effect of the discourse between Gaia and Zeus is relational *and* systematically misogynistic. The methodical suppression, or situating, of positions in discourse maintains the apparent "naturalness" and stability of a hierarchy, camouflaging an ideological relationship in the terms of the apparently inevitable. In the *Theogony's* several-tiered class structure, maleness marks the position of the *hupokei-menon*, or speaking subject. In that position the male articulates discursively (apart from the content of his speech) the rule by which all value in the Greek Kosmos is dispersed and managed. Gilbert Murray even describes the gods in general as a decadent bourgeoisie: "Do they practice trades and industries?" he asks. "Not a bit of it. Why should they do any honest work? They find it easier to live on the revenues" (45). It is clear that Zeus appropriates the position as speaking subject to serve a global order when he overthrows the Titans, creating, in effect, a working class consisting of the humans. (Odysseus, for example, labors under the gods without adequate knowledge of or access to the rules that govern him.) Females, in particular, occupy this position. In obvious sympathy with the oppressed people of his narratives, Hesiod in *Works and Days* bitterly indicts the hegemony of the Pantheon and the evident oppression of the powerless: "For the gods [consistently] have hidden and keep hidden / what could have been men's livelihood" (lines 44–45 in Lattimore). The extreme lower classes are made up of the Hundred-Hands (suggesting actual labor), exploited for their strength and then not rewarded according to productivity. Other social levels between these have varying access to the knowledge that Zeus controls.[3]

In the *Theogony*, Zeus's power is derived politically within a system of social and economic oppression, making Zeus a figure much closer to Machiavelli than to Yahweh. Paternal authority in the *Theogony* is also part of a discourse that includes a defaced maternal authority and all that seems to be suppressed in order to institute Zeus's regime. In *Hesiod* (1988) Robert Lamberton accurately reflects the picture of Zeus as all powerful when he describes "Zeus's power and omniscience" as "givens" of this poetry—formulaic conventions of its language and fundamental notions of the society that was its historical context (100). Perhaps so; but from my perspective Lamberton misses an important dimension of the poem when he adds, "These givens are immune to the demands of narrative, though they do not stand in the way of narratives with which they are inconsistent" (100). Lamberton's view is that the ideal version of Zeus successfully suppresses the articulation of Zeus in the performative dimension of narrative. By contrast, I am arguing that Zeus cannot be actually removed from the narrative medium: if not *in* narrative, where would he be? In focusing on what is suppressed ideologically in this text as a narrative—on Gaia's maternal position in relation to the idealized claims made for fatherhood—we begin to see the gender discourse that situates fatherhood (*patris*) as "central" to the poem. The father's hegemony in this text can be located as a position produced *in*, and an effect of, but not encompassing the text. This misogynistic emphasis on *patris* is also an "effect," a way of interpreting this text.

The Paternal Romance

I am arguing not just for a way of interpreting hierarchy and authority in the *Theogony*, but also for a way of viewing some dimensions of value in Greek culture that can too easily be "forgotten." The French anthropologist and classicist Louis Gernet once wrote, "There are some human activities, such as law and economics, whose intellectual nature it is possible to forget" (73). In this warning he meant literally "forgetting," but in a broader context he also meant that the rationale of cultural practices can be missed, neglected, "forgotten" in the sense of not being "seen" at all. Our cultural practices often make us "forget"—or misrecognize—what we are doing in material and functional terms. Gernet's statement could also be taken to suggest that some practices of understanding are even constituted by such a "forgetting." These hidden dimensions are discoverable, but they may be diminished or defaced if the mechanism for producing them is not kept somehow hidden. Part of their function involves forgottenness *as a function*, being hidden from view and taken as natural while an "effect" is registered.

This is Pierre Bourdieu's point, too, when he says that "every power which manages to impose meanings and to impose them as legitimate" does so by "concealing the power relations which are the basis of its force." The textual power that imposes order necessarily "adds its own specifically symbolic force to those power relations" as part of the necessity to obscure the very nature of imposed order (Bourdieu vi). Such textual mechanisms necessarily operate behind a veil of obscurity, here called "symbolic force." Without such a veiled origin, those mechanisms would be denatured, alien, or simply disappear.

Gernet's idea about cultural "forgetting" highlights something important about a fluctuation between, and an obscuring of, two versions of fatherhood in the *Theogony*. Hovering over the entire poem is the father of epithets and idealized pronouncements—a figure grand in stature but profoundly artificial, like one of the blank-eyed, frozen Greek statues that W. B. Yeats describes. This figure of a monumental great father serves to guarantee the poem's cultural underpinnings and legitimacy and to insure its deference to and promotion of certain values—ultimately men and male authority as signifying the conventional "law" (*nomos*) in religion and social structure. And then there is Zeus as flawed, the father who is an active agent in a gendered discourse and who is circumscribed by his situation and his relations with females and those over whom he attempts to exercise power. Zeus is certainly both of these figures, but never simultaneously; he operates virtually in contradiction with himself. In any specific passage in the poem, one of these versions of the father comes forward while the other is momentarily repressed in the distant background of narrative—"forgotten" in the narrative action. The apparent naturalness of this fluctuation in textual forgetting, and the ease with which the poem orchestrates the movements of two distinctly different Zeuses, begins to make evident the pervasive "symbolic force" of paternal assumptions and ideology.

The specific textual operations of the *Theogony* clearly substantify the larger cultural relations described in Gerda Lerner's *Creation of Patriarchy* (1985). Lerner chronicles "male" culture as derived from a patriarchal order of values that has taken over 2500 years to develop (212). Eva C. Keuls in *The Reign of the Phallus* (1985) gives a vivid account of later Greek cultural practices that evince the same "forgetting" about the constructed nature of paternal authority. She shows that fifth-century Athenian society, like the Greek Pantheon, was governed by a "phallocracy" (2) calculated to promote men and their interests in all social and political spheres. Not focusing so much on religion, she examines legal and private documents, decorative vases, various erotica, and adorned objects of everyday life to establish that the human race in Athens was conceived and depicted as mono-sexual, essentially *male*. Women, like Gaia, were defined as defaced men who rightly exist on the margins of culture. Keuls documents "phallic exposure and female invisibility on the Athenian scene" (13) in her discussions of statecraft, the arts, and family life. She shows, for example, that the public display of actual erect penises in squares, baths, and other civic places was common and "natural."

Keuls focuses her discussion of the phallocracy on the "fateful year of 415 B.C.," the year of Euripides' *Trojan Women*, the Athenian invasion of Sicily, and the legendary "mutilation" of the "Herms," the aforementioned overtly phallic statues in Athens. The "castration" of the statues took place on the eve of the invasion of Sicily; indeed, the Athenians actually postponed the attack because of the bad omen of so many dismembered—"defeated"—penises. She shows that this year of cultural revolution created a division for the Greek world between an earlier period "marked by extreme phallicism" and a subsequent one of lessened phallic oppression (13). In effect, in fifth-century Athens a partially successful sexual revolution occurred, precipitating a decline of phallic cultism and militarism associated with it. Keuls also demonstrates the existence of patriarchal, Greek phallicism in cultural areas not so evidently reflected in "mythic" and religious texts.

Eric A. Havelock, too, documents a largely philosophical "forgetting" about paternal authority in ancient Greece. He notes great diversity in fifth-century Athenian assumptions about paternal authority and the fixity or static ordering of culture. Havelock shows that a cadre of playwrights and philosophers—including Aeschylus, Democritus, and Antiphon—held that, since humans are contingently "historical" in their nature, without "a fixed quantity" or unchanging essence, they should strive to live in political and social environments that outwardly display culture as in flux, "in which power-patterns [exist] pragmatically and temporarily" (*The Liberal Temper* 379).

More pointedly, such Sophists as Gorgias, Protagoras, Phaedrus, Hippias, and Isocrates—much maligned in the Western tradition—advanced rich and varied political schemes generally marked by a tendency toward decentralization and anti-authoritarianism and anti-paternalism. Political authority, they argued, should not be deposited in "permanent" schemes connected with the polis. They feared the institutionalization of state authority and ideology as "natural" or divinely sanctioned—which is exactly how the ancient and Western worlds have developed. Havelock notes that "Aristotle's vigorous and successful purpose [was] to kill this [anti-patriarchal] theory and replace it with statehood" conceived in models dictating "permanent patterns of power" (379). Virtually "haunted"—as was Plato before him—"by the figure of the *paterfamilias*, the [potential of an] authoritarian" father (297), Aristotle depicted state power in the *Politics* as necessarily replicating the patriarchal authority of the family. In so doing, Aristotle gave formal and decisive expression to patriarchalism as a privileged metaphor of Western politics.

Havelock's cultural reframing and reinterpretation of the Sophists bear directly on our views of the origins of Western paternal authority in ancient Greece. In strong agreement with Havelock, Susan C. Jarratt has recently extended this renovation of the Sophists' reputation in *Rereading the Sophists*; so have others, such as Sharon Crowley. Jarratt sees the Sophists as exemplary practitioners of "the art of verbal persuasion as the mechanism allowing for the functioning of social organizations," thus recognizing their fundamentally ethical and political dimension, their culturally situated view of rhetoric. Their rhetorical practice derives from their belief that the "only permanent reality is the historical process through which social structures and the values which undergird them are developed" (10). In these assumptions and others, the Sophists share much with contemporary cultural theorists. Sophistic texts evince "encompassing and mixed discourses, fully in charge of the power of patriarchal logic, [and even] calling it into play on occasion" (72). And instead of focusing on cultural law or conventions according to the fixity of *logos*, the Sophists exploited the sense of *nomos* as representing "provisional codes (habits or customs) of social and political behavior, socially constructed and historically (even geographically) specific" assumptions (74). Jarratt even takes the Sophistic style of discourse, varied and readily adaptable, as suggestive of *écriture féminine* and claims that the Sophists, who traveled frequently and had to adapt their cultural and rhetorical models to many cultures, were the "first multiculturalists" (11).

By contrast, Aristotle and Plato advanced what the Greeks considered to be a pro-paternal (fixed and centralized) as opposed to what they took to be an anti-paternal (fluid and decentralized) approach to the institutions of culture and power. Aristotle shows in numerous ways that he wanted Greek culture to accept the supremacy of paternal authority for the state and to view fatherhood as the central reference of a polis that itself stood at the center of all cultural, political, and religious life—in effect, the center of the Kosmos. The assumptions regarding this patriarchal order, precisely those ideas that are focused upon by the Sophists, are what is repressed in the philosophical enthusiasms of the fifth and fourth centuries B.C.

This cultural "forgetting" and lack of alignment between the two Zeuses, or between the generation of knowledge and action as conflicting cultural products, does not necessarily constitute a tragic split or vision in the *Theogony*, or in Greek culture generally. However, this conflict over paternal authority is an *aporía*, an impasse. Greek culture disguises the impasse by defining the conditions of the father's authority in a way that *seems* natural, in line with the structure of the Kosmos itself. The strategy is to order knowledge and action in a hierarchy that privileges the law and the cultural order signified by the idealized Zeus. It is at times tempting to "forget" about the other Zeus, as when C. Kerenyi writes about the tradition in German scholarship of noting the "'monotheistic impulse in polytheism' that showed itself in the Zeus religion" (xv). But whatever claims may be made about monotheism in the Greek world, Zeus in the *Theogony*, in the *Odyssey*, and in *The Iliad* is not a mono-deity on his own; he is not yet like Yahweh. The myth of exclusive male power, while suggested by epithets about Zeus, is undermined by the very same Greek religious texts that advance that ideal stature.

Notes

1. *Echesamía*, as Arthur Bernard Cook reports in *Zeus: A Study in Ancient Religion*, p. 6, is not a well-known designation for Zeus, but it is an important illustration of Zeus as a signifier of interdiction.

2. For a discussion of the tradition of postulating the chronological priority of matriarchy over patriarchy, see S. Pembroke, "Women in Charge."

3. For a critique of class in the ancient world from a Marxist perspective, see G. E. M. de Ste. Croix, *The Class Struggle in the Ancient World*.

CHAPTER TWO

The *Odyssey* and the Noble Father

What if his great father [*patēr esthlon*]
came from the unknown world and drove these men
like dead leaves through the place, recovering
honor and lordship in his own domaine?
—Homer, Odyssey

Nothing is truly one.
—Aristotle, Metaphysics

In the previous chapter a question briefly arose concerning the
Theogony as a text older than the *Odyssey*. Martin Bernal in *Black
Athena* (1987) has argued for placing Hesiod "in the 10th century
and [Homer] around the turn of the 9th" (88), and this controversy
may never be resolved. However, the gender and cultural considerations raised by the paternal romance are not questions restricted to
chronology, and the *Odyssey*, whenever it was written, is surely an
important expansion of the *Theogony* in its enlargement of four major
issues.

First, the *Theogony* focuses on paternal authority in a global
sense as establishing ordering principles for the Kosmos. It narrates
a male figure's stepping forward against a backdrop of familial, communal, and cosmic events, and then his coming to dominate those
events. Hesiod's poem creates a mode of inquiry defined largely by
its focus on male subjectivity; the intent of this narrative is to explain
the inevitability of that domination, the "naturalness" of paternal
order and its consonance with the cosmic order.

There is also a tactical dimension of the *Theogony* as it explores
the contrariety and logical implications of male and female relations.
As a tactic for rationalizing male dominance, the poem attempts to
describe *how* males come, and supposedly must come, to dominate

the world around them, including females. The *Theogony* also opens a view of the ontological purpose of its own constructions—the *effect* of promoting males in a patriarchal regime, a view of what the *Theogony* as a cultural document actually produces and brings to bear on its culture.

The last issue concerns the foregrounding of the paternal romance itself. The *Theogony* advances the interests of paternal authority and places considerable cultural weight on the paternal metaphor, not as an isolated development but in support of a larger cultural practice reflected in many other texts.

The *Odyssey* develops as a narrative by enlarging on precisely these four areas. Whereas the *Theogony* offers a huge accounting of the beginnings of the Kosmos, the hierarchical ordering of cosmic powers and the institution of culture, the *Odyssey* narrates the fortunes of Odysseus as he moves through a microcosmic reenactment of the same process. The *Theogony* shows the effects of Zeus's hegemonic relations with the Kosmos; the *Odyssey* focuses on the detailed playing out of those relations at prior and subsequent moments of their development, particularly regarding the process of reinstituting Odysseus's rule. The *Odyssey* also explores male/female relations and follows the process of subjugating females en route to achieving effects of male dominance similar to those in the *Theogony.* Finally, the *Odyssey* possesses an ontological dimension: its advancing of male concerns brings into being a cultural pattern, the construction of the paternal metaphor.

The *Odyssey*'s success in creating the effect of inevitability for paternal authority explains much about this epic's influence and traditionally accorded status, and it is for this reason that the *Odyssey* as a text of the father-in-effect has a central place in this study. This "success" is most evident in the complex narrative that, like a painting with effective three-dimensional effects, has lines of development that appear to lead back naturally and inevitably to a core of values and representations associated with paternity. The construction of character, particularly of Odysseus, contributes to this sense of a world that must inevitability reorient to paternal references. This epic "succeeds," finally, in the construction of a comprehensive paternal metaphor fashioned from complex narrative material, so much so that the evocation of cultural law seems unavoidably tied to the narrative's paternal themes. On the other hand, the exposure of the poem's ideological dimensions, its methods and working assumptions in the construction of certain effects of value, will foreground the precise workings of the paternal romance. The *Odyssey* stands as a primary

text both for demonstrating the achieved effects of the paternal
romance and for critiquing it.

The *Odyssey* is also highly influential because it is traditionally
regarded as an important record of eighth-century Greece, a reservoir
of information about law, government, and family life for culture in
an important part of the classical world. Furthermore, it transmits
the values that will reemerge later (in a different guise) as the philosophical formulations of "justice," "law," and "nature" in the work
of Anaximander, the Sophists, Plato, and Aristotle. The *Odyssey* is
a prime reference of Greek culture, what Eric Havelock calls "the
oral encyclopedia of the maritime complex" (*Justice* 177), the "cultural
encyclopedia" of ancient Greece (56).

The exploration of paternal authority that makes the *Odyssey*
a key text for understanding the paternal romance also may restrict
its ability to speak about Greek values in the plainest philosophical
terms. This, in any case, is the argument developed in Havelock's
The Greek Concept of Justice (1978). Havelock discusses the poem's
formulaic structure not as a philosophical text with "statements of
principles or laws abstracted from an activist situation" (*Justice* 122)
but as a fundamentally "oral" poem that tends less toward abstract
formulation, or definition, and is structured largely by the repetition
of formulaic phrasing. Conventional descriptions—"wine-dark sea,"
"grey-eyed Athena"—are situated amidst narrative patterns also conventional and formulaic, such as the heroic test of a riddle (e.g.,
about the "secret" of Penelope's bed) and the use of special weapons
(Odysseus's "great bow"). The hero's exploration of exotic lands
includes Mediterranean port stops known to Homer's audience from
other poetry and from common knowledge of trade routes.

While this formulaic structure does not detract from the *Odyssey*
as a "cultural encyclopedia," Havelock argues that the poem's oral
shape inhibits schematic (what can be called "spatial") clarity of the
sort associated with written texts in which concepts are intricately
and precisely related to each other. He even posits that the understandable lack of precision in this poem reflects Greek culture itself
at this stage, especially a measure of vagueness concerning justice
(*dikē*) and Zeus's association with concepts that later will be important to Greek philosophy, especially law (*nomos*) and nature (*phusis*).

Havelock does argue that Homer's poem has its own way of
advancing the concept of justice and, by implication, the concerns
of the paternal romance. He begins with the assumption that a poem
with oral structure cannot be exact in its formulation of abstract or

highly complex concepts. For Homer, as for Hesiod, "the conditions of narrative syntax required for memorization [in "oral" poetry] still prevailed, particularly as they limited the usage of the verb 'to be,' and so made definition impossible" (*Justice* 14). Oral narratives, which must be memorizable, cannot rely heavily on pure abstractions, on formulations creating the distance necessary for isolating "topics" and abstract entities. Not until Plato's work, especially in the *Republic*, is a crucial concept such as "justice" articulated *as a concept*—"as a topic," as Havelock says, "converting it into a conceptual entity and making it a normative principle" (*Justice* 14).

Plato will even associate the prior historical failure to conceptualize topics such as justice with the "poetry" of epic narrative, as opposed to "philosophy" and its abstract fifth- and fourth-century formulations. In effect, Plato dismisses the structure and limitation of a certain oral tradition embodied in "poetry." His subsequent banning of poetry from the model state as an unsuitable "vehicle for the definition and description of justice" (in *The Republic*) seems less eccentric in light of his perception of a chaotic version of orality in poetry, as opposed to the clear schematizations of philosophy (*Justice* 14).

Havelock is severe in judging the conceptual limits imposed on a poem like the *Odyssey* as a result of oral structure. Ultimately he argues that this epic, and oral poetry in general, will develop narrative scenarios built on rigid polarizations between unambiguously good and bad characters and forces. While such poetry never operates entirely mechanically (even the *Theogony* is not entirely a list), this tendency toward rigidity shapes the *Odyssey* so much that the "main action" is polarized and marked with sensationalist moments of strife to the point that the poem is culturally non-ethical. This poem reflects "a level of behavior in early Hellenism more primitive than the procedures followed in the *Iliad*" (149). In short, Havelock believes that the Law as a concept does not prevail in the *Odyssey*. In the Homeric texts generally, he asserts, "justice does not find a place," at least not in the conceptual sense of moral and political philosophy common to the Greeks later as a "regulative *principle*" (13). Paternal authority as law is not evident in any ethical sense in these texts, and "both epics," Havelock goes on, despite what they may show about Greek justice, "are very far from identifying 'justice' as a principle with a priori foundations, whether conceived as the necessary 'rule of law' or as a moral sense in man" (180). He eventually pushes this point to conclude, with apparent exaggeration, that "there is no concept of justice in Greek epics, in our sense of that word" (192)—no focus of interest, if we take him literally, on the complex of values and commitments that make up the concept of culture.

But even by Havelock's standards, the *Odyssey* does articulate some strategies for indicating standards and values that constitute what is "just" in the Kosmos. This is accomplished, in part, through the repetition of formulaic constructions larger than individual phrases to give a sense of what is "expected" or customarily "just" (*dikaios*) in certain cultural and political contexts. When Telémakhos says to the suitors, "I beg Zeus you shall get what you deserve: / a slaughter here, and nothing paid for it" (2:144–45), this expresses a more abstract formulation, as even Havelock argues, about how "heaven's anger will turn against crimes" (*Justice* 121). This precept is not advanced explicitly as a tenet, and it is not expressed completely in the one line in the text. Nevertheless, it and others are embedded in the pattern of repeated formulae that are "larger than is applicable to the term 'formula'" as "used by metrical analysts" (118).

Havelock wants to say that, in place of abstract precepts or definitions, the *Odyssey* advances such "nomos-ethos" (law/custom) constellations in brief sequences that convey predispositions toward ideas and not fully developed concepts. Despite the lack of abstract formulation in the *Odyssey*, "Homeric *dikē* remains faithful to that sense of social propriety which surrounds its legal usages." The concept is expressed without abstract formulation; Homeric "justice" prevails, as Havelock admits, in an atmospheric sense of "what one has a 'right' to expect, what it is 'just' to expect, of given persons in given situations" (183). This sense of justice is conveyed not overtly, but performatively (and vaguely, Havelock argues) in what he calls "the dynamism of epic narrative" (122).

Havelock argues that Greek culture progresses over several centuries from "orality" and the metaphorical expressions of narrative ("poetry," in Plato's term) toward "written" culture and the literal definitions and dialectics of philosophy. "Oral" culture continued until approximately the seventh century B.C., and then "written" culture and philosophy began in earnest with Anaximander and the rise of philosophy in the sixth century B.C. Subsequently, the change from "oral" to "written" meant a movement away from the latent and mute, non-discursive, significance of narrative and toward the overt articulations of discourse and dialogue—from implicit *and* poetic to explicit *and* philosophic. Philosophy in the late sixth century was the more explicitly formulated outgrowth and elaboration of the values and propositions advanced only implicitly in narrative.

Greek culture developed its characteristic identity—the Western formulation of a "golden age" in civilization—only when philosophy found its voice from the sixth through the fourth centuries, developing a kind of "speech" within written texts to address the abstract nature and significance of cultural values. The rise of writing, Havelock and others claim, was a principal occasion and cause for the enhancement of Greek culture, and surely for the explicit formulations of paternal authority as we know it.

A consistent though unstated assumption in Havelock's analysis is that Greek texts are deciphered and interpreted accurately in terms of propositional logic—at the level, in other words, at which a text functions primarily to advance abstract propositions. A series of narrative details in the *Odyssey* can be reduced to the proposition of, in Havelock's example, "heaven's anger will turn against crimes." A fourth-century philosopher, in contrast, would pursue the idea of discomfort and ill fortune produced by excessive pride through rational argument, dialogue, and dialectics. Homer may render this same proposition richly in a pattern of narrative events, but he cannot clarify the nature of "pride" as Aristotle can, in abstract and exacting terms. Since Havelock's standard for measuring "precision" in the establishment of cultural relevance and significance relies on the form of rational propositions, Aristotle automatically fares better. Homer-the-poet can give only approximate versions of propositions, in a "poetic" medium that is not amenable to shaping exclusively by the structure of logical propositions.

I raise these issues not so much to focus on Havelock's view of the *Odyssey* as because Havelock's position, his identification of oral formulae and other cultural conventions of language in the *Odyssey*, represents the central modern approach to "oral" narratives of this period. His stance is the third of three large-scale attempts to answer the Homeric Question, that is, the question concerning the great difficulty of relating two disparate propositions. The first proposition is that the *Odyssey* was originally an oral performance sung by a man named Homer, as well as by others who drew on oral narrative material from a repertoire developed by previous singers. The second proposition is that the *Odyssey* as we know it, the only way we have ever known it, is a written document, a transcription of the original oral performance that has come down to us through some unknown process. Given both propositions, how can we regard and read this poem "correctly"? That is, how can we connect two such disparate statements about the poem? The Homeric Question specifically concerns the interpretive criteria that should be applied to a written transcription of an oral performance. A similar dilemma involves reviewing a playscript without ever being able to see the performance of that play.

This order of question about texts in relation to the circumstances of composition develops from the same impulse as the nineteenth-century question about the "higher" criticism of the Bible and concurrent philological approaches to written texts. In fact, the first major posing of the Homeric Question occurs in the nineteenth and early twentieth centuries, in the work of scholars called the Analysts. The Analysts read the *Odyssey*, for example, as a sedimented layering of oral composition and subsequent alterations and additions as the poem made the complex transition from oral to written form. The Analysts tended to dismiss the possibility of a single author for such a poem. "Given [the Analysts'] assumption that no one man could have composed the Homeric epics," as Jenny Strauss Clay notes in *The Wrath of Athena*, "they resolved all problems of internal inconsistencies by resorting to theories of multiple authorship" (4). The approach of the Analysts was similar to Havelock's, in that they dismissed problems of structural intention in the poem as resulting from the lack of patterning produced by so many authors.

Subsequently, in the twentieth century, another group of scholars known as the Unitarians argued for a single-author theory of the *Odyssey*, wherein the discrepancies of an ancient text were explained by the overdeterminations and multiple sources of the oral tradition itself. This approach does posit single authorship, and the Unitarians tended to imagine the single and integrated original narrative as altered and revised through the details and accidents of the tradition that transmitted it. Mid-century examples of the Unitarian approach are Denys Page's *The Homeric Odyssey* (1955) and Geoffrey S. Kirk's *The Songs of Homer* (1962), both of which argue for later additions to an earlier Ur poem by Homer. The essence of the Unitarian approach is summed up by Page: "I do believe that somewhere in the dimly seen past there lived a great poet, who fashioned from traditional songs an *Odyssey*" (159).[1] The Unitarians then become reconciled, to a degree, with the Analysts through the work of later scholars who reemphasize the "oral" nature of Homeric poetry. (Havelock is an important representative of this later approach.) Influenced strongly by Milman Parry's *The Making of Homeric Verse: The Collected Papers of Milman Parry* (1971), these scholars of what can be called the Oral Hypothesis attempt to identify the threads of oral tradition woven by the many singers and tellers who have contributed to single narratives. The emphasis on orality and the pure metrical utility of epithets only marginally resumes the focus on intention and poetic vision in local passages and tends not to insist (though does not preclude) that the *Odyssey* could be the work of a single author. In any event, the prospects of single versus multiple authorship or even the poem's structural, or cultural, intention remain largely unresolved in this approach.

For a contemporary reader—that is, one coming after Claude Lévi-Strauss and structural anthropology, and after semiotics and the critique of structuralism—the mere locating of implied propositions, insightful as Havelock's reading of this epic may be, is not necessarily persuasive as a basis for narrative analysis. The abstractions of "logic" may constitute a philosophical discourse and can be intelligible in such terms, but a poem is not intelligible *as a text* if it is reduced to the level of rational propositions in linear sequence. Missing from the strict oral analysis (and I am using Havelock as only representative here) is the consideration of narrative codes—particularly that of value encoded, even encoded problematically, within narrative development. The sense in which the *Odyssey* "speaks" about and represents its culture cannot be limited to the supposed evocation of ideas in brief narrative passages, formulaic conventions of phrasing, and embedded propositions. Havelock focuses on these passages individually and judges them to be virtually undeveloped sections of texts and "primitive" attempts at philosophy as failed (because "before" philosophy) dialectics. He measures this poem against the standard of philosophy as a model implicitly "normal," "clear," "natural," and "civilized," and then judges the Homeric text to be deficient.

It is certainly possible to identify cultural and narrative codes in this poem. Even Havelock and other principal critics agree, in one fashion or another, that motivated action in the *Odyssey* is undertaken within the "just" order of a *polis* run by patriarchs, the city-state as religious, cultural, and political order—the earthly counterpart of the Kosmos and the appropriate discovery of the ethical and moral "good." The frame for these grand orders within the polis is the family; indeed, as Eric Havelock has it, the polis is "the family writ large" (*Liberal Temper* 321). Odysseus oversees the accommodation, or translation, of moral "good" into the ethical dimensions of communal practice. The "noble father" for Homer, thus, is a manifestation of the *ratio divina* (the substance of what the gods know) on earth, the divine intention inherent throughout the Kosmos and (with important qualifications) the ultimate cultural authority of Greek culture. Investigating this poem to apprehend the ultimate values that comprise it as a narrative is what Aristotle calls a "substantial" inquiry, an investigation of form (*eídos*) in the poem, as opposed to accidents that have no impact on narrative structure (issues "quantitative" and "qualitative" in Aristotle's terms) that may not be resolvable anyway.

When Homer calls Odysseus a "noble father," for example, he gives a name to institutional authority in light of the cultural commitments of the Greek world. The person who strives toward the "good" and "noble" life, toward what Plato will describe much later as the classical version of "doing one's own thing" (*Justice* 182), strives toward the good defined by Zeus as "justice" (*dikē*), both the reality of the world's order, how things are, and the need to live in accord with that order. The noble father as a locus of value is an ethical, moral, and epistemological reference in a hierarchy of Greek cultural values that extends from the grandness of the Pantheon and the Kosmos to the intimate ties of family life. This narrative displays a hierarchy of such relationships, and their organization can be deciphered in the act of reading the poem as a narrative. Certainly the structural "authority" to read in a particular way will itself be a cultural effect incomprehensible outside the cultural encodings that Havelock highlights, as well as those that we bring to bear in our own reading strategies.

In what follows, I shall consider four principal narrative units of the *Odyssey*, large structural units that organize the action and situate the cultural values that motivate it. These units correspond to 1) the opening scenes with the gods, where Zeus decides to let Odysseus proceed home; 2) the four books of the Telemakhiad and the presentation of Odysseus as *polutropos*, or man of "many turns," as he wanders in distant lands before returning to Ithaka; 3) the *nostos*, or actual return home, as Odysseus defeats the suitors and reclaims his position as Ithaka's king; and 4) Odysseus's resituated position as patriarch and king in Ithaka. This procedure cannot be divorced from the specific cultural issues Havelock raises about the epic, but it can foreground the act of reading this narrative constituted by what we can call large-scale *lexemes*, the rhetorical and narrative concerns that show the *Odyssey*'s involvement with issues of cultural authority and domination that define the paternal romance.

Zeus Intervenes

The opening lines of the poem establish a tranquil scene in the gods' hall on Olympos. Members of Zeus's own family and officers of state are positioned comfortably around this hall, conversing as they conduct business. Zeus casually meditates on old misfortunes of the Trojan War, long ago ended, and remarks on "Aigisthos, dead / by the hand of Agamemnon's son, Orestes" (1:35–36). This peaceful court scene—peaceful with Zeus himself positioned harmoniously in a community untroubled by major disruption—contrasts sharply with Zeus's memories of Orestes and deep family strife. Poseidon is currently at odds with the other gods over Odysseus's return home, but "now that that god / had gone far off among the sunburnt races" (1:25–26) there is no reason why Odysseus cannot return to Ithaka. So even the one minor conflict that intrudes into this communal scene appears to be under Zeus's control. Zeus continues to think about the death of Aigisthos, the usurper of Agamemnon's household; this thought connects thematically to Athena's entry and her plea for Odysseus, whose house is also marked by domestic strife. In Odysseus's case, too, usurpers need to be routed from a home, and as the narrative sequence of this passage implies, the justice visited upon Aigisthos is also potentially applicable to the suitors in Odysseus's home in Ithaka. Zeus readily grants that Odysseus may return to Ithaka, and Athena begins immediately to set changes in motion.

These well-known opening events of the poem are conventionalized in form and preliminary to the major action. While minor, they are also crucial for establishing motivation and a rationale for the narrative generally. The initial scene on Olympos institutes a decisive viewpoint and frame of communal values for the rest of the poem. This scene shows a hierarchically arranged and integrated community: a patriarch is in charge, and those beneath him are positioned around the court in order of their priority in the Pantheon. This portrait of a successful and functioning community is, of course, exactly the obverse of the broken and disordered Ithaka that will be glimpsed in the next few lines and that will emerge fully in the Telemakhiad. The strong orientation provided by the Olympian community is defined unmistakably by Zeus's preeminent position in it. This opening scene serves as an important reference for the community that Odysseus is trying to reconstitute in his quest to recapture his throne.

This initial scene, in short, immediately creates an implicit contrast between Zeus's Olympian community and Odysseus's Ithakan home and kingdom. In *Archery at the Dark of the Moon* Norman Austin calls this contrast the poem's tendency toward "structural relationships" (85), including an implied but strong reliance on the figure of "contrariety" (121). Jenny Strauss Clay also refers to the logically "contradictory views" that "run deep into the fabric of the poem" (*The Wrath of Athena* 229). The opening opposition, again, as it happens, is a contradictory relation between a community well ordered and one in extreme disarray—between communal generation and destruction. This is the sort of relationship that Aristotle calls *substantial*, in that it characterizes the general state of a subject of inquiry. Through this opposition, the poem implicitly and quickly questions Ithaka's potential as a "generative" and healthy community. This effect is accomplished largely rhetorically as the poem's early lines pose a question that the rest of the poem will answer as Odysseus reaches home, routs the suitors, and reunites his family and kingdom. The *Odyssey* here functions as a kind of commentary on the *Theogony*, the key difference being that Zeus gains his paternal stature almost *sui generis* (although he has lots of help), while Odysseus will recover a *lost* stature, one modeled on the preexistent example of the gods. The poem's large question will be fully resolved when Odysseus's community comes to approximate, at least in broad structural terms, the initial paradigm of a well-functioning community as seen on Olympos in the opening lines.

The contrariety of communities in this initial opposition is quite evident but, at this point, undeveloped. Striking, though, is the power and clarity of the perspective on community. The harmony of the Olympian hall, the assessment of Poseidon's waning objection to Odysseus's return home, and the actual decision to permit that return all situate certain values and a normative viewpoint, established as fundamentally Zeus's perspective. Other perspectives will develop in relation to this "subjectivity" as an important first position. As T. W. Adorno and Max Horkheimer have suggested, this view is a proto-model of bourgeois individualism extremely influential in later Western culture (see their *Dialectic of Enlightenment*). Within the first 200 lines, Zeus's values and communal standards are already established as normative, and his "natural" situating in this position is precisely the gesture of the paternal romance—privileging the paternal metaphor in a way that disguises the privilege.

The Son Responds

Further into the Telemakhiad, the focus is not on the thematics of fatherhood and paternal authority but on the dilemmas of sonship, as this first book appears to restate the initial opposition between communities in terms of a contrast between son and father. Telemakhos is trying to guard his father's interests at home during and after the Trojan War. At first he is demoralized, and we find him staring at an empty horizon as he anticipates his father's return. Athena then appears before him and asks, "Who is your father?"— a question that will continue to circulate in the poem regarding the nature of cultural authority and the world's origin. Her question also coincides with Odysseus's release from Kalypso's island and Penélopê's rekindled anticipation of her husband's return. The poem focuses on a contrast between the son's predicament and the promise of the father's return, and also on the contrast between Ithaka's current degenerative state and the promise of its regeneration when Odysseus returns.

The narrative then moves to Telémakhos's separation from his father, the son's desire for his father's return, and the simultaneous evocation of Odysseus as an absence in the poem. Soon the epic begins to articulate a series of related domestic problems—Penélopê's isolation, Ithaka's falling into ruin—that reiterate the initial situation, giving an increasingly strong sense of the problems that Odysseus's return will solve. The narrative's beginning also concentrates on the fact that Telémakhos's home and land are violated by his mother's suitors; like competing brothers, they ravage the estate and try to murder him. He is not strong enough to disperse them, and his attempts to locate his father have failed. To survive while he waits for Odysseus, Telémakhos emphasizes that he is Odysseus's heir, which would involve calling an "*agora*," or town meeting, and delivering a public appeal for the suitors to stop their pillage (*Justice* 140). At the beginning of the first four books, Telémakhos-as-a-son is defined by his powerlessness.

The source of his paralysis is explained in part by his reply to Athena. After she asks if he is "Odysseus' boy," he replies: "I know not / surely. Who has known his own engendering?" (1:207; 215–16). He thus highlights his father's absence and claims that, though he cannot know his own origin absolutely, he connects the knowledge of origins with fatherhood. One has knowledge, the passage says, by virtue of knowing one's own father; yet paternal absence makes it impossible to gain such true knowledge. So the initial emphasis of the Telemakhiad is on the problematics of sonship. Furthermore, since no less than the first four books of the epic present Telémakhos's domestic troubles, and since the twenty-four books of the epic, as Robert Fitzgerald notes, divide into six "waves of action" (four books in each), one full portion of the poem (one sixth of the whole) shows Telémakhos struggling with the suitors (Fitzgerald, *Odyssey* 494).[2] As we consider that the action of the twenty-four books will mount until Odysseus acts decisively to regain his family and throne in

Books 21–24, it is puzzling that so much space is given to Telémakhos' domestic frustration, which will not directly advance the major action of Odysseus's return. Only in Book 5 will attention shift abruptly away from Telémakhos and toward Odysseus, never really returning to the son.

The emphasis is explained in part by the epic's association of the problematics of sonship with an oppositional relationship. Odysseus, for example, eventually acts to take back his home, but in most respects he is also restricted in action. For blinding the Kyklopes and angering Poseidon, who blocks Odysseus from going home, Odysseus is stranded outside his home, much as his son is imprisoned within it. So whereas his first responsibility as a leader-in-exile is to return to community and family in order to rule again, he cannot do so.

Although Odysseus has been kept from returning to Ithaka because of Poseidon, there is also good reason for Zeus and Athena to be reluctant to help him. The opening lines of the poem say, "Sing in me, Muse, and through me tell the story / of that man skilled in all ways of contending, / the wanderer, harried for years on end, / after he plundered the stronghold / on the proud height of Troy" (1:1–5). Zeus sponsors the administration of justice in the Kosmos and is the official protector of the order of civilization. Athena, likewise, is Goddess of the City and a protector of culture. Both become angry when Odysseus, Sacker of Cities, steals the Trojan Palladion, "the fatal image of Pallas Athena on the possession of which the luck of [Troy] depended" (Rose 238). Odysseus is stranded partly as the result of his own arrogance in announcing his name to the Kyklopes he blinded, but he is blocked from going home primarily because he violated the gods' protection of Troy. Odysseus violated the gods' tie to the polis and to culture itself—the basis of Greek civilization. The Greeks do win the war, but since Odysseus went too far in taking the Palladion and violating the gods' contract with the human community, he must be punished and reoriented. Otherwise, there is little rationale for the "justice" of the gods' detaining him while all others are allowed to go home.

Through his own actions, then, Odysseus has become a cultural outlaw who must find his way back to civilization. Zeus judges that crimes against the fundamental order of culture (dikē itself) do not go unpunished. As a consequence, Odysseus wanders through the many possibilities of human community—the odyssey—into the fringes of civilization. He expiates himself by rediscovering what binds humans together in a community in relation to the gods. Since Odysseus's crime was to deny culture, thereby plundering it, retribution entails wandering through the world to refind the lost foundation on which culture rests.

Therefore, the poem's initial opposition entails more than the terms of father and son, and it is for good reason that Odysseus's dilemma is not essentially different from his son's. Just as Telémakhos waits for Odysseus to return, Odysseus waits for Zeus to intervene on his behalf. Strongly reminiscent of Telémakhos in the first four books, Odysseus sits "with eyes wet / scanning the bare horizon of the sea" (5:86–87), awaiting the actions of paternal authority that he cannot control. As the epic opens on Odysseus in Book 5, he remains a prisoner on Kalypso's island and waits for Zeus to decide when he may proceed to the next step of his education.

If Odysseus is initially positioned in the narrative as being as helpless as Telémakhos, as a "son," then the epic is pointing to the nature of passivity and powerlessness as a prelude to the action that will follow. Initially incapable of suffering the discipline of restraint in Troy, of respecting the "law" that structures the community, Odysseus gains an education by being stranded in exile, as he awaits Zeus's permission to return home. Once he is again positioned in relation to the law, he will have satisfied the text's structural motive and can proceed home. In the later philosophical era of Greek culture, this same emphasis on the instrumental role of passivity as a ground out of which activity grows will be explicit. As G. Verbeke comments, for Aristotle "human activity grows from perfective passivity, through which man's possibilities are actualized" (564)—in the sequence of law, justice, and then human action. Aristotle will even write a treatise, no longer in existence, exploring the relationship of activity and passivity, entitled *Acting and Being Acted Upon* (see *Generation of Animals* 4:4, 768b). Both in Homer's narrative and later in Greek philosophy, passivity as a human posture appropriate for the sublunary world points to the priority of cosmic and communal law in finding one's relation to the "good"—with the emphasis on a higher stability and fixity. In the *Odyssey*, in particular, the ritual of passivity signifies a surrender to the order of justice and the way things are, again suggesting that the passivity accompanying the institution of paternal authority in the poem's early lines creates a crucial reference for knowledge about communal justice and cultural law throughout.

Already in Book 5 it is apparent that Telémakhos's situation is largely Odysseus's; so the seeming leisure of the Telemakhiad's development actually enhances the focus on Odysseus, at least on the structure of Odysseus's position. A "son" begins the epic by gazing toward a fatherless horizon and tries to answer Athena's question

about what it is to know origins. The subsequent narrative oppositions are then charged with questions of value regarding Odysseus's
and Zeus's "absence." Telémakhos's response to paternal absence inau-
gurates the narrative's discourse about the "good" of passivity, or
acquiescence to the law, in relation to paternity. The emphasis on
paternal absence makes the narrative progression appear to originate
with the evocation of fatherhood (*patridos*). That is, the epic creates
a kind of subject position of authority as the narrative's defining
reference from its beginning, and throughout its development a complex of ideas is connected with the father as a manifestation of that
value.

As if to reinforce the importance of the father as the dominant
subject viewpoint, the epic vividly contrasts Odysseus and Telémakhos with characters who want to possess paternal authority without knowing its significance, without positioning it within the polis
or Kosmos, without knowing it as a signifier of communal law.
Whereas Odysseus and Telémakhos are "passive" in a relationship
with the fathers and the invocation of law they await, Penélopê's
suitors reject any such surrender to the law and try to deny their
relationship with Odysseus. With him gone, the suitors could have
chosen, for example, to participate in the reaffirmation of culture
that would be brought about by Odysseus's return (or even by his
failure to return, and the subsequent adherence to ritual and procedure). They would have to protect his empty place at home until
it could be filled by a rightful heir. As Havelock shows, the eight-
step legal procedure for replacing Odysseus as king and husband is
not ambiguous (*Justice* 140–141). Instead, the suitors ransack the
king's home, try to kill Telémakhos, and "illegally" pursue Penélopê,
in each case denying the structural significance of the father's absence
and bypassing the law as a mediating agency. By denying the fact
of Odysseus, who as the visible sign of communal authority administers and preserves "justice," the suitors are acting outside the law
in an absolute sense.

The Law Is Evoked

I have been following the early part of this narrative through the
problematics of sonship. Whether occupied by Telémakhos or Odysseus, the son's position defines a relationship to the law through the
father. In the case of Zeus, the law is explicitly the organizing principles of community in relation to which Telémakhos and Odysseus
are situated. Zeus is a "father" simply in that he organizes the com-

munity of the Pantheon and institutes a system of law that holds the Greek world together. His authority comes originally from Kronos, who rejected the responsibility of procreation by eating Zeus's brothers and sisters (Hestia, Demeter, Hera, Hades, and Poseidon) and who had earlier castrated his own father, Ouranos. When Zeus overthrows Kronos, he does not simply take his father's empty place to eradicate the old order; indeed, his victory does not even destroy his father's authority. Kronos was already trying to destroy "fatherhood" by destroying the children that defined him in that role. By contrast, Zeus actually reinstates the very idea of fatherhood for Kronos by rescuing Kronos's children. In so doing, Zeus reinstates the idea of fatherhood for himself as well, explicitly along the lines of communal order buttressed by familial structure—hence the separateness, but also interdependence, of the family romance and the paternal romance as I discussed them in the Introduction.

In his revolt against Kronos, Zeus even reconstitutes the past as an order by instituting a "cultural" medium in which he can bring back his brothers and sisters. He institutes the new order in which children henceforth will have a position in relation to a scheme of succession in time. Zeus enacts a law of relationality as he breaks Kronos's tyranny and forbids the devouring of children and the destruction of fathers that such devouring brings about. His revolt effects a retrograde reordering of generational relationships, and he creates the possibility for parents' and children's coexistence in a familial order henceforth only partly characterized by temporal succession.

The principle of communal law expressed here says that key oppositions will be deployed to construct hierarchies in the world. Those oppositions serve as formative rules about containment and exclusion, with the "law" at a fundamental level separating past and present, parent and child, king and subject, male and female, and so on, into binary oppositions. When Kronos ate his children, all such oppositions—"difference" itself as a concept—were threatened, and when the Kosmos lacked "difference" it continually relapsed into an order of near Chaos. By defeating Kronos but refusing to destroy him, Zeus thereby instituted difference as succession in time and as a pattern of communal order, instead of the continual obliteration of difference. Opposition and hierarchy organize the Kosmos as an intelligible sphere, so that Zeus effectively re-creates the world for gods and humans alike when he takes control of Olympos, making the Kosmos itself an extended elaboration of the oppositions Zeus institutes in his rule.

The major reinstitution of paternal authority in the *Odyssey* occurs in Odysseus's manner of return from the Trojan War. The precise arrangement of events as he returns to Ithaka is crucial for understanding the significance of this *nostos* and the reinstitution of paternity. On his return, Odysseus first meets Telémakhos and gradually reveals his own identity. Next, disguised as a beggar, he accompanies his son into his own hall and fools the suitors before revealing himself. Assisted by his son, he kills the suitors and turns to purge his household of unloyal serving women. Then, reunited with son and rid of the suitors, Odysseus turns to Penélopê, showing the secret of their marriage bed to prove his identity. (The bed was constructed on a living olive tree.) He visits his old father, Laërtês, while the suitors' angry relatives band together and swear revenge: "we'd be disgraced forever! Mocked for generations / if we cannot avenge our sons' blood, and our brothers!" (24:433–34). Upon Odysseus's return, with a new battle imminent, Athena asks Zeus to "impose a pact on both" Odysseus and the suitors' relatives to bring a lasting peace (24:477). Zeus subsequently answers by proclaiming:

> Odysseus's honor being satisfied,
> let him be king by a sworn pact forever,
> and we, for our part, will blot out the memory
> of sons and daughters slain. . . . (24:482–85)

The fighting barely starts when Zeus, dropping a thunderbolt between the contestants, suddenly halts the dispute. Proclaimed "king in a sworn pact forever," and with the fighting ended, Odysseus is home.

Before Odysseus's return, son and suitors were rivals for dominance in a relationship with Penélopê. Each suitor wanted her hand and her estate, and Telémakhos wanted to make her wait for his father. Without familial hierarchy or communal order and only strife in Ithaka upon his return, Odysseus takes up the conflict as an agent of interdiction on behalf of the polis itself. Killing the suitors, Odysseus invokes the paternal metaphor to make subjects subordinate to him, as if they were sons. Without this interdiction, the killing and the threat of further killing, there would be no law and no social order in the Ithakan community.

Odysseus's gesture only begins to signify the nature of communal law, as is made clear when the suitors' relatives come for another battle. If Odysseus continued to destroy his subjects, as Kronos tried to destroy his children, Odysseus would be destroying community and communal order itself. If the suitors' relatives succeed in killing Odysseus, the ransacked Ithaka ceases to exist as an ordered environment positioned against, in various ways replicating the structure of, Olympos and even the Kosmos. As a conclusion to Odysseus's extended "education," Zeus institutes a new pact for relations between humans and the gods. He replaces the unlimited aggression that made Odysseus an outlaw and almost destroyed his kingdom. Zeus decrees that, since Odysseus has signified the law of priority as a communal order, Odysseus should now honor that law himself by refraining from battle and allowing his subjects to coexist within the realm of the law.

Having in this way killed "sons" to evoke the law of difference, Odysseus served a functional aim. But in such metaphoric constructions "the father . . . too," as Jacques Lacan says, "must submit to the bar [of the law]" (1977, 44). Odysseus himself must then refrain from killing sons, and Zeus's interdiction underlines this necessity in the face of the law. Odysseus and his people are then freed from the burden of past conflict at the very moment the law takes effect, enfranchising the key oppositions of communal order (king/subject, generation/degeneration, etc.). In this way Odysseus's manner of homecoming signifies communal law under the name of paternal authority. By acquiescing to Zeus and by ending the fighting, Odysseus symbolically affirms himself as a son subject to Zeus and cultural authority. In relation to the suitors, Odysseus/father kills son figures but then also refrains from doing so as a means of implementing both dimensions of the paternal metaphor and the law. Odysseus/son, in other words, takes up arms against the suitors and then lays them down to signal obedience to the rule of law by which the community must function. With Zeus, and again with the suitors, Odysseus enacts the principle of opposition and succession through difference that creates communal hierarchies. He signals a relationship of aggression and forbearance (activity and passivity), ultimately deriving his power from his surrender to instituted law. So fundamental is this law that even Zeus binds himself to humans through the principle Odysseus embodies, the very construct of the noble father that Zeus instituted in the revolt against Kronos. This order had to exist prior to Odysseus's return, and it had to be "rediscovered" in the scene of Odysseus's return as a repetition of the law. Otherwise the law would fail to express difference in the oppositions of family and community—thus, the entanglement of cosmic and "personal fate" in Homer's world (Ehnmark 74).

Odysseus Redux

Odysseus's signifying role in reestablishing hierarchies and order in the epic is complex. He is a son in relation to Zeus, a father in relation to Telémakhos and the suitors, a husband to Penélopê, and a mediator between Telémakhos/suitors and Zeus. He is also a son to Laërtês, but this relationship seems less prominent. As he mediates between father and son, Odysseus's functional significance builds on elements drawn from both. In his mediating role as signifier of the law, he occu- a privileged position as the "son" who articulates the connection between father and son and, by extension, the law according to which the community functions. In effect, Odysseus represents a third term in the relations of community. At the epic's beginning Telémakhos alludes to this function when he talks about the import of knowing one's own father, of knowing origins. The character who signifies this knowledge, it turns out, is Odysseus, articulator of the father's law. He represents knowledge about his own engendering in that his return home, as an involved process of signification, articulates the oppo- sitions significant to the cultural origin and stability of the polis.

Odysseus's function in the value system of this poem can be represented in the logic of values imported from Aristotle, a logic implicit in the poem's narrative structure as well. In that oppositional matrix are the "male" ties of the paternal romance, the situating of the father/son opposition, the representation of cultural law, and Odysseus's resituated function in the epic's conclusion (see figure 2). Here the first position (the father) is the subjectivity created not so much in the figure of Zeus, but in the viewpoint associated with values and cultural formations connected with Zeus at the poem's beginning. The position of the son designates not a single character but a relationship to a dominant subject position in the poem—a relationship signified by Telémakhos, Odysseus, and even the suitors (although the suitors finally *fail* to occupy this position). Thereafter, the functional significance of that subject position expressed as cul- tural law is articulated as a key function in the narrative. Finally, the poem's perspective on its own development can be focused on Odysseus's accumulation of signifying functions at its conclusion. Many lines of narrative order pass through him as a character, not because of some mystery surrounding him as a hero, but because his actions signify most directly the cultural order identified with Zeus and the noble father as a concept.

Odysseus's functional role surely signifies not only Zeus's sub- jectivity, but also that of Kronos and the whole line of Greek patri- archs. Odysseus as a character is even related to a visible insignia of the paternal line he represents. Like Kronos, who rejected pro- creation by eating children and actually forestalled the world's emer- gence out of itself, Odysseus once knew a time before struggle. The

1. father   2. son

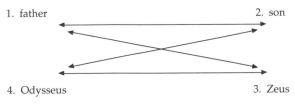

4. Odysseus   3. Zeus

Figure 2.

scar on his leg is a reminder of a childhood event that gave him his
name. This famous sequence is inserted when, disguised as a beggar
on the return to Ithaka, Odysseus sits in his own hall as his old
nurse, Eurýkleia, washes his feet. Following her startled recognition
of her master's identifying scar there appears a narrative interlude
explaining the boy's name and the scar's origin at his first wild boar
hunt.

In this inserted story the maternal grandfather, Autólykos, is
asked to name his grandson. He replies, "Well you know, my hand
/ has been against the world of men and women; / odium and distrust
I've won. Odysseus should be his given name" (19:407–10). The name
can be read as deriving from *odussomai*, in the sense of "angered
at" (*Iliad, Odyssey, and the Epic Tradition* 183), or, as Jenny Strauss
Clay suggests, as *odysasthai*, meaning to have hostile feelings or
enmity toward someone (69–70). In either case, Odysseus is named
as a man of strife and pain, a designation underscored in the boar
hunt that follows.

The hunt scene—still part of this inserted story—is set at Autólykos's home. When Odysseus comes upon a boar, he attacks it and
with his weapon

> . . . had the first shot,
> lunging to stick him; but the boar
> had already charged under the long spear.
> He hooked aslant with one white tusk and ripped out
> flesh above the knee, but missed the bone.
> Odysseus' second thrust went home by luck,
> his bright spear passing through the shoulder joint;
> and the beast fell, moaning as life pulsed away. (19:445–53)

This scene concentrates struggle and reciprocal hurt as Odysseus

thrusts the spear into the boar, and the boar lodges his tusk in
Odysseus's leg. This primal scene of initiation, of sticking and being
stuck, shows the posture of one in fundamental struggle with the
world, playing out the nature of Odysseus's character and presaging
his narrative function at other moments as well. Odysseus's struggle
with the boar suggests activity and passivity in a pattern that will
define his major actions and his substantial development. The opposition between sticking and being stuck will be played out with the
suitors and their relatives in the form of aggression and forbearance.
It is the same activity/passivity schema first played out in Kronos's
revolt against Ouranos, in Kronos's devouring of his children, in
Zeus's rebellion against Kronos, and only later in Odysseus's manner
of reentering Ithaka.

   Odysseus first encounters the terms of his substantial nature as
a kind of subject in relation to communal law under the aegis of
paternal sponsorship at his grandfather's hunt. Autólykos, a paternal
relation but not his father, here sponsors the institution of a rule that
this epic connects to paternal figures. Odysseus's articulation of that
founding relationship in the law of difference is a refinding of, and
a significant channel of reiteration for, paternal authority inscribed
within the structure of narrative.

   By interjecting the boar-hunt incident when Odysseus returns
to Ithaka, the narrative provides an immediate commentary and a
precise comment (Havelock's judgment aside) on the formative nature
of paternal authority as a kind of cultural authorization on several
levels. When Zeus legislates "a sworn pact forever" to stop the fighting
in Ithaka, he reissues the same communal law previously signified
in his own overthrow of Kronos. In effect, as the law's signifier, Zeus
has an origin in a kind of passivity. He also simultaneously "sticks"
and is "stuck" by Kronos, and he repeats that operation when he
rules on the battles in Ithaka—paternal law in this case being, as in
Odysseus's case, a replica, a refinding, of itself in an activity conceived in the terms of (in Aristotle's title) "acting and being acted
upon." Here the convolutions of the father/son opposition suggest
doubling in the reciprocal dimensions of the guest/host relationship:
Telémakhos as host to his disguised guest/father, and Odysseus as
host to the disguised guest/suitors. The suitors will be exposed as
guest/sons, and Zeus will host Ithaka, which is disguised as a community outside of the cosmic order. Douglas J. Stewart describes this
dimension of the *Odyssey* as the "complex study of the possible
ramifications of the guest-host relationship" (188).

   The reiteration of Zeus's and Odysseus's positions in the epic are gestures of a textual positioning of the father's law. The traces of this "law," shown for example in Kronos's reconstituted fatherhood and in the history of Odysseus's scar, suggest an oppositional order intended to "authorize" the noble father as a privileged institution and reference point. Odysseus is passive, yet he mediates the community's dilemma of paternal absence and the subsequent institution of law. His scar is a "bar" of signification: nothing in itself, but a representation of difference associated with the force of paternal authority and prestige in this narrative. That Laërtês believes his son has come home only when he sees the scar on Odysseus's leg pointedly suggests the function of Zeus's subject position as a privileged signifier of values. The dual significance of the scar as an identifying mark functioning as a sign of belonging *and* of castration—of empowerment and loss, activity and passivity—reiterates the two dimensions (sticking and being stuck) of the paternal metaphor.

Beyond the Law

The *Odyssey* is a narrative dedicated to placing the father in the subject's position, the prime gesture of the paternal romance. It does critique the noble father, however, by inscribing cultural discourses not directly governed by the law. Even though the epic clearly dramatizes a particular alignment of communal order and paternal authority, it also shows traces of an order in which the community is not exclusively bound to the oppositions authorized by the great father. This view of a pre- (or even "extra-") paternal world is opened when Odysseus, about to embark on the principal voyage that brings him home, receives sailing instructions from Kirkê, the female god who has turned his men into swine. The most detailed of her instructions concerns the strait of Skylla and Kharybdis. Kirkê explains that, to survive the strait, Odysseus must take note that on the Skylla side

> . . . . is a sharp mountain
> piercing the sky, with stormcloud round the peak
> dissolving never, not in the brightest summer,
> to show heaven's azure there, nor in the fall.
> No mortal man could scale it, nor so much
> as land there, not with twenty hands and feet,
> so sheer the cliffs are—as of polished stone. . . .
> (12:74–80)

The insuperable Skylla cliff houses a female monster (a hydra) that prohibits encroachment on this domain. Humans may sail close to the rock, cautiously maneuvering by, but they can neither ignore nor

conquer it. Also at the top of the cliff is a "stormcloud" that blocks
the sky, so that nothing beyond the rock can be viewed or understood
by "mortal man."

On the other side of the strait, Kirkê continues,

>...........................Kharybdis lurks below
> to swallow down the dark sea tide. Three times
> from dawn to dusk she spews up
> and sucks it down again three times, a whirling
> maelstrom; if you come upon her then
> the god who makes earth tremble could not save you....
>
>   (12:104–9)

Her description of the maelstrom opposes that of the rock. The
maelstrom has moments of relative stability within a cycle of sucking
and spewing; change is its only real "fixity." Where the rock drives
things away and breaks them with its force, the maelstrom accepts
everything to satisfy its appetite.

Frequently in this epic, versions of cultural law are instituted
as repetitions or as archaeological "refindings" of paternal law, and
the strait of Skylla and Kharybdis is one such refinding. Just prior
to his final turn toward home, Odysseus must navigate between the
forceful Skylla and ever-shifting Kharybdis, through a dilemma characterized by fixity and change. This opposition foreshadows the two
sides of the paternal metaphor, even though in Kirkê's description of
Skylla, Kharybdis, and the open strait between them the law as a
function of culture is still ambiguous. Ingesting everything indiscrim-
inately, Kharybdis acts outside the prescribed economy or cultural
pattern of law that has dominated the epic so far. Skylla's rigidity
suggests a generalized sense of interdiction (nothing so specific as
paternal interdiction) in that Skylla is an indiscriminate destroyer
who recognizes no limits. While Homer generally aligns activity with
male and passivity with female, here activity and "aggression" are
female and the maelstrom is male, suggesting that the cultural versions of these forces are not yet fully constructed.

Evident in the Skylla-and-Kharybdis passage is the possibility
of a dimension other than the strictly paternal, an "otherness" of
indeterminant positions not encompassed by paternity as a closed
economy. The otherness of this passage can be seen as even escaping
the father's ordered economy with the contrary assignment of positions. Arthur Lovejoy describes the earliest Greek foreshadowings of
a "great chain of being" in the sense "that all quantities—lines, sur-
faces, solids, motions, and in general time and space—must be continuous, not discrete" (55). Substantial relations must be in harmony

with paternal reference. The escape from paternal order in this narrative is an escape from that linearity and predictability, from the noble father as immutable pattern—a possibility represented here by the economy of chance and a renegade order of the contingent. In the Skylla/Kharybdis passage these references are not paternalized; they represent the possibility of error and deviation, not as mere mishap but as a different order. This passage, in effect, shows a direction away from paternal order, a gap, a moment of free play that functions as the possible marker of an emergent discourse.

Other nonpaternal moments occur in this epic as well. Kirkê, for example, describes the Wandering Rocks, suggesting the thwarting of fixed orientations and the potential of being permanently separated from the cultural order. The Kyklopes, cannibal and transgressor of the polis, is a figure without knowledge of civilization or the law. He has a father in Poseidon and presumably belongs to a community of similar creatures, but the narrative defines him by his violation of those specific communal norms sponsored by Zeus and signified in Odysseus's actions. A specifically a-paternal pattern is depicted in Penélopê's predicament. While Odysseus fights in the Trojan War, waits in exile, and then wanders the Mediterranean on his way home, she is isolated by the onslaught of the suitors. Her own version of "wandering" is figured in her loom, in her weaving in circles, ahead and back, done and undone, woven and unwoven, in an anti-pattern that keeps her free of other schemes. Her marginalization in the paternal order is not voluntary, yet she, by temporizing, demonstrates the potential of an emergent contrary order. Like Kharybdis cycling through random eruptions, Penélopê enacts disruption, a possibility that will be realized as a separate counterorder or assimilated as a momentary lapse back into the paternal economy.

It would be a mistake to view the female, a-linear gestures here as defined merely through exclusion from paternal authority—as merely oppositional. These are emergent attempts to subvert the noble father, suggesting the continual pressure of another order, an emergent discourse existing in relation to a hegemonic one. This other order takes the form of metonymic relations in contrast to a metaphoric, hegemonic order, a relationship simultaneously a "part" of that discourse and yet its "other." Especially the force of Kharybdis attests to an important countersource of resistance in the epic—resistance to the complete appropriation of all orders of difference within a rational scheme. The persistence of a counterforce to Zeus indicates the still emergent nature of this alternative order.

Another sign of an alternative subjectivity or view is Odysseus himself. This key signifier of the noble father lacks a prescribed orientation as he wanders. Odysseus is a prime signifier of Zeus's authority and the law, embodying the principle of community in the epic. At the same time, while on the journey home he lacks an innate sense of (patriarchal) direction and purpose, wandering dangerously until Zeus maneuvers him toward Ithaka. In this mode, resisting paternal authority even as he takes the way back, Odysseus is himself an errant signifier. As such, he also takes up the female's position by moving counter to and away from the noble father. It is as if he is working against linearity and authority; as if, in being lost, he is against returning home. Such a paradox shows Zeus's point about the subordinate nature of humanity when, in Book Eight of the *Iliad*, he characterizes the world as passively without orientation in relation to his own fixed (super-male) point of reference. (I shall discuss this further in the next chapter.) The female order persists as competition for Zeus, but it also stands in opposition to—as the "other" to—the fact of Zeus as a male god. It is part of the logic of ideology in this tradition that the "otherness" of the fourth position either will be reabsorbed into the dominant discourse, or it will break off and form a new discourse. Finally, this view of otherness within the *Odyssey* as assimilable difference or as radical alterity, even in Odysseus's journey home, is not utterly suppressed or obliterated. The noble father, after all, is a fiction, not an all-encompassing force.

An even greater paradox is that the Kosmos only exists by virtue of an inherent opposition to the paternal law, as is shown in the Skylla/Kharybdis scene. The Greek concept of difference depends on the violations of paternal authority; otherwise there is no such thing as difference to be signified by the law. Without difference, the father's power to signify from the position of the speaking subject would have no force, no significance. Gynecological texts of the fifth century, for example, return to this issue with great clarity and address the authority of male doctors to voice truths about female bodies, as the next chapter will demonstrate.

Finally, Odysseus's passivity, and the opposition of passivity and activity as marking the limits of cultural discourse, are evoked explicitly when Odysseus asks Kirkê for final sailing instructions. Her advice on navigating the Skylla/Kharybdis strait is that Odysseus can be destroyed by going too far toward either side, smashed and attacked by the hard rock and hydra or swallowed and crushed by the maelstrom. But, she goes on, there exists no perfect middle course: Odysseus must venture near one side or the other and suffer the loss thus entailed. Her instructions are unequivocal: "hug the cliff of

Skylla" (12:110). As if addressing a subversive female in the Greek world, she tells Odysseus to commit himself to the potential of the law (here not fully realized) even though he will lose men to the hydra: "Better to mourn / six men," Kirkê notes, "than lose them all, and the ship, too" (12:111–12).

Odysseus responds by asking how to overcome Skylla and Kharybdis. Kirkê reaffirms Odysseus's passive role in relation to Zeus as the super "male" and the law: "Must you have battle in your heart forever? / The bloody toil of combat? Old contender, / will you not yield to the immortal gods?" (12:118–20). By heeding her advice and "hugging" the cliff, Odysseus takes an assigned position and assents, "yields," to the paternal metaphor that he will eventually act in accord with. To act in the Kosmos, Kirkê says, means traveling toward the paternal reference and making oneself subject to the fixity of the law inscribed in those relations.

The great achievement of the *Odyssey* resides in its narrative of *apparent* paternal inevitability and inflexibility, an economy of patriarchal values that seems to encompass all possibilities within culture. All patterns of sense and nonsense, the communal and the primitive, the sanctioned and the unsanctioned, lead back, or *appear* to lead back, to the legitimacy of a paternal figure in the speaking subject's position. What is beyond the law in this narrative—Skylla and Kharybdis, women, and aspects of Odysseus's behavior on the journey home—is made to appear insignificant and on the margins of what can be known and acted upon as "paternal." However, the "inevitability" of patriarchal values, even according to this epic, is not a "natural" and immutable feature of *phusis*. Such values are not an unalterable structural feature of nature and narrative, but a specific achievement of the paternal romance in Greek culture.

The paternal romance, finally, is but a cultural artifact given shape and force within this narrative of "many turns." Its apparent inevitability as a cultural force is achieved not through the advance of logical propositions (the structure of the *Odyssey* on which Havelock and others have focused) but by the performative qualities of the narrative itself. That is, the narrative establishes a hierarchy of values that promote patriarchal interests and investments as "natural" and "true." What the *Odyssey* highlights, moreover, is not disinterested knowledge about the father (although Odysseus does seek knowledge) but the institution and exercise of power, the enacting of possibilities that advance the father as a subject and block the attribution of legitimacy to all that lies outside of that association.

This early Western epic promotes the noble father as a reality of the Kosmos and as the inevitable form that the "good" will take in the sublunary world. The *Odyssey* demonstrates, furthermore— if we read it by "remembering" the question of the *father*—the oppositional matrix required for advancing the noble father. Homer shows the appropriation of the world as female matter by the authority of male form. As the *Theogony* also attempted to show, the noble father in the Homeric texts is an effect of power and the playing out *not* of an inevitability, but of an ideological commitment expressed in narrative terms.

Notes

1. Few critics want to be classified as purely Unitarian, or neo-Unitarian, which could imply that they lack the sophisticated techniques of oral analysis. But prominent critics associated with the Unitarian position are B. C. Dietrich in *Death, Fate, and the Gods*; Paolo Vivante in *The Homeric Imagination* and *Homer*; Jasper Griffin in *Homer on Life and Death* and *Homer: The Odyssey*; and George E. Dimock in *The Unity of the "Odyssey."* Surely the most influential neo-Unitarian who also employs oral analysis is Norman Austin in *Archery at the Dark of the Moon*.

2. In *The Homeric Odyssey*, see pp. 52–81, "The Beginning of the *Odyssey*." Page sees great inconsistencies in the narrative of the first two books of the *Odyssey* and believes there is evidence of tampering with the narrative by subsequent editors.

CHAPTER THREE

Aristotle and the Gendered Subject

Tota mulier in utero.
("Woman is nothing but a uterus")
—ANONYMOUS GRECO-LATIN PROVERB

The body sick with desire.
—SORANUS, GYNEAECOLOGY, I, 30

[Aristotle saw that] the relation between men and women is
"political."
—MICHEL FOUCAULT, THE HISTORY OF SEXUALITY, I

This chapter will discuss the classical conception of the "subject" in the specifically Aristotelian sense relating to scientific
inquiry—what can be talked about and known in scientific terms.
This continues the discussion begun in chapter 1. Although I say
"subject," the *hupokeimenon* as the subject of scientific inquiry is not
precisely parallel to the knowing subject of modern philosophy or
cultural studies.

Aristotelian and Western ideas of logic and coherence, seemingly
abstract and austere in their formulation, are ideas that reflect fundamental distinctions Aristotle makes about the Greek model of the
body. While Aristotle argues for canons of logical soundness and
consistency in various texts on logic—particularly in the *Organon*,
the *Physics*, and the *Metaphysics*—he silently draws his arguments
out of the "logic" of bodily form that defines being female or male
in such texts as *Generation of Animals* and *Historia Animalium*.
Drawing on gender differences, he afterward establishes prerequisites
for critical observation and thinking, ultimately canons for logical

rigor that become part of the Western project of scientific thinking—the "self-imposed task," as Evelyn Fox Keller describes of Plato, too, of forging "a theory of knowledge that is immune to the subversive powers of the irrational, that allows mind to achieve transcendence even while it remains compromised by immanence" (22). In what follows I shall examine the logical relations of Aristotle's *hupokeimenon*, the subject as a model of what critical thinking can know. I shall then isolate Aristotle's assumptions about logical "form" (*eídos*) and the body, particularly the female body as known through classical gynecology. Finally, I shall discuss Aristotle's active suppression of the female body in logic and his silent instituting of the male body as the model of scientific and cultural authority. My ultimate goal will be to define the ideological relationships that link scientific rigor and the classical idea of the body—formulations that still contribute to thinking about the subject in modern science and in contemporary versions of cultural studies.[1]

The *Hupokeimenon*

I start with Aristotle on some philosophical problems that at first will seem quite distant from thinking about gender. In defining the scope of scientific knowledge in the *Metaphysics*, for example, Aristotle tries to resolve two pressing epistemological issues before he can define how we know anything scientifically. He allows that the world can be projected in two models: as unchanging and static, or as forever in motion. If unchanging and unyielding of its patterns, either to the senses or to reason, the world forecloses the prospect of critical investigation. Nothing can be known of it. If the world is purely in motion, any subject of inquiry will be unreliable and idiosyncratic "knowledge" about an already changed state of affairs. Whether fixed *or* incessantly in motion, the world will vex a critical observer who then cannot legitimately articulate scientific or critical knowledge about anything.

Within the terms of this dilemma, certainly in the footsteps of Plato, Aristotle creates a dialogue between Parmenides' view of the world as fundamentally "unified" and unchanging and Heraclitus' perspective on a world utterly in flux. Either option will only distort the very world and the relation to form (*eídos*) it was supposed to represent or accurately model. The resultant *aporía* concerns the dilemma of the one unified world as opposed to the many-faceted world-in-flux, the world-as-monolith as opposed to the world-in-continual-motion, and contrasts the knowable *same* (*tauto*) of understanding to the unknowable other, *an* other (*heteron*) of change.

In some logical works, especially the *Metaphysics* and *Physics*, Aristotle then goes on to theorize the subject as it bears on language and logical relations, with no confusion between the subject as *knower* and the subject as *that which is known*. Aristotle does not use *hupokeimenon* to refer to the knowing subject. Yet he takes the "subject" of knowledge as anything but obvious or "given," arguing against the notion of a commonsensical line-of-sight for observation in experience. To approach a "subject" of inquiry in a scientific manner, rather, he specifies a set of operations required for reliable scrutiny, clarifying at every point that these assumptions are open to rational investigation. In contrast to Aristotle's position is that of Parmenides and Plato, particularly Parmenides' notion of the world "Being . . . one and . . . nothing else" (*Metaphysics* 1:5,986b9–987a2). In claiming that unity is manifest directly in the ideas that structure the intelligible world, Parmenides gives the world a single face in a model more monist and unified than even Plato suggests. For Plato, the intelligible world is positioned by perfect ideas regardless of how they are perceived.

Aristotle objects to this approach. If we assume the existence of idealized forms directly in relation to their manifestation, as Parmenides does, then we must also assume the continual recreation of new ideas in order to account for the emergence of new appearances in the world, the ongoing fact of new discoveries and knowledge. Without the generation of new ideas, which neither Parmenides nor Plato proposes, there would be no explanation for emergent knowledge. Aristotle sees this problem as the inevitable result of Plato's and Parmenides' position concerning the world's closed system of forms (*Metaphysics* 1:6,988a).

At the other extreme is Heraclitus' position on the instability of knowledge. In the *Metaphysics*, Aristotle describes Heraclitus's position by saying "that the whole sensible world is always in a state of flux" and that from this viewpoint "no scientific knowledge [*epistēmē*] of [the world]" is possible (1:6,987b). Aristotle even notes that from Heraclitus' viewpoint not only can one not "enter the same river twice"—it "cannot be done even once" (4:5,1010a).

It seems odd at first that Aristotle does not dispute this position; indeed, he grants "that there is nothing permanent in respect of quantity" in phenomena (4:5,1010a). In the absence of a well-defined subject, "predications [*katēgoríai*] must proceed to infinity" (*Metaphysics* 4:4,1007b). Heraclitus is apparently right in claiming that indeterminacy reflects a certain epistemological slippage in the world, the Kosmos' failure to ground directly what Aristotle calls the quantitative

and qualitative characteristics of anything. However, when we put
a set of substantial relations in place—in effect, defining a subject
of inquiry, what it is fundamentally we are looking at in order
to connect the accidents of experience—the attribution of quantity
to a subject under inspection then expresses not the accidents of detail
but the aspects of form that actually make up that phenomenon.
Aristotle's argument is that scientific knowledge cannot be of details
and accidents, because these are infinite in their variety and can be
investigated without end. Investigation must be of the natural representation of form itself, for "it is by the *form* [*eídos*] that we
recognize everything" (4:5,1010a). In this qualification of Heraclitus'
position, indeterminacy and the subsequent infinite regress of *quantity* in apprehension result from the lack of a definition of what is
be-ing investigated (the *hupokeimenon*) and an absence of clear pre-
suppositions about what will be of ongoing interest to scientific
investigation.

Aristotle then settles the issue of indeterminacy, still without
actually contradicting Heraclitus, by positing the existence of a scientific viewpoint that scrutinizes a subject of inquiry. That viewpoint
will consistently take a particular—I will argue "male"—form. As
definitions, both the scientific perspective and the subject of inquiry
are invariant in their structure, while they remain adaptable to the
specifics of particular phenomena and texts. Aristotle's notion of a
scientific subject of investigation, what John Peter Anton aptly calls
the subject as "distributive being" (10), draws on the strengths but
not the weaknesses of both the Parmenidean and the Heraclitean
positions. It implies a subject predictable in form but able to respond
to and, in a sense, encompass diversity—unchanging in form (*eídos*),
but reformulable in terms of accidents related to form (quantity and
quality). This "subject" can encompass the "substrate" or "matter"
of an argument, providing a matrix of assumptions and delimitations
that governs the diverse possibilities for representing a particular text
or series of propositions. Details (quantity) do not ground knowledge
with any certainty, as Heraclitus also said. In fact, in their
ungrounded state, mere details allow an infinite regress of interpretive
frames and conclusions. Aristotle adds, however, that patterns (*eídos*)
of understanding do situate the matrix of a subject as a definition of
something to know. That situating establishes a stable frame for
critical and scientific inquiry.

Thus the character, or particular qualities of a scientific subject,
will reside in its form. Within the idea of form, suggested in the word
eídos, is what Aristotle calls the subject's "substance" (*ousía*), a central

set of recognized logical operations displayed in the pattern of what Aristotle calls "contradiction." "Contradiction" formally describes the state of tension wherein two terms cannot coexist; one must be canceled for the other to be deployed, as in the contradictions (*antiphasis*) of just versus unjust, generation versus degeneration, good versus bad. That is, the *substance* of a general pattern of a subject cannot be both "just" and "unjust" at the same time. Qualitative distinctions (light and heavy, wet and dry, cold and hot) and quantitative distinctions about completeness and incompleteness in number (e.g., a person with two arms, two legs, etc.) contribute to the relations of this substance, but they cannot in themselves effect its definition as something to be known. A "substantial" or structural change—what Aristotle calls *metabolē*—will always revise the largest contradictory opposition (the polarized states) that actually defines a subject's substance or structure (*Physics* E:1,225a1).

In the *Categories*, Aristotle designates the subject in a further sense. He distinguishes between the limited sense of the *hupokeimenon* as the grammatical subject in a sentence and the larger sense of subject as a whole constellation of opposed relations, "subject" here being what Anton calls "the locus of processes" (60). Aristotle identifies this "first principle" of oppositional relations as occurring at the moment of instituting a contrary relation (*Metaphysics* 1:5,986b) and, in fact, gives "male" and "female" as the primary examples of a contrary opposition (9:8,1058a). The first position of the contrary relationship, ideally considered, actually creates the logical channels for all subsequent developments—only after the "contrary" relation has been articulated can the other oppositional relations form in sequence. Aristotle is quite clear on this issue when he says, in *The Generation of Animals*, that "there is nothing in any argument which does not start from the first principles belonging to the particular subject" (2:8,748a). By this he means the initiation of the subject-in-process (the subject as what is known) in the first contrary relationship.

This emphasis on the first position of the sequence is consonant with attempts—by St. Thomas Aquinas, for example—to view Aristotle's work on oppositional logic as a theory of language understood discursively as "enunciative speech," scientific understanding as the articulation of an utterance within a particular context of utterances and the critical relations within which such utterances are situated (see Schleifer 1987). (Aquinas, in his commentary on *On Interpretation*, even suggests the alternative title of "Enunciative Speech" for this work; see Oesterle 1962.) Aquinas and Cardinal Cajetan (thirteenth- and fifteenth-century editors of Aristotle) highlight Aristotle's sequence of oppositions as a cross-indexed interpretive grid of the "natural" relations of critical understanding. They follow Aristotle's own suggestions for a discursive heuristic given in examples such as the "Man is just" case from *On Interpretation* (10:19b–20a), where Aristotle advances his logical procedures as a general interpretive algorithm, as follows. (Here I am using Harold P. Cook's emendation of the passage in the Loeb edition.)

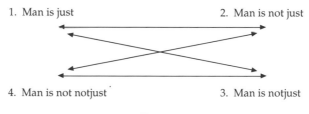

Figure 3.

This arrangement does not precisely match the other logical sequences Aristotle develops, and Aristotle did advance several variations on this logical progression. In each version, however, usually the first two propositions are "universal" considerations, and the third proposition is affirmative as a "particular" consideration. The second proposition is the "universal" contrary, and the fourth is the "particular" double negative. Evident in most instances is the same sequence of contrariety and contradiction and then a double negation in the final proposition ("not notjust").

An especially telling example for showing the importance of value orientation in the positions in the square is Aristotle's "All men are white" example from *On Interpretation* (7:17b16). Reading the propositions clockwise shows their relation to each other in three kinds of binary opposition. Between propositions 1 and 2 a contrary relationship (in this case, privative) creates a double relationship of disjunction based on the presence or absence of whiteness. Between 1 and 3 is a contradictory relationship (the substantial dimension of a subject) with no mediation possible. And between 1 and 4 there is a shared situation of competing propositions; that is, they make assertions that are not logical antitheses of each other.

The first proposition in the sequence dictates the value relations that give form to the others. What is being discussed is presented

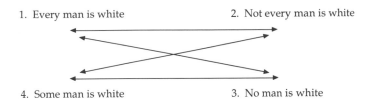

Figure 4.

with an angle on or interpretation of meaning as it will be articulated through the square's other three positions. In this way, the square as a whole structure plays out the logical relations of the first proposition as they can be realized on the square's other three corners.

The second proposition of this example, "Not every man is white," has the specific function of providing "limits and extremities" for relations in the square (Anton 57). The second term in this case lacks the feature of complete whiteness. In this lack it establishes a set composed of white and non-white men, but it excludes the option of *only* white men. Adding the second position to the first creates a range of reference larger than that implicit in the first and, in this case, negates the exclusive set without differences, what Aristotle calls "*isonomoi*"—"citizens" or "men who are the same." "White men" then reemerges as a member in a set, along with other possibilities.

The third proposition then "contradicts" "Every man is white" with "No man is white." This contradiction specifies two distinct states in relation to which degrees of change (articulated on the first axis) could be seen. Here "Every man is white" and "No man is white" are opposed, as are "generation" and "destruction" in more generally applicable terms, to the idea of the subject's "substance." The principle of contradiction defines the subject's "substantial" relations. "Some man is white" completes the square with a specific contradiction of the second proposition on the first level. The fourth term draws structural relations from the other positions into a new position, therein neutralizing the opposition of the other three in what is essentially a new primary reference. This furthest reach of the square closes its logical operation by putting into play an ultimate logical possibility. It also goes beyond the square's logic as if to "escape" the other oppositional relations. By this I mean that this

proposition raises the possibility of a completely new set of oppositions in relation to a new "subject" reference and a new set of
(heterogeneous) positions *other than*—contradictory to—the ones
articulated on this square's first level. The fourth position can also
be interpreted as the complement of the first proposition. Remember
here Aristotle's prior dismissal of the fourth term as a logical necessity
but a practical impossibility.

The square's positions form a scaffolding of opposition rising
above, suppressing, and escaping the expanse of the heterogeneous
possibilities they channel and control. "Some man is white" comes
into the square as the specific instance of interpretation in a new set,
the potentially disruptive but also neutralizing instance that the
square was suppressing through its formal oppositions. The square's
logic, thus, generates the fourth position even while the entailment
of that position creates an opening to escape the rectilinear certainties
of the square's other relations. This example demonstrates how values
inevitably are hierarchicalized in oppositional relations in that each
of the square's propositions marks off and reorients a previous reference, which, in turn, enables a further relational reorientation. The
analysis generated by this reorientation is formally restricted. The
square's oppositional "system," as Anton says, renders difference intelligible by submitting "all the differences to . . . the [rational] principle
of contrariety, which in turn becomes the pivot-point for relating,
organizing, and systematizing differences" (86). The result is a "system" of values arranged in a hierarchy of functions, all with different
positions in relation to the first, the position that initiates the structuring of the other relations.

Even Aristotle's choice of "Every man is white" as a test case
is not value free. This example in itself is a statement of value and
reveals a cultural orientation. Page duBois shows, in her analysis of
Greek art and ideology, that "male" and "white" are particularly
revealing selections as the primary terms in a set of oppositions
generated by Athenian culture as "male/female," "light/dark,"
"Greek/barbarian," and "human/animal." The superior first term in
each case promotes the ideological position of (white) Athenian males
over the non-white, non-Athenian, non-male possibilities (4).
Whereas Aristotle's example has the appearance of notional inno-
cence, duBois argues that its articulation is aligned to advance political ends.

Aristotle's oppositional thinking here reflects the influence of
the pre-Socratics, particularly Pythagoras, as evidenced in the
Pythagorean Table of Opposites. Pythagoras composed a grand

scheme of oppositions that were supposed to serve as the scaffolding for the structure of all knowledge. This Table of "all" significant oppositions was advanced by the pre-Socratic philosophers to represent the "oppositional" form of the Kosmos itself, exactly the oppositional underpinning of reality and intelligibility. Their source could well have been Hesiod, particularly in the *Theogony*, where so many genealogies proceed by some variant of opposition. These oppositions—finite/infinite, odd/even, one/many, right/left, male/female, resting/moving, straight/curved, light/darkness, good/bad, and square/rectangular—as G. E. R. Lloyd notes in *Polarity and Analogy*, line up in large "opposed" groups so that we see "right, male and light on the side of limit and the good, and . . . left, female and darkness on the side of the unlimited and evil" (48). This double alignment points up the structural conditions that would automatically advance the "rightness" and natural priority given to maleness in defining a subject of inquiry and also the privileged scientific perspective, or ultimate cultural authority, in interpretive procedures.

Insofar as the *hupokeimenon* is the "subject" of propositions, it is an abstract pattern of relations, including the entailments of those relations. The *hupokeimenon* specifies that which may be also a site of scientific speech in a cultural text as it creates the form of knowledge and what can actually be communicated, the site where priorities are established in a given text as the form for cultural (scientific) speech. As a matrix, or substratum of discourse, the *hupokeimenon* coordinates what can be said initially in relation to what can be said later, or what is implied initially in relation to what cannot be said later or at any particular moment. The *hupokeimenon*, in other words, specifies that which may be "spoken" and also "heard" from a text in a particular culture. "Allowed" and culturally legitimate speech and knowledge, the *hupokeimenon* is what can actually be "voiced" in relation to the boundaries of representation in culture. When the *hupokeimenon* as the subject of science speaks, it is speech necessarily *for* the culture to which it belongs. As speech, this voicing is the perceptible embodiment or representation of cultural authority, the possibility of speech that gives access to sanctioned values and reigning ideological commitments.

In *On Interpretation* and the *Metaphysics*, in sum, Aristotle advanced that an act of understanding, properly conceived, is a complex series of abstract affirmations and negations capable of engaging with and describing the world. The Greek notion of "fate" as the speech of the gods—said or advanced as a decree by Zeus or Moira—captures this dimension of privileged understanding or voicing in the *hupokeimenon*. The linear logic of such reasoning is what Susan Handelman calls the "Greco-Christian ontotheological mode of thinking" (168)—Aristotle's fundamental belief that everything "sayable" is a quality or quantity in the economy of the subject as what can be known in critical terms.

Aristotle's logical texts are surprisingly clear in their constitution of a theory of the subject as the "scientific" arrangement within a hierarchy of values, so that each dimension of oppositional relations is a formalized utterance in speech. The subject is a "locus of processes" and logical functions, and insofar as that constellation is the ordered, syntactical speech of cultural representation, the subject itself is structured as a text of oppositional relations. Each proposition as a syntactical juncture corresponds to a cultural position of value, meaning that the voicings of the *hupokeimenon* are aligned with assigned values that actually anchor and identify aspects of Greek culture. We can readily reconfigure Aristotle's oppositional relations as the positions of enunciative speech and the directional relations among those positions.

Figure 5 displays the progression of contrary, contradictory, and double-negative relations apparent in other such versions of Aristotle's oppositional square. Here the first position of the speaking subject ("I who speak") is hierarchically privileged in that what follows unfolds the entailments of that position. The values assigned to each of the three succeeding positions have the double relation of a movement *away from* the first position of the speaking subject and *toward* the fulfillment of the subject's logical potential. Placing "male," "female," and other such terms in this grid of relations, we would discover that these positions signify actual cultural priorities and values for the agents that occupy those positions. The emphasis here on discourse, the relations of subject and object (though Aristotle

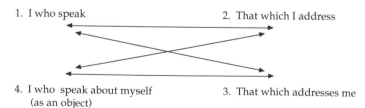

Figure 5.

does not oppose subject and object as such), and the discourse between the subject and its other (*heteron*) reiterate oppositionally, and "scientifically," what can be known in the situating of cultural values.

Just as Aristotle's sequence of relations can interpret the positions of cultural voicing, or "enunciation" as Aquinas wants to say, it can allegorically represent the same positions in epic narration. (This is, in fact, what I tried to show in the *Odyssey* in the previous chapter.) In figure 6, the position of "I who speak" identifies the function, if not always the exact mode, of the hero in narrative— the hero as the point of convergence for different strands of thematic and narrative development, the hero as the privileged "locus of processes." "That which I address" then defines the hero's mode of action, perhaps in relation to a companion, but also indicating how the hero is situated in a particular *agon* or situation. The object a hero struggles in relation to, including what the hero stands to achieve, points to the narration's ultimate motive or reason for being. "That which addresses me" functionally identifies the donation of power from some external source and substantial change in the hero so that he can overcome the object-dilemma posed in the narrative. "I who speak about myself" describes the hero's fortune as a final situating and understanding of the initial predicament or endeavor—more precisely, the final disclosure of the hero as a locus of reconfigured relations. In this way, "enunciative" logic is also the logic of narrative positioning and voicing.

Aristotle's formal handling of oppositional relations in his theory of the subject potentially answers the difficulty of reconciling Parmenides with Heraclitus. Classical epistemology generally holds the belief that "the object of knowing" and "the intuition of the knowing subject must be stable" for the critical acquisition of knowledge to

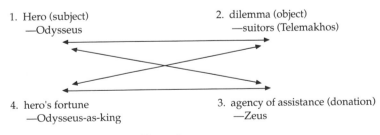

Figure 6.

be possible, which is to say that the act of "knowing may not be affected by movements of the body nor by passionate elements" (Verbeke 560). Knowledge (*epistēmē*) must possess a stable quality precisely because it stands in relation to the "good," and the "good" is not in a state of becoming. If knowledge is to approximate the state of the good, therefore, it must copy the fixity of the good, even if the act of doing so necessarily takes place in a world of apparent motion. God's perspective on substantial relations, if it could only be adopted, would automatically show that there is truth and pleasure to be taken "more in stability than in movement" (Verbeke 563).

For Aristotle, I am arguing, there is a homology between the idea of a first position or foundation in logic and the ontological foundation of the "good" in the world, the "good" and the *hupokeimenon* being logical representations of ontological and epistemological firstness. This is not to say that Aristotle makes this association explicitly, or that he in any way deliberately advances such a connection. Rather, it is the logic of the subject to be centered as a prime reference in the hierarchies of reasoning and rational interpretation, a significant model in epistemology for the centeredness and hierarchical organization of the polis as well as the Kosmos. The logic of the subject even suggests a foundation for the institution of cultural law, for without the subject there is no critical discrimination (*diakresis*) about the significance of difference and the subsequent elaborations of culture and truth as they are known to Greek culture. And without the apprehension of difference, there is simply no hierarchy of values and no cultural law. The *hupokeimenon* as a construct catches the sense of cultural order in the most local and also in the broadest cultural terms.

The Logic of Gender

I have been discussing Aristotle's conception of the subject in *On Interpretation* and the *Metaphysics* and several other texts—logical texts that, I will show, draw their principal references from Greek gynecology and theories of the body. Along with temple practitioners under Asclepius (the God of Healing) and teachers in the gymnasia, philosophers such as Aristotle (also the son of a physician) could contribute significantly to the general store of Greek theory and knowledge about medicine. His contributions coincide largely with medical science as compiled by the followers of Hippocrates (460–380 B.C.), the great doctor of antiquity from Cos. Let us look, for example, at *The Generation of Animals*, where Aristotle addresses human physiology and anatomy to establish principles for understanding the medical practices employed by Greek doctors. In his discussion of male and female bodies, Aristotle shows the intrinsic importance of gender discourse not only for Hippocratic medicine but also, more importantly, for his conception of scientific knowledge—that is, his ideas about science and cultural authority.

Like Hippocrates and the doctors writing under that name, Aristotle posits the order of gender as establishing a fundamental hierarchy of male over female. His general precept is that a woman's body, with weak and ineffective muscles, is a vastly inferior version of a man's, with a marked tendency toward illness and malfunctions and limited internal structuring or order. He notes frequent illness among women, which he attributes largely to a relative lack of body heat, the fact that "male animals are hotter than female ones" (*Generation of Animals* 4:1,765b). The woman's experience of blood loss during menstruation and the apparent abundance of blood in women at other times could suggest the contrary: since blood is hot and a woman has a lot of blood, a woman might have an especially warm body. The error here, Aristotle says, can be explained by the diluted state, or lack of purity, in a woman's bodily fluids. Women actually have too little pure blood and, thus, less body heat (4:1,765b).

He draws on a similar argument about body heat when he says that the human body, male and female, is naturally given "form" (*eidos*) through the presence of semen (*sperma*). The "concoction" of semen is the result of heat, and the body produces semen only when it is hot enough to do so. Since "the fact that it has been concocted means that it has been set and compacted . . . the more compacted semen is, the more fertile it is" (4:1,765b). The very warm male body, then, "is that which is able to concoct, to cause to take shape, and to discharge, semen possessing the 'principle' of the 'form'" (4:1,765b). By "principle" he means the "*first motive principle*," that which "is able to act thus in itself or in something else" (4:1,765b). The "female is that which [only] receives the semen but is unable to cause semen to take shape or to discharge it" (4:1,765b). Males, it turns out, can do precisely these things owing to their active and ample production of semen, and the male as an active agent actually embodies a "*first motive principle*" of form. The female produces and discharges some semen, too, but with her lower body temperature she produces only an adulterated substance not "in a pure condition" (4:1,765b). In *Historia Animalium*, Aristotle adds that only the male emits semen "into another individual," whereas the female "will emit semen [only] into itself" (1:3,489a), suggesting the transactional nature of the male in sexual reproduction and the self-contained state of the female. The female, in other words, is not characterized particularly as possessing form or as being able to produce it.

With her lower body temperature and without much semen, a woman really cannot possess the same form, "motive principle," dynamic force, or sense of general "firstness" as a man. Hence a woman's robustness in worldly action and in sex—her ability to achieve orgasm, for example—will be a drastically diminished version of a man's (evidence that contradicts Tireisius' testimony about male compared to female orgasms). Aristotle speculates that even a man severely "deficient of heat" and unable to produce adequate amounts of semen would eventually lose the male "principle" and would at last "of necessity change over into [the] opposite condition," in effect, becoming a woman (*Generation* 4:1,765b). The person of too little semen, whether male or female, is a kind of castrato—an infertile male. (For a similar distinction, see Plato's *Timaeus* 90E–91E.) The connection here is form (*eídos*) as a natural and intrinsic expression of maleness.

Not always in agreement with Aristotle, Hippocrates (or writers under his name) in *Diseases of Women* elaborates the same doctrine of inherent weakness in the female body owing to its poor physical "form." He differs with Aristotle on the issue of body heat, believing that a woman *does* have an especially warm body. However, this text still provides a context for Aristotle's comments by attempting to offer visible proof, for example, of female deficiency in that a man's body has "more solid [muscle] flesh than a woman" (Lefkowitz and Fant, eds. 1982, 89). Smaller amounts of semen cause women to be smaller and weaker overall, but the most vivid example of a woman's lack of solidity and strength, and a cornerstone of Hippocratic gyne-cology, is the phenomenon of the "displaced uterus"—the "wandering womb." From the fourth century B.C. through the second century A.D. there prevailed the medical notion that serious female disorders frequently arose because the uterus was not anchored. It could become "displaced" and "wander" through the body's cavities, espe-cially the chest and lower abdomen. Depending on where the uterus wandered, a woman could be ill with suffocation, general body limp-ness ("atony"), headaches, or liver pains; she could even die from this problem.

With the resulting illness, whether minor or fatal, it was the male physician's task to track the errant uterus and discover how to put it back behind the vagina. Several Hippocratic texts contain lengthy explanations about the regions into which the uterus wanders and what ailments are then produced. Particularly dangerous are movements of the uterus around the lungs. A woman might miss up to two menstrual periods because her uterus has lodged between the lungs; in this condition, the text says flatly, "she cannot survive" because the accumulated menstrual fluid will fill the lungs and drown her (Lefkowitz and Fant, eds. 1982, 90). Less alarming is the situation in which the uterus moves to the upper abdomen and causes nonfatal suffocation, a loss of voice, drowsiness, and chattering teeth (93). On the order of a minor danger is the problem of older women and those who are sexually inactive. A dormant uterus becomes "empty and light" (from aging and abstinence) and then turns until "it hits the liver"; both then might "strike the abdomen." The uterus hitting the liver "produces sudden [but minor] suffocation as it occupies the breathing passage round the belly" (90–91). This condition, causing only minor suffocation and painful urination, responds well to treatment. The least serious ailment occurs when, because of a woman's "hard work or lack of food," the uterus "falls toward the lower back or toward the hips" (91). The Hippocratic text explains reassuringly that this afflication is temporary and usually self-correcting. Hippocratic doctors often came to these conclusions based on abstract theory. What little clinical knowledge they possessed seems to have come from "midwives" who had considerable experience and information based on their own observations.[2]

Remedies cover a wide range of treatments. If the woman has a marginally displaced uterus, she might be washed with warm water, given several herbal preparations (orally and vaginally), and then directed to "have intercourse with her husband" (94). Severe problems require repeated vaginal insertion of "pessaries," or suppositories, powerfully sweet ones to draw the uterus close and fetid or pungent ones to move it away. Along with prescribing warm baths, intercourse, and fragrant oils for the nose, the physician applies the pessaries and massages the woman's body to coerce the uterus back into place before a fatal condition can develop.

The misogynist character of the Hippocratic texts emerges particularly through their attribution of a kind of spiritual and physical animism, a belief in the willfully perverse motivation of the woman's body as it chooses to go astray, becoming ill instead of remaining healthy. Perverse intent is centered in the uterus, as is shown in the following Greco-Latin text by Aretaeus of Cappadocia. A late text of the second century A.D., this passage nonetheless foregrounds the very conceit of female animism and highlights the metaphors fundamental to that tradition since the time of the earliest Hippocratic writers:

> In the middle of the flanks of women lies the womb, a female viscus, closely resembling an animal; for it is moved of itself hither and thither in the flanks, also upwards in a direct line to below the cartilage of the thorax, and also obliquely to the right or to the left, either to the liver or spleen; and it like-wise is subject to prolapsus downwards, and, in a word, it is altogether erratic. It delights, also, in fragrant smells, and advances towards them; and it has an aversion to fetid smells, and flees from them; and, on the whole, the womb is like an animal within an animal. (*The Extant Works of Aretaeus, the Cappadocian*, 285–87)

The passage summarizes many of the precepts of Hippocratic gynecology, highlighting the perverse independence of the female body as it takes a kind of animal pleasure in violating its own order of health. Possessing the independent volition of "an animal within an animal," the uterus actually wishes to propel itself away from where it should be according to medical wisdom—all because its aims are not consonant with those of bodily health as communicated by the male gynecologist. Aretaeus, the Hippocratic doctor, actually condemns the uterus as a primitive and uncooperative organ, errant and rebellious.

The idea of "an animal within an animal" renders the woman doubly passive. Unable to control her uterus, she is made passive while the uterus follows its own dictates, its inner "animal" urge to go astray. When the woman becomes ill, she becomes passive again as the gynecologist supplies the uterine orientation that the woman supposedly lacks in herself. The woman's body, lacking form, is divided into an errant, rebellious part, a kind of dark frontier of incivility and formlessness, and a malleable, colonized part that, while not well formed, is nonetheless capable of being structured and made healthy by the gynecologist. The woman can be saved and cured, in a sense exorcised of error in the flesh, if the rebellious spirit within her can be kept under control.

These texts are not "gynocritical" in the sense of involving women as the producers of knowledge (see Rousselle 1980 and 1983 for a discussion of producing as opposed to appropriating knowledge about women's bodies in Greek gynecology). The woman's body in each case is not properly her own concern. She cannot prevent the uterus from becoming displaced, does not know where it wanders to, and does not know how to reposition it. She knows only that she needs the doctor's guidance (or conceivably the "midwife's" help) when the condition develops. The male doctor—all doctors are male— steps in to position the woman's uterus and to reposition her as a female subject. The gynecologist frames the woman's viewpoint with "gynecology," in effect deploying a male technology to displace female knowledge or self-awareness. From this viewpoint, the woman with no access to a "midwife" would have no occasion to minister to her own body, for patent in these texts is the assumption of a doctor's mastery of the female-as-a-body and of the female as a body-of-knowledge.

To return to Aristotle, he argues that the woman is in this predicament because she is constitutionally inadequate owing to her lack of warmth and firmness. Her condition keeps her weak because her natural state is to be soft and less well "formed" than a man. The doctor's job, *as doctor,* is to provide the structuring or "form" of health that a woman cannot provide for herself—to *make* her healthy. The male's supposed ability as "that which is able to concoct" semen, and the supposed fact that semen possesses "the 'principle' of the 'form'" (*archēn tou eidous*), aligns and marks the male "naturally" and irrevocably with form—*eidos* (*Generation* 4:1,765b). Other "facts" of gender, such as Aristotle's disclosure that a health deficiency in the parents' fluids will "tend to produce females" (4:2,766b), also clarify the significant tie between being male and having the proper *form* of one ontotheologically well suited for life in the Kosmos.

Aristotle argues quite clearly that the same form (*eidos*) that is the essence of maleness is the form that structures the logical relations of the *hupokeimenon* and scientific inquiry. The male virtually fulfills cultural destiny by aligning his scientific thinking and actions with the dictates of what is taken to be his own body and physiology. The female is not only alienated from form by her nature as a woman; "sick with desire" (as Soranus describes her) in that the amorphous nature of femaleness renders her dysfunctional, she will be healthier in her dealings with the world to the extent that she receives the impression of male form, which a male must somehow impart to her. Thomas Laqueur describes an abstract version of this gynecological scenario in *Making Sex* (1990) when he says that "conception is for the male to have an idea, an artistic or artisanal conception, in the brain-uterus of the female" (42).

I am making this same connection between the gendered body and ideas and thinking. For Aristotle, the woman's body/brain is a poor receptacle, and the natural limits of her constitution will keep

her from succeeding past a certain point. By contrast, the male—
who actually *possesses* form—can naturally make critical observations leading to scientific knowledge. For Aristotle there is an intrinsic
congruence between the *hupokeimenon* as a matrix underlying representation, and maleness as embodied in *sperma* as a form-giving
substance in the construction of gender. This line of thought shows
that the logic of the subject, conceived as scientific rigor, is a logic
of the gendered subject conceived principally as male.

Conceptually akin to the practice of gynecology in its general
operations, and an equally dramatic example of the Greek institution
of the male as defining the natural perspective on the *hupokeimenon*
in cultural representation, is the practice of the *gunaikonomoi*, the
"regulators of women." In fourth-century Athens and other city-
states, including Sparta, Syracuse, and Boeotia, the *gunaikonomoi*
were communally sponsored magistrates, individuals and boards of
men who (at Boeotia, for example) had the responsibility of monitoring and supervising women, particularly married women, during
public ceremonies. The *gunaikonomoi* in Athens and Syracuse were
specifically charged with "the surveillance of meal ordinances" and
empowered to set and enforce "the rules imposed on women, particularly in matters of dress" (Wehrli 36). The mandated responsibility
of the *gunaikonomoi* was generally to set standards for female behavior in public meetings and celebrations, civil and religious, and otherwise overtly "regulate" women's public demeanor (Vatin 254–61).

The practice of "regulating" women as an official institution in
Greek culture is already evident in the assumptions and practices of
medicine. But the "regulators," along with the gynecologists, are a
dramatic externalization of the social and political orders reflected
quite clearly in the *Theogony* and the *Odyssey*. The *gunaikonomoi*
performed their tasks to monitor anti-paternal ("feminine") elements,
especially among rich men who could overdress their wives and
socially overpromote them as a way of displaying their own pros-
perity and importance (see Pomeroy 131). Like Zeus in the Pantheon
and the gynecologists in medical practice, the *gunaikonomoi* were
cultural agents committed to monitoring the violations of form associated with women and with being non-male, and to advancing men
and the oppositional structure created to promote them.

The relationship of the *gunaikonomoi* to women closely replicates the relations of power in other dimensions of Greek culture.
First, the cultural perspective of the "regulators" was that of the law
as the "universal" truth of Greek culture from a prescribed perspective, a fixed reference for religion and civil society. And while the

regulators were enforcers of the law as conceived by men, these women were immediately dependent on the regulators—or on the authority they represented—to sponsor their participation in Greek culture. Finally, the relationship of males as the law and women as marked by their violation of the law is established through the utility, the instrumental nature, of female transgression. When an improperly dressed or misbehaving woman is corrected, her compliance necessarily reinscribes the authority of patriarchal ritual and celebration. In short, the women monitored by the regulators were being defined in terms of their proclivity to error—as that which "naturally" counters and opposes men and paternal authority and therefore needs male correction. Women again are associated with perversity, with a willful counter to the order of proper form. Male regulators and women together inscribe law and deviance along the lines of gender— the potential of veering from the "first motive principle" that, in fact, affirms the law's importance.

Women in this circumstance are involved in a scene of indeterminate and repressed non-paternal power. Political and cultural authority as figured in the *gunaikonomoi* is a closed system—the "law" as a fixed reference for women. As in the *Theogony*, women are positioned to reflect a supposedly "open" economy of chance— the possibility of error that, in turn, defines the law. As the *Theogony* and the *Odyssey* showed, too, that which is "beyond" the law has no absolute separation from paternal authority. As the law's avatar, but also by participating in a discourse with Gaia and the other gods, Zeus is implicated in the non-paternal "feminine" order as well. Odysseus, likewise, represents the law but "errs" in his passive wanderings away from it. Existing only to correct women, the regulators are defined by discourse in the same reciprocal dependence of law and deviation as evidenced in the perfect (as opposed to the imperfect) version of Zeus that is so important to the structure of Greek culture. In effect, the regulators, too, are made passive by acting in relation to the "deviant" women. This dynamic again suggests the functioning discourse of the paternal romance, the operation of a system for the articulation of male power under the guise of a natural and civilized order.

In this classical view, women are positioned to reflect a supposedly "open" economy of chance—the certainty of "female" error that, in turn, functions to define being male as having scientific rigor. The figures of the *gunaikonomoi* and the gynecologists evoke and confirm cultural authority in the assumption of an immovable reference of underlying form (*eídos*)—form that stands in relation to an

amorphous female, suggesting the male as a the stable stylus writing
on the soft, feminine slate of the woman's body. Along this same
line, G.E.R. Lloyd writes that the Greek "world-whole" is a Kosmos
"subject to orderly and determinate sequences of causes and effects"
expressed in "images and analogies from the legal and political
domain"—the Kosmos as a large "monarchy" (*Magic, Reason, and
Experience* 247). The cosmic monarch's relation to the world in fact
replicates that of the doctor to the malleable body he treats. In *The
History of Sexuality II* (138–39) Michel Foucault also connects medicine and politics, suggesting that Zeus' mission is to doctor the world.
This is the connection, too, concerning Zeus's doctoring in book eight
of the *Iliad*, the earlier-quoted passage in which Zeus has brought
all of the gods to Mount Olympos to warn them about intervention
in the Trojan war. Again, Zeus ends his oration as follows:

> Or prove it this way:
> out of the zenith hang a golden line
> and put your weight on it, all gods and goddesses.
> You will not budge me earthward out of heaven,
> cannot budge the all-highest, mighty Zeus,
> no matter how you try.
> But let my hand
> once close to pull that cable—up you come,
> and with you earth itself comes, and the sea.
> By one end tied around Olympos' top
> I could let all the world swing in mid-heaven!
> That is how far I overwhelm you all,
> both gods and men. (8:18–29)

Here Zeus is positioned alone on Mount Olympos, with a fixed
orientation. He is the only one who can tend to the formless and
inherently chaotic world below. If he chooses to break his tie with
it, the world in all its vastness comes unstuck—precisely as a women's
uterus comes unstuck. This similarity exists because the Kosmos itself
was conceived by the Greeks as a female otherness in relation to
Zeus's position as a super-male agent. (The *Theogony* makes this
point with great force.) Zeus and the gynecologist have the same
approximate relation to the *hupokeimenon* and the discourse that
makes the world knowable. The fixed position of the father/doctor,
as doctor, orients the female body; Zeus as super father/doctor orients
the female world. The technology of gynecology, the pessaries, oils,
and various treatments, are the instruments of this orientation, the
means of its implementation, just as Zeus's "male" technology—
golden cable and his various powers of state—implement his rule and

order the world. The gynecologists and *gunaikonomoi* represent the male's fixed perspective, suggesting the equivalence of the female body and Kosmos in that both are dependent on "male" technology for form. "Gynecology" as cultural reference and technology of power, the rules for a woman's dress and behavior, and the fixity of "Mount Olympos," in effect, are the references of Greek critical authority. In relation to them "womb" and "world" wander without purpose until a male can reposition them. Male technology cures "female problems"—that is, female constitutional inadequacy and disorder.

In the passage from the *Iliad*, paternal authority is a position of speech in a discourse that defines "true" speech for the "other" positions relating to it, much as oppositional relations are established in the logical scaffolding of the *hupokeimenon*. Zeus and the gynecologists define "truth" by seeming to arrange the world's otherwise amorphous matter in relation to form (*eídos*) as a sublunary gesture toward the "good." A dialogic relationship exists in each case between male or paternal authority and that which it shapes and governs. Suppressed is a recognition of the discourse that constitutes the text; each text shows that the "power" of form and maleness is based not in itself, but in the social discourse producing the effects of apparently "natural" male form in that text. That dialogic discourse is made evident only when the oppositions constituting it are brought to light and exposed.

The situating of male authority over women is the impulse of the paternal romance. In making these remarks I assume, as Laqueur says in *Making Sex*, that "the nature of sex [and gender] . . . is the result not of biology but of our needs in speaking about it" (115). Accordingly, I have emphasized the "discourse" and not the natural reality of gender distinctions in my discussion. The discourse of these texts, finally, tends to articulate a central axiom of Western sexual mythology—what Thomas Aquinas later will assert in the formula of woman as "matter" and man as "form," raw material and mold. (In the misogyny of a Greco-Latin aphorism, *Tota mulier in utero*— "Woman is nothing but a uterus.") The question of the great father's relation to women cannot be left behind if we are to understand the paternal romance in early Western culture, a question that will reappear with particular significance in the Christian definition and theory of the Father in the next chapter.

Aristotle on the Paternal Romance

Aristotle's texts demonstrate how the effect of enfranchising paternity in narrative exists alongside counter possibilities, the "contrary" and "contradictory" propositions. Never "all" or "everything," as he is described in the epithets, the noble father is an effect in the practice of the paternal romance. Zeus and the derivatives of his authority constitute a privileged reference for Greek culture, the ontological angle (the ontological "male") according to which the economy of the Kosmos expresses its values. Night, Moira, the Furies, Gaia, and other such "anti-paternal" figures exist in a contrary relationship to Zeus's authority; even so, in this "contrariness" they expose the logic of the father as an agent taking up a textual position.

This epistemological construct, the Greek implicit ideal version of a critical and true perspective, is elaborated in the fifth and fourth centuries b.c. This era saw the rise of philosophy and science, accompanied by a widespread formal recognition of critical procedures, a powerful sense of how systems of interpretation function. There was a new sense of an analytical dimension of cultural knowing "beyond" the older epic narratives, such as the *Iliad*, the *Odyssey*, and cosmogonies such as the *Theogony*. There was a growing belief that formal "logic" functions in cultural texts far more comprehensively and deeply, and in closer conjunction with the "good," than the older narratives *as narratives* could possibly reveal.

Particularly in the fourth century, there is a strong investment in seeing in discourse an operation that functions "beyond" narrative facts and structures. Legitimate knowledge, above all, must have a cognitive and stable quality in order to coincide with the "good" in the Kosmos. At the same time, Aristotle saw the need to account for differences, alterations, and other imperfections newly manifest in the world of philosophy and critical rigor. He reasoned that, if a moral being attempts to realize the "good" already constituted—but unrealized—in its nature, that being must grasp the relation of events in motion so as to enhance their approach to the ultimate "good" that is not in motion. There is a need, in short, to grasp the world as world (the "realism" of Aristotle) in order to realize the "good's" stable and constant nature. His strategy was to postulate the invariant "good" of knowing as existing apart from the apparent mutability of the world.

The position from which one sees the ultimate "good" must be based, in an analytical sense, "outside" apparent motion, at least "outside" sublunary imperfection. That scientific position of knowing can be occupied fully only by those who can see into the natural order of this world. For Homer, the stable viewpoints belonged to Zeus and those in the Pantheon; for Aristotle, they involved the scientific perspective and subject of inquiry. Aristotle's wager is that in any instance of interpretation or knowing there must be a "first mover," and the existence of this perspective addresses the problem of indeterminacy in the world. If *more* than one such authoritative perspective existed, "the series of [subsequent] movers and movables," as G. Verbeke notes, would "be infinite too." And since "an infinite movement cannot be realized [as knowledge] in a limited time" of human understanding, the lack of a prime knower would likewise make any knowing impossible (548). Aristotle's scientific undertaking demands the postulation of an inherently stable scientific perspective, the perspective coordinated by the *hupokeimenon*.

If we could fully occupy it, this viewpoint of the prime mover would allow us to take pleasure, as Verbeke says, "more in stability than in movement" (Verbeke 563). We lack that viewpoint, so we must content ourselves by devising schemes for understanding the world in relation to the postulated stasis of the *epistēmē* as a gradually perfectible understanding. The critical approach to the *hupokeimenon* then allows us to chart the ratios of earthly imperfection in relation to what we supposedly can assume is ultimately stable and perfect. It becomes possible to imagine a system of interpretation wherein one can separate mere quantitative and qualitative differences from substantial patterns to find a model of human understanding that approximates, or at least is on its way toward an appreciation of, true and reliable knowledge.

The argument of the logical treatises leads finally to the conclusion that knowledge and power, language and politics, are constitutionally implicated in each other. Aristotle's commentary is crucial for framing the textual and interpretive conflicts generated by the interactions of language and power. In his logical and gender treatises, Aristotle tried to show the potential for constant and reliable interpretation and to indicate why logical possibilities necessarily move along certain "oppositional" lines of development and not others. If the interpretation of texts could not be conventionalized at some level, then change could go unnoticed, lost in the mundane proliferation of heterogeneity and chance. And "there can be no demonstrative knowledge," as Aristotle says in the *Posterior Analytics,* "of the fortuitous [chance]" (1:30,87b). Contrariety as a trope serves the single aim of contextualizing chance within substantial patterns and foregrounding intelligible differences, rather than infinite regression.

The move to align the male body with scientific "logic," as if doing so were natural and inevitable, is a key strategic move of the paternal romance. The nature of this strategy helps explain how the strength or weakness of particular manifestations of paternal authority may do little to change the paternal romance itself. Paternal "power" lies in the economy of positioning as Aristotle defines that scheme in the *hupokeimenon*, in the institutionalization of the speaking subject's position *as a male position*, and in the Western tradition of this institutionalization. The authority of the paternal romance derives from a fundamentally discursive practice: from privileging the father and father surrogates as ideal knowers and the ones who speak of and *for* knowledge—for form as instituted in their own bodies. This covert privileging (Aristotle overtly advances *no* such claims) has deep ties to Greek science and notions of coherence and reasoning, and Aristotle's texts cannot help but provide the conceptual frames for critiquing and undoing them as well.

Notes

1. Introductory texts about classical Greek science that discuss Aristotle include Benjamin Farrington, *Greek Science*, and Morris R. Cohen and I. E. Drabkin, *A Source Book in Greek Science*. Standard texts on this subject by G. E. R. Lloyd include *Early Greek Science; The Revolutions of Wisdom*; and *Magic, Reason, and Experience*. More specialized but highly influential, particularly on contemporary French classical studies, is Lloyd's *Polarity and Analogy*.

Other specialized discussions include *Science and Speculation*, ed. Jonathan Barnes et al.; Lloyd's *Science and Morality in Greco-Roman Antiquity*; and Ludwig Edelstein's *Ancient Medicine*.

2. For a discussion of the relationship of "midwives" and male gynecologists, see Paola Manuli, *Fisiologia e patologia*. See also Aline Rousselle, *Porneia* and "Observation féminine et ideologie masculine." About the "midwives," Rousselle says in *Porneia:* "The ancient doctors whose writings have come down to us owe their knowledge about women's ailments to these women, but in the hands of the doctors the knowledge acquired by these midwives lost much of its observational basis" (25). Citing Manuli, Rousselle adds that "the training of [ancient Greek] doctors in medical theory in fact resulted in women knowing less about their bodies than they had in previous eras" (25).

CHAPTER FOUR

Father Tetragrammaton,
Lord of the World

In the beginning was the Word, and the Word was with God,
and the Word was God.
—GOSPEL ACCORDING TO JOHN

Una substantia, tres persona.
—ATHANASIAN CREED

One, two, three—but where, my dear Timaeus, is the
fourth . . . ?
—PLATO, *TIMAEUS*

Hallmarks of Greek theology, as we have seen, are the breaks
that exist between Zeus and the Pantheon and between Zeus and the
whole Kosmos. At some moments the former *seems* resolved in monotheism and at others in polytheism. There is also a "resolution" of
sorts when the socially productive law of Zeus's Olympic regime goes
into effect and stabilizes the social order as a divinely sanctioned polis.
The tension between the two orders, however, persists throughout
major Greek texts, and the conflict between Zeus, the Pantheon, and
the rest of the Kosmos reflects many issues of cultural authority in
Greek texts. Even though Zeus as patriarch does not create the world
ex nihilo, as he claims—neither does he "contain" the Kosmos within
himself—he does succeed in creating an effective political coalition
and the model for a civil society. We also know that his suppression of a female economy produces a principal dramatic interest in
Greek religion and narrative. Although they are self-contradictory,
Zeus's claims for monotheism and omnipotence, finally—although self-
contradictory—play a significant role in accounting for his status in
Greek texts.

The rise of a Christian Father owes much to the Greek noble father that I have been discussing. St. Paul warned the Colossians about the Greek error and "the empty deception of [Greek] philosophy" (Colossians 2:8), aiming particularly to point out the falseness of the Greek father. But the rise of God in Patristic literature and the New Testament does not always succeed in negating Zeus's "legitimacy"; indeed, it builds in many ways upon what the Greeks believed. This process of transition from a pre-Christian to a Christian version of the father extends up through the thirteenth-century elaboration of Church doctrine.

The doctrinal disputes of this lengthy period concentrate much effort on attempts to "mediate" the opposition of father and son—the tension of One (Zeus) and Many (Pantheon) also inherent to Greek theology. The Church's claim to moral, ethical, and philosophical authority comes to rest on its ability to effect this mediation. The result is the doctrine of Christ's accommodation—or "dispensation"—of God to man, the connecting of (finite) humans with the (infinite) Father through the intermediary of the "incarnation" and the Son. That is, in the paradox of Christ's twofold position as son of man *and* of God, the principle of mediation between father and son is contained—much like the rule of opposition that "mediates" between Zeus and the Pantheon, the principle that St. Augustine expresses as a paradox of difference and identity. The Father and the Son "are two different things"; at the same time, "there is no difference in their substance," because the distinction between them is relational and structural. Relationality as the basis for establishing these positions is everything, and the "relation is no accident because it is not changeable" (180).

The assertion of an "unchangeable relation" at the core of the world, essential to Christianity's advocacy of its own version of a "noble father," is itself an indication of the extent of Greek influence on Christian doctrine. This influence, as Edwin Hatch notes (280), occurs in three principal domains: (1) the assimilation of Greek metaphysics in a very broad sense and a tendency, subsequently, to abstraction in doctrinal formulations; (2) the assumption of a "chasm between spirit and matter—[and] the tendency to interpose powers [or mediators] between the Creator and His creation"; (3) the assumption of God's perfect being, which explains the general high valuation of "perfection" as embodied in perfect stability and stasis—the assumption, finally, that "rest is better than motion, that passionlessness is better than feeling, that changelessness [as Augustine conveys] is better than change" (281). These influences all bear directly on Christian "authority" and dogma, and thus on the foundations of Christian thought. They are closely tied to the issue of "Father-hood," Zeus's in regard to the Kosmos and Yahweh's in relation to the creation. At issue in Greek culture's impact on Christianity is the particular form, the representation, of authority. How much of Zeus survives in Yahweh and in "God"? And how does the Greco-Christian investment in authority shape the Western tradition of paternal authority, what I am calling the paternal romance?

I cannot pretend to answer this question completely, but I can begin by looking at Yahweh. In the early Church, owing to Jewish and pre-Christian influences, the conception of "atonement" as a ransom paid to keep away the devil presupposes an actively menacing "paternal" force. An "evil" father existed prior to the development of an elaborated Christology and the identification of Christ with sinful humanity. As Christianity develops, a shift occurs: what was once a relationship in which ransom is paid to keep away a threatening, dark father becomes a channel to knowledge about a divine father. As the concept of atonement develops, especially in St. Paul's thinking, satisfaction through "ransom" gives way to the idea of justification by faith. As E. O. James explains, "the victorious death and resurrection of Christ [produce] a new status of sonship by securing justification and reconciliation" with the father (120–24). The Church, in other words, develops an alternative to the angry god who could be bought off only for the moment (as with the Old Testament "jealous" God—Yahweh), offering instead the benevolent Father/God for whom one could want to strive to be a good "child."

Sacrifice

This evolving relationship with and conception of a benevolent God is given important expression in the practice of ritual sacrifice. This symbolic representation of connection with the Father appears in an early or "primitive" mode and a later Christian or symbolic mode. Sacrifice "in its primitive mode of expression" is devoid of any moral and ethical qualities in the modern sense; nevertheless, although sin is regarded as a ritual defilement, its expiation is a sacramental process of restoration of the state of religious purity and holiness on which the continuance of divine beneficence depends (James 106). Its purpose is to raise mankind (either individually or collectively) to a higher spiritual status where the transcendent exercises control over the physical and human, and the eternal over the temporal and mutable, but always through human agents and material instruments. Strongly biased in this association of Christianity with "a higher spiritual status" than what precedes it and with a "legitimate" (as opposed to non-Christian "illegitimate") morality, many theorists of sacrifice and related practices assume that "restoration of the state of religious purity" involves symbolic reinsertion into an original "unity," which entails the existence of (or the retrograde projection of) an unspoiled "origin."

Implicit here is that the origin of sacrifice as an institution lies in a founding act of creation. Functionally this involves a kind of doubling, wherein a single god with a single spirit becomes two. The unity of the origin is lost when the god travels outside himself to create the being of another. The god must implicitly renounce his own sacred being in order, as Henri Hubert and Marcel Mauss explain, to bring "about the existence of things" (93). There is a "sacrifice" of perfect unity for the sake of a "world." The "first" sacrifice, therefore, is an act of both creation and destruction, the god committing suicide through the offspring created as an "other" self. The manifold spectre of doubling and suicide that underlies most "origin" stories also overcomes the difficulty of explaining how a powerful god can be destroyed or slain. By presenting an "other" god "in the guise of an evil spirit [,] it is the spirit who is put to death, and from it emerges the god" (Hubert and Mauss 91).

Precisely this commemoration of a god's suicide is manifest in the reenactment of sacrifice, where "a part of the self," as David Bakan says, "is made into an 'it' for the seeming preservation [or creation] of the remainder" (125). The goal of sacrifice is to renew contact with a holy agent. In the case of a father sacrificing a first-born child (the traditional biblical and non-biblical case of human sacrifice), the father gives the child in order to put himself in direct contact with god, with what is sacred and life renewing. This "bloody" ritual (as opposed to the later "bloodless" taking of the Host) displays atonement for past sins through the regaining of god's lost attention and approval, removing the "obstacle" of a fallen state as represented by the life of the child. In the terms of Aristotle's theory of the *hupokeimenon*, bloody sacrifice is a case of the father insisting on control of what goes in the first position in subject relations. This opens the possibility of idealism and "romance" (hence the paternal romance) of an eternally new beginning in the Father. However, the latent "motive" for this tyrannical act must be, as Kierkegaard stipulated, hate for the child, or for what the child represents: the father performing the sacrifice desires the son's death so that he can stand without rival or intermediary before god (84). The

father himself thus dictates the subject relations that define an understanding of the world.

Infanticide does, in a way, "overcome" opposition in the restoration of unity, but it brings with it a devastating contradiction.
Without a son, the father not only ceases to be a father; without the
mediation through sonship as a concept, he also loses the relation
to the divine father. In killing his son, the father kills himself as a
"son" and destroys his own father's fatherhood. In this cycle, because
he loses his children, even god himself is destroyed *as a father*—in
effect, loses his own subject relations to the world. In thus seeking
the role of preeminent son to god-the-father, without mediation, the
father usurps (or attempts to usurp) god's position and ends up negating paternity over three generations, culminating in an act of theocide.

In the Jewish tradition, it was sometime after the destruction
of the Jewish Temple in A.D. 70 that sacrifice became a kind of
symbolic or totemic expression of God's suicide. "The ancient blood
ritual" of sacrifice "underwent a fundamental change in character so
that the concept of life-giving became that of self-oblation, the sacrifice of the lips instead of that of the calves" (James 74). Whereas
human and animal "bloody" sacrifice attempted to reenact, in the
form of ransom paid, god's suicide when he created the world, the
"sacrifice of the lips" became a symbolic expression of the yielding
of a whole life as love for God-the-Father. By taking in the Host, the
communicant symbolically signifies an unrepeatable act, an act for
which God is the only author.

The communicant also accedes to the death of God, who then
only lives through the life of Spirit in the world. By one's voluntarily
ingesting the Host (Spirit), a circle is completed: a human now mediates the opposition of Father and Son by returning to the Father (in
a kind of resurrection of the Father) the connection of love which
He first gave to humans through the Son. Through love, the subjectivity of life in the world, where Christ lived, is returned to its source,
the Father toward whom all life and love travels as, in Augustine's
words, "a kind of life which couples together or seeks to couple some
two entities, the lover and the loved" (Burnaby 54).

The sacrificial structure inherent in the Catholic mass brings
with it the assumption of the opposition between Father and Son as
mediated by the ritual recognition of a "dead father." Whereas in pre-
Christian sacrifice the father "killed" his father (symbolically) by
killing his son, in communion a father recognizes that his father,
God, already "died" when he created the image of the Son. A

"bloody" sacrifice need not be repeated; indeed, it would constitute a sacrifice, an attempt to usurp God's role. In fact, the full recognition for Christianity is that God has died twice, first when he left his solitary state to create the possibility of the Son, the "Word"/world, and again when the Son died for humanity, a sacrifice made so that, through divine retribution the Holy Spirit, love, would be infused in the world. (Or as the Church Father Origen argued—with some debt to Plato's *Timaeus*—God caused the world to be; Christ caused it to be "rational," or ordered, in relation to God's image [Hatch 205].)

In each case the accommodation of God to humans, in the incarnation of Christ and in the commemoration of Christ's death in the ingestion of the Host, is focused on a totem that signifies the temporalization of the sacred. The incarnation and communion, that is, are part of "a sacramental system in which the [totemic] material is the instrument and channel of the spiritual" (James 237). Through the agency of the so-called material totem of sacrifice, nearly identical to the signifier of the "dead father" to which Freud refers (*Totem and Taboo* 143), a timeless and "lost" primal unity is signified in time by the performance of a ritually enacted "narrative." The Mass is the "narrative" structure that articulates the totem and signifies the absence (or death) of the Father. The Father's death is necessary for the totem to have its signifying function, a "function" invested with the special privilege of absolute authority (derived from an "unchangeable relation")—again, suggesting part of Christianity's own version of the "noble father."

The Trinity

The other important dimension of Christianity's version of a "noble father" is the doctrine of the Trinity. The New Testament mentions this only obliquely when it says, "Go ye therefore, and teach all nations, baptizing them in the name of the Father, and of the Son, and of the Holy Ghost" (Matthew 28:19). The Trinity is developed in the work of the Church Fathers and is ultimately codified in the formula of the Athanasian Creed (ca. A.D. 500)—*una substantia, tres persona:* one substance in three persons; a formulation based on a Platonic theory of mind that is worked out in lengthy Patristic debate, a gradual process of adoption and rejection of doctrine from the first through the fifth centuries.

For instance, in the third century Sabellius proposed a "Trinity" of "persons" whose names indicated modes of a single being, in reality a "single" God. In this theory, called "Modalism," a single God manifested himself in the expressions of Father, Son, and Holy Spirit. The Church judged Modalism to be heretical and rejected it because of the emphasis on the unity of the Trinity to the exclusion of the separateness of the three persons. The whole point of mediating the *human* and *divine* was being lost. In the fourth century, on the other hand, Arius proposed a hierarchy of descending authority from Father to Son to Spirit. This maintained the separateness of the three persons, but in so doing ranked the Son and the Spirit *below* the Father. This doctrine, termed Monarchianism, necessarily implied that, contrary to St. Paul's belief, there was a time when the Son did not exist (Armstrong and Markus 23). The Church rejected Monarchianism as heresy at the Council of Nicaea in A.D. 325 because it was thought that a "hierarchy" of persons in the Trinity created too much separation. Monarchianism also contradicted the tenet of Christ's "preexistence," an idea grounded in the opening verses of the Gospel of John and accepted by the Church, as can be seen in Paul's Letter to the Philippians.

A Trinitarian doctrine acceptable to the Church came at Nicaea with the formulation of the Son as "of one substance" (*homoousios*) with the Father—the Father being the "principle" according to which the Son "proceeds" into the world and according to which the Spirit "spirates" out of the Son, the last two persons being "emanations" of but "equal" to the first. The official doctrine, stipulating that Christ is in this way "begotten" of ("procreated" by) and not "made" by the Father, is given full expression in St. Augustine's *De Trinitate*, where it is merged with a theory of "Mind" in a neo-Platonic psychology. It is safe to say that the essential framework here is borrowed wholesale from the works of Plotinus, the third-century "father of Platonism" (see "On the Three Primary Hypostases" in *Ennead* 5:1). The doctrine is further elaborated at the Council of Chalcedon (A.D. 451) and then is codified fully by St. Thomas Aquinas in *Summa Theologica* in the thirteenth century.

The official Trinitarian doctrine that emerges, especially as influenced by St. Augustine, is a structuralism for the analysis of object relations in the world, with particular emphasis on the dynamics of psychological interpretation. Like the theory of sacrifice, for example, the Trinity begins with the construct of formal opposition. Above all else, as the Church Father Irenaeus says, the Son is "knowledge of the Father" (Hatch 262), knowledge founded, however, on the recognition of a principle of difference and exclusion. "Exclusion" is essential because to "know" the Father the Son must be "excluded" from the Father's immediate presence. He cannot share the Father's being if he is to be the "Mind" (as Augustine says) that has an object of awareness outside of itself. Hence the Son's obligatory exclusion from and "opposition" to the Father.

Augustine then imagines that the relationship of the Father as an original One and the Son as Mind, following Plotinus, distinguishes "within the external world of spiritual reality a 'trinity' of One, Mind, and Soul or life, in which Soul forms the link between spirit and matter, eternal and temporal. Soul is both one and many and is itself a product of the activity of self-conscious Mind—mind thinking itself; whereas Mind in turn derives from the ultimate and absolute Unity in which there is no distinction of subject and object" (Burnaby 20). In one sense the Trinity is an outgrowth of the "ultimate and absolute Unity" of the Father, except that by himself (if such a state can be imagined) the Father is a kind of "absence." He could be viewed as a divine predication of "is," as Plutarch argued before the Christian era (or at least before Christianity had established any significant intellectual tradition), unable to be temporalized or made directly manifest in the "human" world—that is, bounded by human birth and death (Hatch 242). Even to say something apparently notional, such as that the Father *is*, "would be to give [Him] a second attribute in addition to [His] one-ness" (20). Such a contradictory gesture would "imprison" God in time, as if He were human. (The notion that God cannot even be described as being has its roots— as does all "negative theology"—in the latter two-thirds of Plato's *Parmenides*.)

It is unclear what it means to say that the Father is known by the Son if the Father is an absence or "nothing" to begin with. What can the son know? The Father's Greek name—"tetragrammaton" (the "four-letter-word") or *YHWH*—means simply "he that is" (Yahweh). He is primary in being, without contingency, irreducible to any "prior" state or being. "God" cannot have a name as such—hence the initials of the tetragrammaton—for, as Hatch explains, "a name implies the existence of something prior to that to which a name is given, whereas He is prior to all things" (251). The Father in his "primary" state cannot be articulated because, as is evident, without any contingency he is without difference from anything else, and without being subject to difference he cannot have an identity in the usual sense. It is appropriate, therefore, that theologians use the integer "One" to designate God because One expresses his fundamentally solitary state.

Like "to be," though, the figure of One touches off another contradiction. The metaphor of "One" only superficially and incompletely expresses God's solitude; strictly speaking, there can be no such thing as a solitary "One." If we take "One" as an integer, we must grant that it already stipulates an arithmetic principle of ordinality and has meaning only in relation to other integers. An integer is part of a differential system, as Frege and others show and as mathematicians have long known (see especially Macrobius' *Commentarious in Somnium Scipionis* I,6,8). A single integer is meaningless outside of its holding a position in relation to the "two" (and then the succession of integers) that it is not. As we grant a difference between "one" and "two" based on their opposition, a third thing— a relationship—has come into being, the arithmetic "principle" of enfranchisement through opposition and difference. Thereafter, "zero," because it is not an integer—though it holds an integer's place—will mark the principle of difference that relates integers (see Wilden in Lacan 1968:178–88). The paternal romance replaces such "positionality" with the "effect," or illusion, of originality—with a non-textual grounding for paternity. Here we can see the "progress," or further staging, of the paternal romance by the Christian Fathers. In their view, God stands for the Father as origin and not position— outside of all relationship—with authority that is absolute. Their reasoning is as follows: the meaning of the Father as One is grasped only *within* the relationship of opposition, namely, within the sequential Trinitarian relationship that the Catholic church defines as One, Mind, and Life. The Father as a solitary One—like a number—is indeed unknowable, except as he is found in a relationship with the Son, with two. The Father and Son are separate, like integers. Rising from their opposition is a principle of relationship expressible in a third term, one which literally unites them as common signifiers of the difference that initially separated them.

Still, it cannot be quite clear what the Son *knows* if the Father by himself is nothing. In many theories of sacrifice, it was the god's re-creation of himself in a double (an offspring) that created the world of things. The double, or Mind (in Augustine's term), is nothing except an awareness of the Father. It must follow that the Son is Mind thinking of itself *as nothing*. But how can an awareness of nothing be an awareness at all? It is helpful here to imagine the relationship of Father and Son so that the Father appears as a featureless black surface, one without the distinction of subject or object, top or bottom. The Son then comes out of the Father like a "disk" cut and removed from the blackness—a something where before there was nothing. Before the disk is cut out, there are no distinctions or features; the Father "fills" everything with himself, with his "nothingness." The disk, by being cut out, is excluded from the Father's blankness, and the Father's nonsignifying state is broken. Furthermore, removal of the disk creates a relationship between the disk and the absence (now a particular feature, a locus) of the Father that the removal creates. The disk cannot stand in relation to the total (featureless) surface of the Father, which is without distinction and "unknowable" anyway, but only in relation to the "absence," or the position, actually created by its removal. In short, as the disk breaks off from the blackness, there is suddenly something to know in the absence (different from a nothingness) that is left. "Absence" itself necessarily creates the knowledge of absence as a relationship, and it follows that this relationship of Mind and Father is a primary "object" of awareness—the creation of a world of things. (These ideas reflect Meister Eckhart's commentary about the soul and godhead as both "nothing"—see *Meister Eckhart* [1981].)

In assuming that relationship itself is an originary or primary "thing," primal *ousía*, or an *archē*, Augustine merges his theory of mind with an epistemology and an ontology. This strategy emphasizes the Father in Christianity as a total "structure" of meaning—a "noble father" at the level of perception and meaning as well as of being.

God and Zeus

This abstracted picture of God closely resembles Zeus in a number of important ways, especially regarding the relation to power. The origin of Zeus's authority, for example, is in his victory over the Titans—the manner in which Zeus outmaneuvers them with the help of Gaia, the Hundred-Hands, and other such allies. Zeus triumphs primarily because he understands the nature of power in the pre-Olympian and Olympian world. From the succession of castrated patriarchs who follow Ouranos, Zeus learns the impossibility of escaping the law (especially as the *Odyssey* defines it)—that is, of escaping identity through "difference" as manifested oppositionally in the patriarchal signifier of castration. Zeus correctly assesses the law and chooses not to resist it. Instead, he swallows Metis, "intelligence," and becomes knowledge of and a representative for the law. Thereafter he cannot fall subject to the law because he has already "fallen," subjecting himself to the law by becoming its signifier.

Once accomplished, this "fall"—symbolically a "castration," or act of destruction—need not be repeated. Zeus will exist henceforth under the sign of "law"—the rule that in Zeus's case will be always already implemented, always "in place" in relation to him. Recognition of the law's centrality in the Pantheon allows Zeus to be at the structural center of the Kosmos so as not to be harmfully, unstably, subject to the law's implementation in the future. It is important to remember, though, that Zeus only *signifies* the law, situates himself in the position of the speaking subject, and is not "himself" the rule by which the world functions, as his inability to save his son Sarpedon shows. But he succeeds in situating himself in advantageous close proximity to the law (in the subject position) by claiming it as "knowledge"—in much the same sense that the Christian Son is "knowledge" of the Father/law.

Zeus's rise to power also closely parallels God's progress through the sacrificial cycle and operation in the Trinity. As I described earlier, God first "falls" out of himself to fashion the "otherness" of the world in the Son/Word. He does this again when, through the Son's agency, He saves the world by allowing the Spirit to inhabit and transform it through the "love" made possible by the act of transubstantiation. God's "fall" into time (and the theatricalization of that "fall" in the Eden story) is a primordial event that need not be repeated and will henceforward "authorize" ritual celebrations, signifying re-enactments of the world's creation such as in the Catholic Mass. God's function as a "person" in the Trinity, as I discussed earlier, is also such a fall into time and into the complex relations of the Trinitarian "persons." This is Zeus's situation, too, when he becomes an avatar for and subject to the law. It is not surprising that the conception of "trinitarian" structure describes both Christian doctrine, the relationship of Father/Son/Spirit, and the Greek "God/Form/Matter" relationship that is the prototype for the Christian Trinity (Hatch 181).

Furthermore, these two versions of the "Trinity" operate according to a common version of the law. In the Homeric formula of Father/Son/Knowledge (Odysseus as "knowledge"), as in the broader Greek cultural formula of God/Form/Matter, the Father becomes associated with the principle of difference generated out of opposition and elaborated in the conflict between Zeus, the Pantheon, and the rest of the Kosmos. The law is most clearly implemented regarding questions of world order, fate, and death. Zeus frequently represents the law on questions of governance, whereas Moira and the Erinys (and the Olympians collectively) tend to represent or defend the autonomy of death and the moment of its arrival. On the question of death, they keep Zeus honest. The law governs personal psychology and identity, too, but (as we saw in the *Odyssey*) individual "personality" for the Greeks is subsumed as a facet of communal responsibility and public identity, with very little sense of the reductively personal in the modern sense.

The situation is similar but in an important way changed in the Mass's sacrificial structure and in the doctrine of the Trinity. In Christianity the Father is, literally *is*, the principle of difference out of which the world proceeds *ex nihilo*, out of "nothing" save the principle of the Father itself. As in the Greek world, the Father's law is the authority for earthly versions of justice and order and (more strongly than for the Greeks) for the fact of death and fate according to the dictates of Providence. The involuted Augustinian paradox of paternal authority, wherein the Father is an absence engendering a "principle" of difference, describes the Christian Father, therefore, not as a sign of the law (*Diosemia*) but *as the law itself*, as Augustine insists repeatedly in *The Trinity*. Unlike Zeus, God does not merely "signify" difference or a rule for its implementation. God *is* that all-important difference, the *archē* itself. This distinguishes him from Zeus and decisively separates the Christian Father from the Greek noble father and the Greek notion of authority from the Christian.

The issue of the distinction between Zeus and God can be applied to presentations of these gods. Popular graphic depictions of both often show the same older, bearded man with long hair dressed in a peasant robe, as can be seen in the Otricoli bust of Zeus and in several of Michelangelo's portraits of God. As Dio Chrysostom interpreted the icons of this traditional "philosopher" figure, the unshaven face expresses a protest against vanity and excessive concern with personal appearance. The peasant robe—frequently of rough, "uncomfortable" cloth—indicates the holy man's askesis and a "warning and rebuke to common men" to forgo the sensual life and to tend to the spiritual (Hatch 151). This anthropomorphic depiction of divinity, while quite appropriate for Zeus, is not really fitting for God. Zeus is a "sign" of the law and represents it more often than any other Olympian, but still he is only an important but conventional representative—the *Diosemia*. A stylized "portrait" of Zeus, as in the Otricoli bust or in sketches of the Colossus at Tarentum, therefore, shows a conventional representation *of* a sign for law, the law being non-identical with the paternal character who supposedly lived on Olympos. The same cannot be said of God in that the conventional "philosopher" portrait of him suggests representation and, therefore, a separation of signifier (image) and signified (law). God, though, is precisely not a representation of anything—not a sign but, as defined by Trinitarian doctrine, a nonrepresentable "principle" that the world operates by and tries (imperfectly) to imitate.

This difference between Zeus and God is far reaching in its implications. Zeus is a politician, a Machiavellian figure who takes power and governs much of the Kosmos; God, according to Christian doctrine, is not a "figure" but the very essence from which the world is made, not merely what the Greeks termed *ousia* (substance) but, as John Damacene said, the *huperousios* essence—the "super-substantial" and noncontingent "essence" that all other essences derive from (Shiel 77).

There is, however, an ample foundation for seeing the Christian concept of the "super-substantial" in Greek thought. In the sixth century b.c., as Hatch explains, Greek philosophy developed several notions, embodied earlier in theogonies like Hesiod's, about the world's absolute beginning. *"Hulozoism"* was "the belief that life and matter were the same" (Hatch 175). Anaximander identified the "hulozoistic" stuff as the world's *apeiron* (infinity)—the "unbounded, inexhaustible reservoir of living stuff" (Armstrong and Markus 10). These and other such ideas about the world's absolute and "original" radical unity eventually began to crystallize around the idea of a "maker" (*demiourgos*) and even an "owner" of the *apeiron*—the growing belief, as Roy Kenneth Hack notes, "that the cosmogenetic divine substance" belonged to the "supreme divine power" (40). Someone had to put together the unity of the world, and if it could be made, then it was probably owned by someone as well. However, the idea of "owning" the world (perhaps implicit in Socrates' argument against suicide in the *Phaedo*) is never seriously incorporated in the Greek concept of divinity—say, as attributed to Zeus as the world's "owner."

On the other hand, the essential identity of God becomes invested with such idealized authority as the *huperousios* essence, the *apeiron* that God owns because it is an expression of the divine— as the Patristic writers define it, the perfect mix of "everything" (matter and form as "of one substance"). The mix of "everything" in God as *law* also sets boundaries for what humans can understand of the world, for how one may read the "book" of nature to "know" God and "read" the Bible to "know" his intent. In the Judaic tradition, Yahweh's ultimate unknowability was expressed in his lack of a name sayable by humankind. The tetragrammaton is precisely not a name (cannot be "said" as such), and it expressed both the Judaic view of God's transcendent authority and the recognition that he cannot be grasped by humans. Instead, the "four-letter word," literally a cryptographic and gapped text, is deciphered through supplemental, "interpretive" meanings that provide the voicing the "text" otherwise lacks.

This conception of the tetragrammaton as flawed text—or the human grasp of it as flawed—is dramatized in the late Christian misreading of it as "Jehovah." In Hebrew, vowel sounds are indicated by diacritical dots placed around consonants. The Jews intentionally wrote the tetragrammaton, however, with the wrong vowel dots— those for "Adonai," Lord, instead of "Yahweh"—so as to insure that the tetragrammaton would remain unsayable. The Renaissance translators of the Bible misinterpreted those marks and translated Yahweh as "Jehovah," inadvertently confirming, through their error, the Judaic sense of the tetragrammaton's fundamental indeterminacy.

Such acts of interpretation suggest at the very least that textual decipherment is a fundamentally ongoing activity, repeatable but not perfectible. In fact, as Susan Handelman argues, the "Rabbinic tradition," as distinct from the Patristic, "based itself on the principles of multiple meaning and endless interpretability, maintaining that interpretation and text were not only inseparable, but that interpretation—as opposed to incarnation ["enlightened" and privileged interpretation]—was the central divine act" (xiv). The Rabbinic "central . . . act," a transitory and always partial filling of interpretive gaps, is never adequate in itself as a single and unique act. In this tradition, interpretation necessarily means the reiteration of interpretation, and so on. In this specific sense, wherein the Rabbinic tradition does not essentialize or freeze the act of interpretation, Rabbinic "reading" is anti-paternal in its fundamental reliance on radical recursivity.

The interpretive stance of the Rabbinic tradition reflects one view of the Judeo-Christian God's transcendence, that of *extra flammantia moenia mundi*—the manner in which God fills "the infinite space which surrounds and contains all the spheres of material existence" (Hatch 244). In this pantheistic version of transcendence, God is immanent but infinite. A second view of transcendence is the recognizably Christian one wherein God "passes beyond all the classes into which sensible phenomena are divisible" as a ubiquitous "pure Mind," the set of anthropological and psychological relations in the Trinity that are not bound "in" any one thing but order all things (244). This version of transcendence sets a completely different set of boundaries for what a text of any sort may mean. It gives a different expectation of what the noble father, or Christianity's God, will enfranchise as "intention" in interpretation.

In this version of transcendence, and the interpretive strategies that follow from it, the "patristic" reading of the Bible as text, for example, is seen as embodying the very Word of God and, ultimately, the principle of divinity that is God. To effect this reading of a text, the Church Fathers brought together two traditional explanations of meaning. On the one hand is the Hebrew concept of *davar*, which literally means "word" but denotes (as Handelman quotes Isaac Rabinowitz) "'reality in its most concentrated, compacted, essential form'" (Handelman 32). Here "word" essentially means reality. The Church Fathers conflated *davar* with the Greek notion of *ousía* (substance), both of which construct the world's irreducible *eídos*. In this way, the Patristic writers "took the Hebraic concept of the word as essential reality and combined it with Greek concepts of substance and being, and developed the idea of the incarnation—the word-become-flesh, *thing* in a literal sense" (Handelman 32).

The interpretive stance derived from this new concept eschews "interpretation" as the imperfect and repeatable *activity* projected by the Rabbinic tradition, and on this point the Rabbinic tradition *cannot* be taken as part of the paternal romance. The Patristic approach, rather, defines reading the text ("text" as the written word and as the "book" of nature) as divine anabasis. God steps forward in the material of a text and the Word comes forth "revealed" (not only "interpreted") in the one true light of heaven. In an important sense, the Church Fathers actually asserted that God steps forward in a text for the reader when the Word is present. Such exegetical absolutism, scarcely "interpretive" in the Rabbinic sense, "discovers" God's idealized authority as "revealed" in the text and projects the text as signifying nothing outside itself. The Father is the permanent and insuperable occupant of the subject position and the dictator of the way that text will be read—the most perfect version of the "romantic" hero as substantial self. From the Patristic viewpoint, the biblical text will hereafter be seen as the vehicle carrying the substantial being (the Word)—the essence of what can be revealed to humans of the "truth" that is God.

This model of paternal authority combines various elements of the Greek noble father having to do with epistemological and ontological authority and "power." These attributes are variously distilled as a "procession" out of the Father. This authority is officially incarnate in the Word "without remainder," particularly in light of the Trinitarian proviso prohibiting subordination of the Word to the Father (or of Spirit to Word). God's authority allows no epistemological monarchianism. The supreme Christian Father, with far greater range and depth of authority than Zeus, embodies the relations that constitute the world, but with no (or very little) hint of the Greek polytheism suggested in heretical descriptions of the Trinity, particularly by Arius. Whereas Zeus swallowed Metis and became incarnate "knowledge" of the law, the Christian Father has, in effect, swallowed the law itself in the form of the Word. He is the super-transcendent epitome (*huper-ousios*, or "super-substantial" essence, as John Damacene said) of all authority.

The "Logic" of Christian Paternity

As Christianity paradoxically shows, the incarnation is not accomplished "without remainder." In fact, the divine incarnation creates a "remaindered" counter-version of itself in the "world." The "created world," the Kosmos at the greatest remove from God's presence, exists in addition to God who (as a cosmic agent) is its opposite—"*un*created," "*un*born," "*un*dying," and "*un*contained." The "created world" known to humans is the antithesis of these divine characteristics and exists only as a contingent supplement to God, in what some contemporary theologians call its "extra" status (Armstrong and Markus 24). This state is also suggested by the prophecy in Revelation of the world's expendability, nonexistence, after the Millennium. Strongly tied to the created world in time is Satan, whose "supplemental" status to God is shown by the confinement of his fortunes to this world.

Satan, in fact, bears strong similarities to Christ. Both were rejected as sons and "excluded" from an original union with God. While they preexist the human world, clearly both have important missions *in* it. (According to one Gnostic belief, Satan not only falls into the world first; he is also God's first born [Jung, *Psychology and Religion* 170].) There is even a fairly widespread heretical tradition of insisting on Satan's virtual membership in the Trinity as a fourth "person." This view entails reimagining the Athanasian Creed as a "*quaternarium*," the Trinity-plus-Satan. From this view would come the assertion that God's supposed pouring of himself into the World "without remainder" is a twofold act that positions a "remainder" (the profane world) in a different register. This act offers the possibility of a simultaneously effaced yet persistent worldly presence, which is precisely the status of "evil" Satan and his taboo domain in the fallen world.

The quaternarium thesis can be approached analytically through Aristotle's square of opposition, an accurate blueprint, especially as interpreted by St. Thomas and Cardinal Cajetan, of the logic of ideology inherent in paternal authority and the paternal romance. Aristotle's "square," as I discussed earlier, consists of two levels of opposition. In one version of this logic in *On Interpretation* Aristotle stipulates that on the first level are the universal affirmative and negative positions, and on the second level are "particular" affirmative and negative positions (the "subaltern" level). His use of these terms, as I explained in the last chapter, offers a method for analyzing the inherent logic of a proposition or concept in its general and specific dimensions.

For instance, the logic of trinitarian relations, plus Satan, can be analyzed on the square as in Figure 7. This "rigid," logical progression from one proposition to another is made possible by the reductionism of the law of non-contradiction as "the firmest of all principles" (Handelman 13), the result of which is a "straitjacketing of logic" and interpretation in the underlying precepts of the paternal romance (13). But precisely because of its limitations, because it models the ideological content of the paternal romance, Aristotle's interpretive logic provides an invaluable display of "rational" and strictly oppositional formulations that make up a paternal decorum— in this case, the Trinity and the repressed Catholic idea of Satan as a "fourth" person.

The square's "founding" opposition of Father and Son, particularly following Aristotle's idea of how relations develop from the *hupokeimenon*, eventually requires the positing and situating of a double negation as shown in Satan's existence. As Trinitarian theory already shows and as the square's analysis reemphasizes, the Father by himself (the first term) is "nothing," a nonrelation about which nothing can be known or said. The introduction of the second term and the "opposition" it creates in relation to the first institutes difference through mutual exclusion, but not negation. The resulting

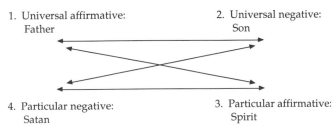

1. Universal affirmative:
   Father

2. Universal negative:
   Son

4. Particular negative:
   Satan

3. Particular affirmative:
   Spirit

Figure 7.

system of two positions generates an economy of knowledge, a knowing whose immediate product is the square's third position—in this
case, the rule of Christian relationality as expressed in the Spirit.

The third term on the subaltern level is the product of the first
two and articulates their relationship. It also negates the first in that
the Spirit is invested in the created world, while the Father is the
created world's antithesis. The Father is "unborn" and "undying," but
the Spirit's mission—even granting its "preexistence"—is "spiration"
in the created world. The Spirit is not so much "opposed" to or
"different" from the Father (the relationship created through the Son);
rather, the Spirit subsumes the relationship of "difference" and goes
farther, negating the Father as "non-Father." The "opposition" of the
first two terms on the square here allows one (by instituting "difference") to think the third term's negation of "non-Father," or everything
other than the Father. While twice removed from the first, the third
position is still tied to the Father through its elaboration of difference.
Hence the economy, or interrelatedness, of the three positions.

The Athanasian Creed and St. Augustine's *Trinity* stipulate
that the Trinitarian positions form a unity without remainder, a perfect equilateral triangle, suggesting that no relation—in effect, no
"reality"—exists outside the three "persons" and their interdependence. (Even Jung, who writes extensively on this subject, follows the
orthodox view when he makes the untenable claim that the "Trinity
contains no opposition of any kind, but is, on the contrary, a complete harmony in itself" [*Psychology and Religion,* 130].) The logic
of Aristotle's square requires a fourth term, however. Initially the
second term instituted the relation of "difference" from the Father;
the third term (through negation) then indicated the rule of relationship in *all* that is not the Father, which seemingly left no other
possibility for a relation (another "person") within the square.

A further radical relation does exist. That which neither differs
from nor negates the Father can evade similarity and difference as
defined in this paternal economy. This fourth term emblematizes not
just opposition to or negation of the Father, but a total rejection of
his articulated relations. I am speaking of actual "oblivion" and
"breakdown," the radical negation of linear logic and the law of
noncontradiction, precisely the instance of the extra-paternal formulation that the Father's totalizing law aims to exclude. These ideas
about the "failure" of relation, loss of the relations of the other three
positions, is required by the logic of a correlative to the Trinity's
"success."

Paradoxically, the relation of "failure" (of no relation), while radically extra-paternal, as opposed to anti-paternal or nonpaternal, also possesses its own distant tie to the Father. The function of the fourth position is actually to re-enact the lack of relation inherent to, but hidden inside, the first position—the Father's status as "*un*born" and "*un*created" nonrelationality. The fourth position is radically and simultaneously "foreign," yet it offers the conclusion to (and "closure" of) the square's oppositional logic.

As befits the fourth term, Satan's (non-)position in, or "negative affinity" to, the Trinity is necessary yet simultaneously is effaced, in the sense of being generated by but excluded from the site of the other terms. The fourth term is repressed in that, as radical transgressor, it exists outside of and cannot be articulated in the square's other terms—hence its abject, "foreign," and "evil" status. A similar repression of the quaternarium is evident in Plato's recognition, in the *Timaeus*, of a recalcitrant fourth in relation to a triadic and otherwise balanced intellectual schema. The quaternarium possibility also arises in the Pythagorean theory of the Soul with a nature that is both rectangular and triune. Such is Goethe's implied reformulation of the Trinity as a mythic allegory of consciousness in the famous Cabiri scene in *Faust, Part II:*

> *Three we brought with us,*
> *The fourth would not come.*
> *He was the right one*
> *Who thought for them all.*
>   (2:2,8186–8189; italics in original)[1]

The fourth "thought for them all" in that its target of denial, and hence its (denied) origin, is the whole structure of Trinitarian relations—including the critique implied by the radical fourth. That "fourth," as Goethe appears to say, follows its own logic in remaining excluded from other relations. There is always a radical de-negation, or complete rejection, of those possibilities created in oppositional relations. This is certainly true in the case of the Trinity, where opposite the Son is the "negative" position diagonally adjacent, or "contradictory," to the Word.

In fact, a good deal in the square must "not come" forward, as Goethe says, and cannot formally enter logical progression without destroying or transforming it. Aristotle explains the logic here when he says that the repressive function of the square is evident in the privileged, initiatory status afforded to the logic of "opposition," the sense in which the "speech" of a proposition is truly "enunciative," or legitimate, only if "there is truth or falsity" in it—that is, only if the square's first two terms are organized as strict binary oppositions (*On Interpretation* 7:17a2–17a5).

In a revealing fifteenth-century commentary on "opposition" in the square, Cardinal Cajetan completed the commentary begun by Aquinas on Aristotle's *On Interpretation*. Cajetan recognizes the inevitable but unwanted intrusion of non-oppositional, "relative" relations in the square (what could be called "analog" relations) and ironically affirms the possibility of a sense of the world that is not purely rational in this classical sense. Could there be non-oppositional, relational paths of association? He quickly forecloses this possibility, somewhat tautologically, and insists that "significations are not opposed relatively . . . the only way they can be opposed is contrarily" (*On Interpretation* 1962, 234). Cajetan's commitment here, affirmed by the structural intention of the square, is to exclude as illicit anything posited "relatively" instead of "oppositionally"—all that does not conform to the formalism of oppositional relations. This is a revealing moment in the history of interpretation, wherein the drama of violent exclusion is overtly played out by a medieval commentator on Aristotle. In Cajetan's rejection of the possibility of nonrational interpretive meaning, we glimpse a deliberate suppression of material that could well and will return as the effaced "fourth" term in the square.

It is also clear that the "logic" of the fourth is a logic of suppression. Suppression establishes the formal relations of the other three terms and the nature of the fourth as the unrepresentable term in the square's economy. The square's formal reliance on opposition, in fact, depends upon the effacement, or repression, of radical negativity—what Cardinal Cajetan so hastily and authoritatively dismisses as the merely "relational" terms that do not reflect opposition and that are *absolutely* other to the decorum of the square, not inscribable within it. That which rejects altogether, in other words, has no place as a formulated principle in a rational economy.

Non-oppositional terms are inherently problematic to the logic of the paternal romance. They introduce contingencies and discrepancies within relationships that cannot be known in advance; this is a problem, because the whole point of the oppositional square is to allow prediction of the form and direction relations will take. Such control renders the logic of interpretation uniform and predictable instead of contingent. If contingency were to reign, little could be categorized or controlled. In the *Posterior Analytics* Aristotle asserts simply and emphatically that there can be no "science of the contingent," a way of knowing that is polymorphous and irrational, unpredictable and corrosive—that is, no science of the *extra-* or *a*-paternal. Such a science would dismantle and destroy paternal logic and the important certainties it achieves. Aristotle's "science of the contingent," in fact, accurately looks forward to the deconstructive "sciences" of Nietzsche, Michel Foucault, Sarah Kofman, and Jacques Derrida, and it is appropriate that all four are strongly anti-paternal, anti-rational, and anti-philosophical in the classical sense.

The "logic" of suppression, then, creates the appearance or effect of uniformity and continuity—of an unencumbered and natural logical advance through the terms of the square. The obstacle to this advance, as if a deferred debt—the "extra," or remainder, accompanying suppression—will be repaid as that lost material is reclaimed in the problematic fourth position. The act of suppression that produces the square's and the father's authority at the same time resituates and diminishes that authority in relation to a counter force ("debt") in the fourth position. The more the square operates according to its own strict rule of suppression, the more it will accrue a debt at an "other" site. The Father by necessity brings about his own murder in the "other," radically negative, site of his own repression.

Christianity's supreme paternal authority is caught in this reversal. Power to embody truth is continually being undermined and diminished by the usurpation of an extra-paternal otherness. This ongoing "reversal" suggests that the Christian version of the noble father, within the "square" of his own repressive logic, must continually dismantle and destroy himself. Time itself, and the dynamics of ideology and time in history, do not respect the professed permanence of the paternal romance.

Christian doctrine also reaches this conclusion. Earlier I mentioned God's double death in the creation of the world and Word. Now, in contrast to the perfect incarnation "without remainder," there is also the doctrinal scenario wherein—as Paul shows in the Epistle to the Romans—the Father's law and Satan's sin derive from a common, heterogeneous source, ultimately from an incarnation "with remainder." Paul speculates on the heterogeneous or contaminated "origin" for law and sin when he wonders about the etiology of sin and asks rather boldly, "Is the law sin?" Is not the law, in other words, part of the same economy of relations that produces sin? He reasons that it must be so; otherwise, he pleads, he could "not [have] known sin, but by the law: for I had not known lust, except the law said, Thou shalt not covet." The law and sin, he concludes, have a mutual derivation, just as do Christ and Satan, existing on adjacent ends of an oppositional set of relations.

Finally, in a decisive and revealing moment of doctrinal decon-struction, this Church Father actually posits dynamic, structural inter-action between substance and remainder within a Christian framework and concludes, rather poignantly, that "without the law sin was dead" (7:7–12). Extremes meet at precisely the point where law and sin—ultimately, God and Satan—create each other within the same ideological discourse. In more strictly logical terms, the existence of Satan presupposes that of God. This conclusion is Paul's succinct recognition of the mechanism in Christianity that situates the Father in the subject position and tries to forget that act of positioning—the Christian narrative version of what I am calling the paternal romance.

The fact of a tie based on logical presupposition does not deny the difference between the Father and Satan, or Christ and Satan. Rather, it strengthens the idea that the "Father"—whether "uncreated," super-substance, law, or tetragrammaton—is at base and essentially a *text*, an articulation (more accurately, an interpretation of an artic-ulation) in a hierarchical system of differences. As the case of God makes most clear, paternal authority is structured like a text and is itself a structure within a text. We can see this in the Mass's and the Trinity's vivid demonstration of strategies—and in the history of these strategies—for interpreting paternal authority. In official Church read-ings, in Patristic interpretation, there is the ideologically based assumption that the Father will always be the *hupokeimenon*, in the subject position. This assumption is intended to substantialize the Father as "sacred" and give Him prestige above all other possible subjects. This claim for privileged, sacred interpretation can be resub-jected to a critique. The predictable and uniform significance of "Father" is effected through the arbitrary suppression of possibilities that do not fit the formal requirements of paternal logic. And yet it is not, in any defensible way, inevitable.

Christian paternal authority, in short, comes in two forms, as does the Greek. The first is God as a kind of noble father who claims absolute power over the world. This is the *huperousia* who cannot be represented and who is at once the world essence and the "owner" of its cosmogenetic material. He is the essence of what is "emptied" into the world and of what is returned perfectly to its origin (in Him) through the agency of the Spirit. This ideal of the paternal romance is a tremendous enhancement (and distillation) of key characteristics that defined Zeus, particularly regarding the origin of the cosmic pattern and the force for implementing that pattern in the creation of a world. In this version He is the noncontingent center, or navel, for the world and exists in relation to nothing outside himself. His unpronounceable name (*YHWH*) stands as an indication of his uncontained and transcendent (non-), thus perfect, existence. He is so grand in his infinite perfection that, like Northrop Frye's ersatz version of Zeus, the whole world emanates from him and could fit back inside him. Truly the "noble father" in a sense superior to the way the Greeks used that concept, Yahweh is (seems to be) "everything."

The second form of Yahweh is the "Father" as a concept of order that can be analyzed on Aristotle's square of opposition. This Father is emptied into the world *with remainder* and is embedded in a matrix of relationships and significations of "other" meanings and possibilities in what is generally called a "text." His existence is found within, and is completely dependent on, a textual system of relations—an environment of relationships wherein He "exists" only insofar as He is an interpretation of certain textual structures. He is neither perfect nor infinite. The manner of "reading" Him is also limited and imperfect; hence the need for recursive interpretation, as shown in the tradition of the Rabbinic reading of texts. This God does not contain the world but is contained by it and is situated in particular texts as an interpretive "effect." This God claims to be "everything," but that claim must be viewed as a distinguishing characteristic of a figure contained within texts, not as a transcendent "truth" about texts.

The Illogic of Christian Paternity

In an important sense, therefore, the Christian Father duplicates or merely continues the dilemma presented by the Greek noble father. In both cases a repressive version of paternal authority presents itself as the creator and owner of the world. The strategy for promoting this notion (as in Greek gynecological texts, the *Odyssey,* and the Aristotelian analysis of the Trinity show) is itself a sustained act of suppression—a method for discounting all that does not fit the prescribed form of the paternal romance. A text that functions to promote the monologism (in Mikhail Bakhtin's sense) of a privileged version of paternal authority must be viewed as deeply engaged in a political act of suppression.

The concept of the Christian Father not only duplicates the dilemma of the Greek noble father; it also deepens the inherent contradictions of Greek paternal authority in ways that strain the paternal romance as a privileged cultural referent. Whereas the Greeks constantly tested the notion of the father as "everything," encompassing the entire Kosmos, in the end they only claimed that Zeus was a particular cultural force among others, the privileged sign of their cultural investments, especially their notions of justice and law. The conception of God, however, is far more idealized. He *is* the world—the embodiment of "everything," the One who only temporarily withdraws from the world so that He may return love to Himself, so that difference and the many may return to the *same*.

At the same time, as the analysis of Satan in relation to Christ and also to the heretical doctrine of the quaternarium demonstrates, especially as that tradition can be analyzed through the oppositional relations of ideology in the paternal romance, God is separate from the world he owns and administers. Like Zeus, He has two selves: the God of perfect knowledge but also the God of imperfect actions, of the fallen world. Unlike Zeus, however, in God's primary conception He is fully merged into the world he supposedly owns as his own cosmogenetic matter. He loves his own perfect subject self. In this incarnation of the world without remainder, God transcends all mundane value, cultural investment, or ideology. God-the-"everything" should not be amenable to ideological situating, for he is supposed to transcend the world.

The dilemma of Yahweh's position is evident in three areas of his conception, as follows:

1. In the absolute merging of the Father with the concept of the law's function, God as a figure—through Christ—becomes fully equivalent to the "all" of the Kosmos—the world's "everything." God must be at once the supersubstantial stuff of the world, the owner of the *huperousia*, and the system of operation through which the paternal "owner" administers ownership of and interacts with the world. God, in short, is merged "perfectly" with the law; the law is then merged with the world in such a way that the world manifests the law. The Father-as-World encircles the *same*, Himself. He formally admits to no deviance from or error within what must be a perfect incarnation.

2. The paternal "logic" that Christianity inherits from the Greeks, and on which the concept of the Christian Father is founded, clearly positions the Father within a hierarchy of textual relations. Trinitarian doctrine and ironic generation of a quaternarium are incontrovertible evidence of this situating. Henceforth the Father is necessarily grasped within those relations as a limited "effect" of discourse. But such a view of the Father contradicts the Father as an ideal. Like the "perfect" and absolute version of Zeus that arises from the Greek popular epithets, the "absolute" version of God negates

his evident functioning in theological formulation and doctrine—his performative function in Christian narratives. A "function" of necessity is relational and contingent, unable to be absolute in the sense of God's standing free of all relations. The hierarchical and oppositional view of paternity is not compatible with the concept of the Father as an absolute (non-)entity—an infinite "being" absolved of all relational contingency. He is the One to whom "is" would add the contradictory attribute of being to that of infinity. Like Zeus, God cannot simultaneously "be" a perfect unity and "function" in texts that are situated in the fallen world.

3. Christianity's theoretical resolution for this dilemma is quite different from that of Greek religion. The Greeks project Zeus as the *Diosemia*, or the mere signifier of the law, whereas God is said to effect a supposedly perfect incarnation of himself into the Word "without remainder," consummating his status as the perfect "all." But the *performance* of this step generates precisely the "remainder" that is generated by all performance and semiosis, a remainder connected with the logical necessity of what I have been calling the "fourth." The Christian equation of God with the law blocks God from recognizing the "fourth" of Satan, or evil, chance (non-oppositional relations), mortality, or even woman—in short, blocks God from the world. Removed from and situated against the world, wholly "other" to it, Christianity "solves" the Western problem of paternity by radically denying the possibility of any performative efficacy to the Father. But as the contemporary Catholic philosopher Edward Schillebeeckx points out, "if God is indeed the 'Wholly Other' without a recognizable immanence in our world, then we would revere him best by saying nothing about him" (Schillebeeckx 627). The great dilemma of God at the elevated height given him by Christianity is that He can "do" nothing in the world from which he withdrew.

God actually dismantles any claim to paternal authority in that he is unable to function—or to recognize and claim his function— in the very world where his performance would be significant. In essence, the Christian definition of paternity as "everything" erases the distinctions between self and world that made the paternal romance a powerful force and agent of cultural intervention to begin with. From the perspective we have created in the analysis of Zeus and the tradition of the paternal romance, God is conceived with deep contradictions about authority—whether it reigns in this world or out of it. Christianity tries to assert that God is the perfect melding of noble father and world, so that the contradictions of One and

Many in the paternal romance are manifested simultaneously, impossibly, as "everything" and "nothing." It is as if God is an attempt to achieve a fantastic ideal of power of which Zeus could only dream.

God, finally, is a playing out of the idealized relations of the paternal romance that exposes it ideologically and removes the mystery surrounding its origin and function. Without this obscurity, as Louis Gernet and Pierre Bourdieu show about ideological systems, the paternal romance will be exposed simply as ideology, rather than the "truth." And then the paternal romance—the mystified and idealized Western projection of power—topples. Once dismantled, the Father no longer looks like the proud and austere bust of Zeus. He now looks more like what Shelley described in "Ozymandias" as "that colossal Wreck, boundless and bare." The persistence of the paternal romance, even as a "colossal Wreck," will be a topic of my final chapter.

Forget the Father

In this chapter I have continued to superimpose the figure of the Greek noble father on a Christian context to critique the idea of a privileged "text" of Western culture, a text gradually modified by the Greeks and then later drastically reformulated by Christianity in Yahweh, Jehovah, and God. In regard to Greek culture, I am articulating a view of the Greek Kosmos as constituted by a framework of the world made up of three tenets. The first is that the universe is a hierarchy of powers organized according to function, value, and rank, the Kosmos constituting a management of power according to social class and ideological configuration. Second is that this hierarchy of powers is not a "natural" order in any sense, but one established through the exploits of an agent, the force of a particular ideology, and expressing the dominance of *phusis* by *themis* and *nomos*. The Kosmos is a cultural construct and a social hierarchy. It is organized by a structural intention within an ideological grid of overdetermined relations. Finally, the world is governed by the exceptional power of Zeus, the Greek father as the supreme agent of politics and not merely of the given *phusis* (see Vernant 1982, 115, for a discussion of this scheme). The Greek philosophical version of this "framework," I contend, is the "subject-in-process" of the oppositional square, the *hupokeimenon* and the relationships that represent and articulate the "substratum," that is, the "subject" that gives definition to all other forms of knowledge in the Kosmos.

The noble father is an effect in narrative that functions as a prime referent for key ideological (what Michael Harrington calls "political") hierarchies in culture, several of which I have discussed. Such hierarchies can be glimpsed with remarkable accuracy in the Pythagorean Table of Opposites. Furthermore, it is the nature of the noble father *as a text* to function in the manner of a textual economy, that is, dynamically and with a margin of indeterminacy. It is true that in Greek texts it is often not clear when paternal authority is formative and when it is not, or whether the noble father represents power or the lack of power. The textual nature of the noble father often exists in conflict with Greek attempts to find stasis and finite meanings in texts that are oriented by the noble father's supposed stability. This conflict finds expression in the two versions of Zeus, the cognitive and performative versions that appear in the *Theogony,* the *Odyssey,* and other major cosmogenetic texts.

In reading these texts it is apparent that Aristotle's formulation of the oppositional square is a key version of the Greek process of interpretation. Most important about the "square," however, is that it foregrounds the concept of positionality, the speaking subject in Greek texts and discourse—the privileged textual matrix on which the concept of ideology rests and from which the father in the paternal romance acquires his privilege. The "noble father" stands as the attempt of Greek culture to make the position of the father the normative and privileged referent of discourse—the "natural" substratum as a "voice" of the Kosmos. This practice of identifying the father with the subject's position in discourse leads the Greeks, finally, to substantialize the noble father as an absolute figure, a primary "substance" (*ousía*) in a romance about a masterful, ideal subjectivity. The noble father is an early version of the cultural narrative of the paternal romance—Western culture's ongoing attempt to privilege the father as the subject of discourse.

Once established, this system of paternal reference has been incredibly resilient and difficult to dislodge. The father and paternal substitutes are easily and customarily returned to the first position of discourse along previously established channels of ideology. It is evident that the overdetermination of paternal references contributes to the fixity of the paternal romance in complex cultural and ideological systems. In the *Theogony* a powerful female figure such as Gaia or Night can temporarily *be* the subject of discourse without challenging the fundamental claim of paternal subjectivity and positioning. This is so because every nonpaternal figure comes into the position of power as previously and already textualized, as already understood in relation to the father and as a paternal substitute. Gaia will tend to be powerful in any context relating to paternal authority, as a figure that is already standing in for the paternal figure.

This scenario of substitution and reversion suggests the paternal romance as a closed system of reference, endorsing Michael Harrington's notion that "God has been a leading conservative in Judeo-Christian society" and culture (1). While the father may begin as the mere institution of an ideological frame, once in place, he constructs the equivalent of a "natural" and "true" reference in the Kosmos. But the father is not "nature" and "truth." The fixed truth of the world and the ideological discourse of the paternal romance would be absolutely unalterable were it not for the instability of the subject in discourse and the fact of continual ontological inadequacy, José Ortega y Gasset's "constitutional inadequacy," or error, within historical discourse itself—that is, indeterminacy and misrecognition within the operation of culture as a semiotic and ideological system. The *Theogony* and the *Odyssey* show that even highly paternalized narratives necessarily evince gaps, fissures, and recesses of signification wherein discourses other than paternal ones find channels in which to operate, and even in which to alter paternal authority. The codes representing male and female authority that circulate through Odysseus as a figure—his wandering and his passivity—show that an otherness, even a "contradictory" version of the father, in Aristotle's terminology, invades a most paternalized figure.

Likewise, the Christian formulation of paternal authority deepens the contradictions of the paternal romance and, in a sense, points toward its dismantling. The contradiction of God's position is evident in all areas of his conception. Michael Harrington advances this view of a dysfunctional god when he begins *The Politics at God's Funeral* (1983) by saying that "God, one of the most important political figures in Western history, is dying" (1). In the modern world, he writes, the Judeo-Christian God-the-Father can no longer "be conjured" (35). Specifically, the Judeo-Christian Father is experiencing a gradual demise as a cultural construct in the modern world. This "is not [an event] simply theological" (1), an issue pertinent only to the technical patterning of religion. Rather, God's absence has an effect on the world, just as his "presence" at one time created theology and therein shaped the world. Blaise Pascal writes in *Pensées*, as if peering ahead to the whole of the fatherless modern age, "The eternal silences of the infinite frighten me." He refers to a largely metaphysical fright in response to absurdity and chaos, what Lucien Goldmann calls the "discovery of infinite geometric space"—the modern "space of rational science" in which "God does not speak anymore." God-the-Father has gone silent in the post-Enlightenment world, Goldmann adds, "because in order to elaborate that [rational] space, man had to renounce every ethical norm," including the grounding of such norms in the very idea of God as an absolute and irrational reference (Harrington 1–2).

Key to the discussion of the paternal romance is a connection between two events: (1) the issue of recognizing the ideological and political dimension of God, the idea of "God" as embodying a particular Western configuration of ideology, (2) and the post-Enlightenment "death" or dismantling of the universal ideal of God as a Western representation of "truth." This is my argument about God's formulation and rise. Harrington maintains that in the advent of the Judeo-Christian version of God there was a temporary loss of any connection between religion and politics, any sense of a God who clearly stands for an understanding of and commitment to material values and the management of power in the world as an inhabited community. "The universal deity of the Jews and Christians," as Harrington describes Yahweh and God, "seemed to become a stateless person" (2), a universalized and transcendent figure not overtly identified with ideology or any situated context.

The history of the paternal romance shows that there is always a "remainder" and an "excess" to power, a plethora of subordinate discourses that do not disappear from the textual economy. Dominant discourses must have subordinate and subaltern discourses as references in order to situate themselves as dominant. Just as a father destroys fatherhood by destroying his children (as was the case with Kronos), dominant discourses cannot destroy subordinate ones without destroying their own hegemony. The *Theogony* and the *Odyssey* as narratives, in other words, are governed by the noble father, but it is entirely possible to retrieve maternal and filial discourses from them.

The possibility of retrieving repressed textual material was the issue I raised in regard to gynecological texts and scientific logic in chapter 3. In the gynecological construction of the female body, for example, the counter to male technology is marked and seemingly dismissed. Ultimately, the stray movements of the entire world (as writ small in the stray movement of the woman's uterus within her body) require correction that, in patriarchal discourse, only a global male authority can provide. The following chapter will show how contemporary feminist discourse acknowledges precisely this "perversity" in the paternal romance. Feminist theorists then attempt to deconstruct the division between the perverse and the rational and,

in so doing, institute a feminist critique that does not so much comment on patriarchal values and practices as contribute to the dismantling and transformation of the paternal romance.

One effect of the feminist critique is to suggest that the continual
positioning of the dominant discourse involves a mediation of contrary relations, as the operation of the oppositional square shows.
The subject of discourse is repeatedly pushed toward greater complexity and inclusiveness, toward more accommodation of difference.
Like a viral mutation, the cumulative effects of semiosis leave traces
in a gradual reconfiguration of the dominant discourse; what is left
out, the "remainder" of ideology, becomes more clearly inscribed
within the texts of official power. The difficulty of effecting the reconciliation of contrary and contradictory relations so as to keep the
dominant ideology in the subject position increases exponentially as
it becomes a far vaster and more difficult cultural operation. The
paternal virus, in other words, eventually becomes far less paternal.
As the reconciliation becomes too difficult to bring about, the
"remainders" of ideology begin to break off and eventually form their
own ideological hierarchies that either compete openly with the dominant discourse or else exist alongside it. Antonio Gramsci has elaborated this process of "subaltern" discourses in competition with
hegemony.

This scenario describes the inevitable failure, or at least the
major modification, of any one ideology. It also describes what has
happened to the paternal romance in ancient Greek religion and in
the rise of Christianity. I commented earlier on Western culture's
tradition of "forgetting" about paternity and the subsequent need to
"remember" repressed and "forgotten" aspects of the father—much
like the need to recall the details of a recurring bad dream so as to
work through and be free of it. This book is an attempt to advance
the full working through and forgetting of the paternal bad dream
and, by letting it go, to obtain real freedom from the paternal romance
and be done with its oppression. Questions and probings about the
Greek and Christian fathers tend to recur in modern culture precisely
in this spirit of a therapeutic "working through," a cultural retrieval
and analysis of repressed material—that which is "remaindered" by
culture and long ago "forgotten" even while it "returns" as the still
evident effects of the "colossal wreck."

The post-Renaissance reframing of the father is a continuation
of the dismantling of the paternal romance that, in a sense, began
in the Christian alteration and idealization of Zeus's essentially political power and authority. Subsequent texts highlight points about the

nature of the father that should bear on the deteriorating fortunes of the paternal romance. Homer's conception of the Greek noble father is a strong demonstration of the genesis and institution of the paternal romance arising out of assumptions specific to Greek culture and history and, thereafter—only as Greek culture itself becomes formative for the West—influential in Western culture quite broadly. This cultural perspective on patriarchalism becomes even stronger as we follow the transformation that takes place in the paternal romance as Christianity develops its version of the noble father through strategic alterations of what the Greek father stands for—in other words, as Zeus "becomes" Yahweh.

Paternal authority is generated from the internal and external interactions of a culture. This point should work to counter a dangerous possibility that exists even now in cultural studies. There is a seductive explanatory power, even now, in sanctioning paternal authority as an obligatory and "natural" dimension of culture, a universal and unalterable function. As this specious line of reasoning runs, culture cannot operate without the paternal romance and still survive *as culture*. But major texts of ancient Greece show that the father's authority in the paternal romance cannot be pure or monolithic, in any way an indivisible expression or demonstration of power. The father, in an important sense, *does not exist*, and he never did. Paternal purity without the traces and signs of a non-paternal otherness has always been an ideological formulation and strategy that belong to the cultural discourse of which the paternal romance is a part. This point is made with particular clarity in Hesiod's *Theogony*, which shows Zeus's interactions with and dependence on the otherness that opposes paternal authority—Zeus's complex and paradoxical relationships with Gaia, the Erinys, and Moira.

Even more dramatic is Homer's depiction of the "feminine" side of Odysseus. As if foreshadowing the "wandering wombs" of Greek gynecological texts, Odysseus wanders through the Greek world until he is oriented, put in his proper place, and given ideological significance by Zeus. In each case paternal authority is an "effect" of the paternal romance within narrative. As Eva Keuls, Page duBois, G. E. R. Lloyd, Sarah Pomeroy, and many others have noted, the hegemony of paternal authority in ancient Greek culture is visible in a preference for oppositional relations and strict hierarchies, what Lloyd calls "polarities," over heterogeneity and fluctuation, the "other" cultural models preferred, as Eric Havelock notes, by the Sophists.

These observations recapitulate the three phases of Jean-Joseph

Goux's historical and ideological reading of Western culture: (1) an "unconscious" epoch in "pre-history" that exists prior to paternal hegemony in Greek culture but which ultimately produces the rectilinear model, (2) an epoch of consolidated patriarchalism and "social contract" from the Renaissance through the Enlightenment, and (3) the modern period of self-critique and the perspectives on the human artifact of "history." I am intending a parallel here between my discussion of the dialogic cultural context of paternal authority in the *Odyssey* and Goux's discussion of the conflicts of an "unconscious" dimension in a "primitive" cultural epoch.

Following Goux and others, I am addressing Western forms of paternal representation, the point being not merely to understand the paternal romance, but to change it. In postmodern culture paternal authority remains, as Donald Barthelme has described it, like "blocks of marble, giant cubes, highly polished" which are "placed squarely in your path." If we attempt "to go around [the father]," we "find that another (winking at the first) has mysteriously appeared athwart the trail. Or maybe it is the same one, moving with the speed of paternity" (129). This wry and dark picture of institutional intractability suggests that the paternal romance is so deeply implicated in Western modes of analysis, logic, and even rhetoric that life under patriarchy appears to be sustained even by direct challenges to and critiques of the paternal romance.

Derrida's idea about the difficulty of looking fathers "in the face" first concerns the problem of being ideologically blind, of succumbing to the "natural" truth of paternity. But there is also the question of finding a foundation of values on which to stand, a place outside the Western tradition from which to examine and critique that tradition. Where should I stand? On what theoretical ground can I stop and regroup in order to effect a critique of the father? Where is this analytical "outside" that will allow me to look the father in the face and stare down the paternal romance and its tradition?

Gilles Deleuze and Felix Guattari try to answer such questions. In *Anti-Oedipus* and *A Thousand Plateaus* they argue for a questioning of paternal authority, one so radical as to entail a critique of the entire underpinning of the Western tradition. They challenge fundamental notions of order and rationality, especially as embodied in the concepts of repression and castration, as "molar," ideologically loaded and open to critique. The "molar" is a cluster of suppressed assumptions united in an ideologically motivated pattern that is taken—mistakenly—to be "scientific" and "naturally" the way humans function. The molar formulation of "castration" conveys not only cultural restraint but a masculine "presence." The buried supposition behind the term castration, Deleuze and Guattari show, is precisely "that there is finally only one sex, the masculine, in relation to which the woman, the feminine, is [also] defined as a lack, an absence" (*Anti-Oedipus* 294). They challenge this hegemonic version of cultural regulation as promulgated to advance an essentialist conception of males. By contrast, the "molecular," non-essentialist conception of the unconscious, like the repression that engenders it, "knows nothing of castration" precisely because castration as such is an ideologically motivated construct (295). Deleuze and Guattari seek to explode the monological concept of castration and speak, instead, of an unconscious that produces positive "multiplicities" and "flows" (295)—potentially not just "two sexes, but *n* sexes," perhaps a "hundred thousand" (296).

These distinctions lead, finally, to their critique of paternal authority via the concept of representation in the West. What allows the constitution of such "molar" conceptions of castration is Freud's conception of the unconscious as a static *representation*. The fact of the unconscious as such, as difference not represented in a manifest text, is not objectionable to them in the critique of psychoanalysis. Indeed, to a certain extent Deleuze and Guattari actually approve of Freud's conception of the unconscious as the site of the "production of desire" and, without irony, call this conception the "great discovery of psychoanalysis" (*Anti-Oedipus* 24). The problem comes in Freud's attempt to bury the unconscious as a productive function "beneath a new brand of idealism" and to associate it with the *representation* (rather than "production") of "a classical theater" of "myth, tragedy, [and] dreams" (24). In short, Freud, and Lacan after him, depict the unconscious in a passage through Greek texts inextricably with the Western *family* and the ideological investments inherent to Western culture. For Freud and Lacan, it follows that the unconscious is not a site of production, a machine capable of various modes of work, but is itself the "essence of representation," constructed in advance "to be a *familial* [and paternalized] representation" (296; emphasis added).

Deleuze and Guattari massively reject this absolute identification of the unconscious with the family and radically reposition the unconscious as a "machinic arrangement" that *can*, but need not, produce the familial and patriarchal organization of narrative as one of its effects. In so doing, they re-situate the "order of desire" in the unconscious not as cultural representation, a static and permanent framing of familial (Oedipal) order, but as cultural *"production"* (296) in all of its possibilities. They then project a "post-Oedipal" world as without the genital and Oedipal organization characteristic of Western culture—in other words, without the father as I have been discussing him. They argue that the loss of the father will yet produce, among many other things, a radically liberated human body—echoing Marx, a "body without organs" (*A Thousand Plateaus* 285). Such a body of energy "flows" and "excesses" is capable of "becoming an animal" in the specific sense that psychoanalysis, with its belief in castration and Oedipal commitments, "doesn't understand" (259). In their cryptic parlance, "becoming an animal" means the dismantling of the concept of Western humanism, *what it means to be human* in Greco-ontotheological terms, certainly a configuration of the "human" subject *other than* what psychoanalysis posits.

In my discussion of the Greek noble father I suggested that we, in fact, can examine Zeus, dissolve his continuous lines, and dismantle his apparently "natural" identity precisely by examining the father as an "effect" of narrative. Because the "paternal romance" is so clearly a narrative construction, an artificial and "made" thing, recognition of it can be part of a strategy by which to challenge paternal authority. Recognizing and critiquing the paternal romance become analytical instruments to be used *against* the father, to avoid being mesmerized by the allure and seduction of "natural" and supposedly inevitable authority. Also, the critique of paternal authority must happen precisely from *within* the cultural frame in which the paternal romance itself is situated, from the position of otherness, especially involving post-patriarchal conceptions of women. That otherness cannot be assimilated into paternal authority; it is often constructed in the spectre of dialogism, whether associated with women or with others who mark the periphery of paternal discourse. The issue here is not the universal superiority or rightness of dialogism and heteroglossia over monologism, but the implications for the paternal romance of denying the existence of dialogism and heteroglossia in relation to texts.

Derrida's skepticism focuses on the fact that the father cannot be examined directly, "in the face," even when we think we are doing so. Accordingly, a critique of the paternal romance circulates through non-paternal dimensions of cultural discourse, through the "other" paths of feminine writing and unconscious enunciation—through the non-paternal otherness that constitutes the cultural discourse within which the paternal romance is situated.

There is a further and useful perspective on the ideological

critique of Western patriarchalism. Goux's idea of history also includes
an articulation of ideology in the self-conscious patterning and analytical projections of contemporary "history," and his analysis suggests a critique concerning the aims and the future of the paternal
romance. The contemporary period Goux characterizes as governed
by the possibility of cultural simulation and synthetic reproduction,
what he calls the world of *"socialized hyper-nature"* (*Freud, Marx*
274). "Hyper-nature" is reproduction as simulation but without an
"original." It is, in short, a "fatherless" world of no fixable origin, a
world characterized by high technology and cultural reconstruction,
micro-storage, corporate management, internationalism, and the
postmodern esthetic. This is the world that already exists, the postmodern "scene" of quantum logic, continual innovation, and situa-
tional reality. But in another sense it is the "future"; it is not locatable
now as a present "world" or "text."

Not descriptive and analytical in the manner of the other three
historical epochs Goux names, and covering the present *and* the
future, this epoch is not a "time" or "place" but Goux's methodological
wager on the possibility of a culture after post-modern culture, a
time for thinking the "unthought," an act of critical imagination
calculated to grasp the cultural mode "beyond" the paternal
romance—to read culture as an emergent, and not yet fully deci-
pherable, text of the historical unconscious. Goux attempts to grasp
the "recalcitrant fourth" of contemporary culture, the repressed text
that at other moments in Western discourse "would not come," the
text that previously, as Goethe said, had "to stay behind or below."
In contemporary glimpses of Nietzschean wonderment and even a
kind of speculative madness, Goux speaks of an attempt to read
traces of a new world, an a-paternal cultural "beyond" itself as a
response to the paternal romance, and also a clarification of what
we have already seen about Zeus's and God's authority, especially as
they remain in dialogue with the "other" and the non-paternal references in cultural discourse.

I can make three principal points about an hypostasized epoch
without the father. The first follows Friedrich Engels in asserting that
"modern times [necessarily] begin with a return to the [ancient]
Greeks" (*Dialectics* 259). The force of the paternal romance, now
coming to an end, began with Greek culture, and so in that sense
this book is an engagement with Engels's important insight. Also,
an endorsement of Engels' claim certainly does not imply looking for
a reinstitution of the noble father or a reinitiation of patriarchy. The
era of a post-paternal romance could well be a privileged and rare

moment of historical opportunity, a time wherein momentous deci-
sions will be made anew. Modernity "begins" with the Greeks in that
the turn to them is an act of analytical "remembering" and a return
to the sites of repression that initially constituted the paternal
romance. (On this point, again, see Adorno and Horkheimer, *The
Dialectic of Enlightenment*.)

Second, such a cultural possibility may now have opened precisely because of historical events in the West involving the role and
importance of language. Since ancient Greece, Western culture has
moved slowly away from belief in substantial and absolute manifestations of authority and toward possibilities for understanding differential and scientific systems that were unavailable previously, at
least as primary modes of thought. I do not mean "science" as such,
but scientific and self-consciously critical modes of thinking such as
language conceived semiotically. Foremost among such developments
is the modern designation of language as cultural "Other," language
and symbols as manifestations of authority, by which I mean authority in place of the traditional "paternal and ideal" version of the
Other in the Father (*Freud, Marx* 257).

The post-Enlightenment and postmodern concern with language
is a "materialistic and dialectical reversal made evident [*se rend lisible*]
through the history of ideologies" (*Freud, Marx* 257). Language as
cultural "Other" in the fourth epoch posits its own configuration of
authority and cultural reference, its own way of projecting and knowing a world, a mode in which the dynamics of language as "Other"
render meaningless repressions that previously enfranchised culture
as paternal. The "feminine" dimensions of culture may now be able
to emerge as a text "*beyond* the phallic symbolism that [previously]
represented it." This emergence, which would mean totally realigning
the relations of gender, would effect a "*materialistic reversal of sexuality*," which is to say, the whole system of gender construction and
sexual interaction and the cultural dynamics representing sexuality
as they are generally known (257).

The alteration in our understanding of the signifier (the way
meaning comes to be) in cultural texts, the "Other" conceived as
"father" or as "language," profoundly shifts all modes of cultural
production. In basic ways it transforms what it means to know
anything and even to be human. As Saussure, Freud, Lacan, Derrida,
and others have advanced previously, language in the modern era
has priority over "mind" in that language creates what we "think."
A shift in the signifier, in the direction from which subjects enter and

situate themselves in relation to other subjects, necessitates a shift in what it means to know anything.

Third, this fourth epoch of culture would be a new "genital stage" wherein the body is reclaimed for erotic yet productive pleasures not confined under the law-of-the-father. Purposely shuttling his ideas in a blur between cultural and biological references, between the body-projected-as-ideology and *the body* as essential object, Goux envisions this new epoch as fatherless. It possesses the possibility of a-paternal creativity, the advent in history of *"engendering without the father"*—that is, procreation without "his principle" of rectilinear domination (274). Such engendering does not mean returning to reformulated (patriarchal) ideals of *"mother-nature,"* but a new projection of *"socialized hyper-nature,"* "nature" as a social construct with ideological implications and still situated squarely within the context of cultural production. In other words, "hyper-nature" is not "nature" under the father's aegis, nature as the romantic projection sponsored by the paternal romance as a "natural" order. Non-paternal nature is "hyper," rather, in that it is free from paternal repression of the sort required by the paternal romance (274).

The dimension of fantasy and utopianism in the conception of this fourth "fatherless" epoch is significant. While the future in some sense is always in the process of becoming visible, ideological and "oppositional" analyses cannot project what will happen, cannot actually see the future. Goux is right, though (as is Harrington), in addressing paternal authority as it derives from Greek and Christian sources, that is, in seeing the father as a manifestation of authority enacted along particular lines of ideology in Western texts. Goux also posits a "future" in a particular ideological configuration in relation to the current eclipse of paternal authority based on the development of Western ideology as he understands it.

The conclusions of Goux's *Freud, Marx: Economie et symbolique* are in harmony with what I have argued in regard to Greek and Christian texts. I have suggested the specific ways in which the Greeks constructed the paternal romance. The Fathers of the Christian Church merged paternity with an idealized law of epistemology and ontology in a super-paternal subject and produced God. The Father was then the absolute and perfect manifestation of Word/World without remainder—a merger so perfect and complete as to be (as St. Paul said) the "end" of the law, the end of finitude and death, and the subsequent beginning of eternity.

But Paul's notion of the end of the law can be read ironically also as the "end"—as the achieved "aim" and the beginning of the end for the paternal romance. In sum, the very deterioration and cultural dismantling of paternal authority becomes observable *within* that tradition. And it is no surprise that Christianity displays the height of the father's self-proclaimed power and also the greatest contradictions in the claims made about paternal authority. Understood in this way, the Christian Father sets the stage for a corporal and cultural "engendering without the father," in lieu of the failure and demise of God-the-Father. Whereas Zeus was a companion and "comforter," an agent of daily life as he altered and shaped the world through his exploits and interventions, God became the infinite and perfect embodiment of the uncreated world itself. In this way he became nowhere evident—*deus absentia.* Christianity, therefore, and the Christian transcendent ideal of procreation, dramatically stage, or at least provide an exemplary narrative for, the Western dismantling of the paternal romance.

This "dismantling" is an important event of Western culture, and I have tried to be unambiguous about my commitment to the ideological critique of the paternal romance. This formulation of *The Paternal Romance* is not intended as a belated or inadvertent homage to paternal authority, a further involvement with and tribute to the father's power—yet another instance of bringing life back to Shelley's "colossal wreck." However, there is no escaping the fact that oppositional thinking and criticism have an effect only if they happen within culture, within competing discourses that affect hegemony. Such participation within cultural discourse may compromise ideological analysis and lessen the impact of intervention. However, the alternative is to fail to engage with the dominant discourse and to "forget the father" in the wrong way—in the forgetfulness of neglect, in eventual passive compliance with the dictates of the paternal romance.

The strategy of this book is to remember correctly and then to "forget the father" by returning to Greek texts, as Engels claimed moderns must do, and rereading God-the-Father and the strategies of the paternal romance as specific deployments of cultural power. It will be possible for postmodern culture to forget the father only when our rereadings foster the renarrating of a history of power and gender relations that constitute the social text. In the next and final chapter, I shall turn to the persistence of the paternal romance and to the process of working through a renarration of power and gender.

Note

1. While I am not comfortable with the archetypal dimensions of his discussion, Carl Jung's fascinating interpretation of the Trinitarian significance of the Cabiri lines in *Faust, Part II* is worth inspection; see *Psychology and Alchemy*, p. 157, and *Psychology and Religion: West and East*, p. 164.

CHAPTER FIVE

Reflections on Post-Paternal Culture

> It is formed, irradiated, disseminated; it is instrumental, it is
> persuasive; it has status, it establishes canons of taste and
> value; it is virtually indistinguishable from certain ideas it
> dignifies as true, and from traditions, perceptions, and
> judgments it forms, transmits, reproduces. Above all,
> authority can, indeed must, be analyzed.
>
> —EDWARD SAID, *ORIENTALISM*

We have seen that Homer's version of Zeus in the *Iliad* and the *Odyssey* gives a useful account of paternal authority as a cultural regime influential throughout the Western tradition. Homer shows how Father Zeus rules the Greek Kosmos as a powerful monarch, one who could rise out of the realm of monarchy altogether into some other sphere, to be "more" than one of the Greek gods. Where can a divine monarch, already at the world's "top," ascend to? Those Greek narratives raise the possibility that Zeus could leave the Kosmos in the same way that one might leave behind a personal possession. Zeus claims even to "own" the Kosmos in that he could shape, control, and dispose of it as he likes, as if it were an extension of his own body and person—precisely as Northrop Frye, in fact, imagined Zeus's relation to the Kosmos.

This possibility of a super-transcendent Zeus—of a god whom the world emanates from, like a mere appendage as if he were subsumed in a higher order—is a view of power apparent, though problematic, in Greek culture through the rise of Christianity. This possibility defines a complex tension between absolute and contingent power in the Greek conception of authority that runs through and structures important religious and philosophical notions in classical culture.

Honor/Murder the Father

In the wake of classical and Christian culture, there have been radical reconceptions of the religious, social, and intellectual dimensions of paternal authority, shifts in culture and the intellectual technology for knowing it. Jean-Joseph Goux calls these a "succession of forms of exchange" (*Freud, Marx* 92), that is, ways for cultures to know, interact with, and conceive of the world in relation to different concepts of authority. In his classic study *The Great Chain of Being*, Arthur O. Lovejoy constructs versions of paternal authority in consolidated patterns from Greek culture and Christianity. Positing Western paradigms, Lovejoy constructs the paternal romance in largely philosophical and religious terms as the "history of an idea," showing a pattern modulated and rationally dispersed as the metaphor of paternal influence in the world, a playing out of God's potential as an agent of value and structure. Lovejoy's subject is specifically the narrative of creation and administration held together by the divine patriarch's rational purpose as it can be described as a great "golden Chain" of paternalized technology, *technē* in the sense of the paternal way of knowing and shaping the world. This technology includes the replicating of hierarchies and the promoting of the Father's hegemonic position, all that links sacred heaven and the profane existence. The Chain that Lovejoy describes organizes "all" that exists so that "everything" imaginable—including the unimaginable specters of chaos—is connected through a complex system of rational gradation and ranking, with the links of the Chain tied ultimately to the immovable, guiding hand of God-the-Father at the Chain's heavenly end.

This scheme of the Great Chain, especially its orientation toward God as its ultimate referent, is based on two guiding principles: the *scala naturae*, and the idea of "measure" or allotted positions on the Chain. The idea of a world "scale" can be traced back at least to Plato's *Symposium* and "a scale or ladder of being" constituting a "graded series of creatures down which the divine life in its overflow had descended." This overflow "might be conceived to constitute also the stages of man's ascent to the divine life"—toward God (Lovejoy 89). The scale extends and connects everything from God-the-Father to Chaos, from the most perfect to the least perfect "substance" (*ousía*) in the world. In between are the angelic, human, animal, vegetable, and mineral orders, each in turn reflecting a scale of organization that ranges from most to least perfect. At the top of the human scale is a king; at the bottom is a beggar, leper, or some other powerless person. At the top of the mineral world is gold; at its bottom are lead and rocks. As values, the king represents the divine father for humans and is to the leper in power as gold (as a marker or sign of God) is to lead. This principle of gradation, wherein the privileged paternal metaphor is key to the order of a hierarchy that structures "everything," gives a particular and modulated (also ideologically informed) value to every item and category included in the Great Chain as a scaffolding for the Kosmos.

Lovejoy claims that the notion of a divine scale is intricately encoded by the seventeenth century. In John Milton's words,

> The scale of nature set
> From center to circumference, whereon
> In contemplation of created things
> By steps we may ascend to God. (Lovejoy 89)

The form of the Great Chain that Milton imagined became so highly complex that every being in the Kosmos could be said to have its own allotted place, or "measure," in the paternal grand scheme—its own connection, however far removed, to the "center" of an economy that the Father signifies. Nothing should be able to fall from the ultra-fine matrix of paternal relations generated from this system, because the Great Chain supported and sponsored every instance of minutia, with even a relation to Chaos. Nothing should be able to elude the Father's grasp because nothing can escape the structure he has provided for the world.

Lovejoy argues generally that the Renaissance and the seventeenth and eighteenth centuries constitute eras in which the father as the privileged marker for a position of power triumphs in elaborated Christian formulations and in the variety of cultural disclosures that Lovejoy associates with the Great Chain. He particularly looks to the Enlightenment period that most preoccupies postmodern theorists, the period that Alice Jardine describes, following Goux, as the time of the "West's conscious [mind]: superphallic, superparanoid, totally phonetic" (Jardine 85). In Europe, it is an era that asserts the balance of perfectly "accurate" representations in language's account of the world, as in the graphic representation of speech sounds and grammar. In an important sense, this is the period of an emerging scientific economy, of a symmetrically coherent and rational world order, perhaps the last era of true strength for the paternal romance. This is the period in which the narrative economy of the paternal romance most successfully creates a manifold simulacrum of what is "real."

This epoch begins in the Renaissance, with the emergence of

the "new world" in liberal speculation and science, a time manifesting a belief in the human acquisition and understanding of the laws that govern the natural world. This is the early phase of triumph for the pre-industrial middle class and the moment of social arrival for shop-keepers and tradesmen. This is the time of mercantilism in the worka-day world. (Robinson Crusoe later shows his discovery of God through the process of accumulating wealth, as he turns his island into an industrial park.) This is the age, too, of Enlightenment ration-alism and empiricism. In the seventeenth and eighteenth centuries, the Father-as-authority is known and disseminated increasingly in secular, communal, and political terms, as a cultural and political force and a representative of secular civilization. The Enlightenment staging of paternal authority increasingly becomes a social function with more secular than divine implications, best represented in the power of the "social contract." "The Enlightenment [gradually] dis-pensed with the patriarchy," as Juliet Flower MacCannell writes in *The Regime of the Brother: After the Patriarchy* (11). "The construc-tion of a political state around liberty, equality and fraternity [become] indeed the very essence, the real hope and glory of modern-ity, the heart of democracy" (12). This institution of a brother in place of a father, however, turns out to be not liberating but oppressive in a different way. It entails the actual reinstitution of the paternal romance, with the surrogate figure of the citizen brother and the bureaucratic regimes of the modern technocracy.

It is a significant commentary on the durability of this neoclassic version of the paternal romance that even Lovejoy's twentieth-century rendition of the Great Chain tends to duplicate it. Not only does Lovejoy present the "classical sign" (*epistēmē*) of logical analysis and rational decorum that make up the Chain; his analytical method it-self exemplifies neo-Enlightenment foundations for cultural theory. Lovejoy's mode of representation presupposes three tenets that under-lie neoclassical thought. The first concerns the certainty of "relation" in the classical model (such as the Great Chain), its positive know-ability and decidability as information, including the positive relations of empirical (and thus incontrovertible) investigation. The interiority of the Great Chain is presented in this model as a mirror of the world's structure, displaying what the Kosmos "really" is. Next, such analyses display certainty about the discrete categories of relation ("types") in the Great Chain. Demarcations such as the division between the sub-lunary and the supra-lunary are presented as dis-tinctive features and marked as "crucial" and "decisive." (The world is mutable and crazy, for example, below the moon and nearer to perfection above it.) The functional authority of such categories is presented as virtually non-problematic. Finally, as Page duBois argues, such neoclassical schematic presentations claim certainty about the origin of relation. The Chain and its authority as an order are "caused" by, created by, quite literally pro-created by, God-the-Father. This is true in Lovejoy's interpretation of the Great Chain *and* in his own view of it. The Father stands behind and absolutely guarantees the order of the Great Chain. He is the very authority of authority, the privileged agent who alone can procreate and who alone can effect the authentic positioning of an ultimate reference, as opposed to the performative activity on a lower order of mutability, such as the activity of giving birth (duBois 58). In this view, the Father is metaphorical certainty, the substratum as embodied in the *hupokeimenon* that underlies "all" that can be known. In contrast, the sublunary Mother is metonymic (relational) uncertainty and chance, as played out in the uncertainties of birthing.

Michel Foucault is in some ways Lovejoy's ideal critic. Certainly, from a perspective such as Foucault's, Lovejoy not only bases his own notion of the Chain on Plato's *scala naturae* but also attempts to duplicate the analytical fixity of Aristotle's and Plato's classical and patriarchal commitment. Whereas Lovejoy assumes, as duBois claims, a "principle of unilinear gradation" (10), Foucault differs from this "history-of-ideas" approach on four crucial and ultimately anti-paternal points. First, Foucault quarrels with the general tendency in neoclassical thought to attribute innovation and "newness" to individuals, to situating innovation with individuals instead of within the cultural matrix. Second, he does not assume that cultural contradictions are reconcilable within a universal paradigm. It is the nature of paradigms, in other words, to be constructed around the spaces of irruption and contradiction. Third, he finds in comparative descriptions of culture a set of divergent texts and not a master or standard model of comparison, no scenario of deviation from a privileged metaphyiscal norm. Foucault, in short, argues against the totalizing of cultural texts into master texts—like the paternal romance—that camouflage difference and blur issues of power. Finally, in the mapping of transformations in culture, Foucault focuses on and analyzes fissures and discontinuities, rather than seeing automatic (linear) "progress" in cultural development.

By contrast, Lovejoy's approach to paternal authority and its manifestations falls within the same rational scheme of efficient and ultimate cause, linear mapping, and paradigmatic validity that the Great Chain signifies to begin with. Foucault warns that unless these analytic underpinnings of classical discourse are challenged—unless, in effect, the father and his power are destroyed, or "murdered," which they are not in Lovejoy's discourse—"no interrogation as to the mode of being implied by the [classical] *cogito* could be articulated" (*Order* 312). If there is no situating of the "cogito," or subject, implicit in the Great Chain's perspective and in our own analytical viewpoint, we merely replicate the partitions, the organizations and ideology, of the classical and neoclassical episteme. Playing the Sophistic part to Lovejoy's Aristotle, Foucault characterizes such studies of epistemology as symptomatic of a residue of post-Enlightenment monologic order, order that promotes absolute and "linear" models suggestive of, and furthering, the *procreative* line of authority represented in the paternal romance.

The Death of the Father

The period since the mid-nineteenth century is a time of decline and dismantling of the paternal romance, the period when "totally phonetic" economies such as the Great Chain of Being are undermined by the lapsing of the authority that underwrites fundamental binary oppositions such as culture/nature, truth/error, inside/outside, health/disease, man/woman, procreation/birthing. These oppositions have previously made the paternal register seem transcendent, somehow existing "beyond" the worldly conditions in which fathers and patriarchal authority are actually inscribed. Also, conceptions such as "God" (as unassailable primary reference and "truth") and the later "dead father," the rhetorical trope of the "paternal metaphor," and other idealized paternal concepts attempt to convey the procreative and transcendent authority traditionally belonging to the father.

In a major anti-paternal discourse in the twentieth century, seeing no "scientific" basis for a unified "Great Chain," Foucault instead posits a matrix of radical ruptures and multiple deployments of power in culture. These ruptures and deployments are neither internally unified nor harmonized with transcendent references. In postmodernism there is no world father and no Father of fathers, no final and absolute "other" as a ground for the world's deeply ironic sense of otherness. This theoretical gesture late in the twentieth century is the serious beginning of the attempt to "forget the father"— not in the inadvertent and merely "forgetful" manner of the Greeks, who acknowledged their own ideological investments to a very limited degree, but in a deliberate, methodical dismantling and dispersal of fixed references. Like the "liberal" Sophists, Foucault argues against the supposed fixed "naturalness" of authority and for a dynamic discourse of constantly changing and seemingly perverse relations understood in dialogical as well as catastrophic terms.

Foucault's analysis of the classical episteme, or mode of signification and knowing, and the implications of his break with the rational, "unilinear" decorum of Lovejoy's highly rational and axiomatic analysis suggest a deep cultural break in the Western tradition and a decisive turn from the procreative authority attributed to the paternal romance. No longer is the originating moment merely "forgotten," "assumed," or unattended to—as Aristotle seems to have wanted. Rather, the fixed origin is the scandalous residue of the classical episteme in modern culture—no longer that which is naturally assumed to be true, but a condition for "truth" that is still in the process of disappearing. This process consists of a virtual dismantling of a privileged institutional referent and a decisive shift in the paternal romance, even a mandate identified with Foucault's critique of the Western episteme that we can discern as a call to "forget the father."

Foucault is but one commentator on these developments. Many facets of modernism and contemporary theoretical discourse can be seen as attempts to understand paternal "murder" and the breakup of the paternal romance. As so many classical texts show, ancient Greece had near amnesia about such conflicts—clearly so regarding the ideological implications in the procreative (prime mover) function of paternity. Partial exceptions are evident in *The Trojan Women* and *Lysistrata*, in which a female viewpoint temporarily challenges the patriarchy as an institution. But even here there is no formulation, no probing into the nature or constitution of paternity as a cultural practice.

The twentieth century, by contrast, is obsessed with remembering what the Greeks forgot and then with "forgetting" paternal hegemony, de-negating the Father in a radical sense. The Father has been analyzed and displaced in four areas: (1) the semiotic revolution in the social sciences and humanities, including the critiques of sign and structure; (2) psychoanalysis and other critiques of "natural" schemes for knowing and interpreting the world, including anti-psychiatry and post-Freudianism; (3) cultural theory that continues from the nineteenth century into the present as sociology and cultural studies, overlapping with the other three critiques; and (4) feminist critiques of the institutions of gender and power (including pedagogy) and their shaping of cultural life. I shall consider briefly the critiques implicit in the first three areas and then discuss more fully the exemplary cases of Hélène Cixous and Gayatri Chakravorty Spivak as they effect feminist critiques of the paternal romance.

Semiotics, for example, as formulated in Ferdinand de Saussure's *Course in General Linguistics*, is a particularly powerful case of a nonsubstantialist (differential) mode of analysis. By this I mean that Saussure proposed a way of analyzing "texts" calculated not to posit a monological (paternal) origin for them. Saussure described the possibility of avoiding self-legitimating constructs ("justice," "truth," "natural order") whose existence necessarily assumes the authority of a prior arche-substantial being or reference. The same can be said about the subsequent modern enterprise of linguistics—including phonology, semantics, and syntax—that postulates "differential" systems of analysis deeply indebted to sign theory. Also out of semiotics comes the large, anti-paternal project of structuralism, especially as elaborated in Claude Lévi-Strauss's structural anthropology, which studies the relations of the Western family and sexuality as "signs and symbols . . . regulated by internal laws of implication and exclusion" (31). Such a view exceeds and recasts the situation of individual people, families, or patriarchs as structural "signs" and "positions," none of which are inherently privileged or "natural" within a cultural text.

The semiotic critique, as absorbed in many other analytical strategies that do not allow for the epistemological foundation required by the "father" as a fixed and absolute reference for procreation, culminates in deconstruction's even more aggressive questioning of substantialism and monologic versions of absolute authority. This critique succeeds to the point of radically—perhaps decisively—questioning the foundations of the paternal romance, what Derrida calls "the Father of Logos." In effect, semiotics and the semiotic enterprises attempt to dismantle the underpinning of the paternal romance by denying the existence of a fixed or "natural" origin for anything. In this way, they hasten the true forgetting and "end" of the father as a primary epistemological referent and a cultural institution.

While in popular culture Freud is associated with the advancing of paternal authority, he usefully articulates aspects of the paternal romance—Oedipus and repression—that could otherwise remain transparent and unassailable. He also helped to shatter the classical episteme when he defined the Oedipal structure *as a structure* in the family romance. In *Totem and Taboo*, for example, the accuracy of his "anthropology" aside, Freud foregrounds the ascendancy of males as a specific historical event in Western culture—an apocalypse engendering civilization as we know it, but an event afterward wherein "God is nothing other than an exalted father" (47). Even granting his preoccupation with privileged male authority, Freud succeeds in focusing on Western institutions and their consistent advancement of men as ultimate and exclusive referents—"the root of every form of religion" (148)—in important moral, psychological, and religious narratives and hierarchies. The great force of Freud's modeling of a theory of mind on the patterns of *Oedipus Rex* and his seeing the father there not as a "natural" *pater familias*, a substantial manifestation of power, but as an agent position in a dynamic psychosexual structure of relations—a position in a text, a "position" that is not always filled by a biological father or even a male—have been catalytic for cultural theory and critiques of gender.

Cultural theory as a discourse dedicated to understanding mechanisms of modern culture can be said, in one sense, to begin with Wilhelm and Friedrich Von Schlegel's early nineteenth-century comparisons of classical Greek society and modern culture. Their thinking about the "romantic" and vital dimensions of classical culture and the enervation taking over post-Enlightenment culture eventually becomes a massive attack on the institutions of Western culture, including capitalist economies, bourgeois cultural practices, and even the traditional conception of the middle-class family. Like Marx, they posit a radically new relationship to authority and a crisis of community that culminates in the virtual disappearance, or "death," of God.

Friedrich Engels investigated the economic origin of the family in ancient Greece and Rome and showed the "lost" economic motives of the family in order to re-examine the family as an economic and social institution, studying how the family served immediate patriarchal ends "conditioned by the class position of the parties" (63). The nineteenth-century crisis of authority, typified by the triumph of "impersonal" science as much as by massive social and economic displacements such as the British Electoral Reform Bill of 1867 and Western industrialization, reflects this decisive decline of centralized, symbolic authority. God "dies" in this conception as a male symbolically representing the patriarchy and as a fixed point of absolute cultural reference. In *Thus Spake Zarathustra*, Nietzsche envisions paternal Time who "must devour his children" (150); Thomas Hardy describes communal orders that "devour" their children. Such imagery signals a virtual collapse of the traditional notion of paternity as a beneficent sponsor and ideal manifestation of cultural order.

These examples indicate the persistence of the paternal romance in nineteenth- and twentieth-century culture. They also indicate the growing conviction that the father as a privileged cultural construct, once riddled with irony, now no longer even exists. These are major "rememberings" of what was "forgotten" in Greek culture about the father and forms of power. If we add to this the past century's advances in classical studies, including recent French rereadings of classical texts under the sign of contemporary rhetoric and theory, we can discern a huge effort to "remember" what the Greeks forgot. Cultures often depend on strategic omissions and "forgetting," on amnesia about the deepest communal commitments. But the modern concern with Greek culture has prompted such questions in order to make other inquiries into the psychological, political, and gender dimensions of current cultural relations.

The evidence for such a radical "forgetting" of the father is predominantly semiotic, or post-semiotic. Semiotics postulates "knowledge" and "truth" not as natural expressions, but as messages encoded within differential systems, semiotic "texts" always found in a medium of cultural practice and not grounded in nature. In an important sense, psychoanalytic, feminist, and post-structuralist theory are all pedagogical moments in the modern appropriation of oppositional theory—that is, theory deployed as a teaching about values moving away from the paternal romance. These are all "oppositional" teachings, in other words. Given these global erosions of monological authority, it is surprising that the paternal romance still exists. It does continue to exist, however, even while being deeply divided with the irony of the already accomplished "failure" and "fall" of the Father from the heights charted by Greek religion and Christianity.

The rise of modernism's fragmented sense of culture and irrationalism even signals, at a fundamental level, an already accomplished displacement of the effects of the paternal romance—a tremendous decay of paternal institutions in private and public life. This is the beginning of the true demise of the exclusive power once exemplified in Zeus's and Jehovah's authority. Large cultural transformations can be indexed to radical shifts in the paternal signifier. For example, our own is an era in which the supposedly incontrovertible "fact" of "Man" is projected, in Foucault's figure, as merely an "invention of recent date, an invention perhaps nearing its end." Foucault adds that "if the arrangements of knowledge, which brought this 'invention' to the fore, were to disappear as they appeared, then one could certainly wager that man would be erased, like a face drawn in sand at the edge of the sea" (*Order* 386–87). This shift in the relations of authority and the shattering of the classical episteme that Foucault correlates with the cultural legitimation of the "unthought" in textuality (326) can, in fact, be seen as encompassing an array of major developments in the human sciences—the modern/ postmodern project, as I define it, "to forget" the father.

Major instances of this "forgetting," within the broad context of cultural theory, are the practices that have merged as oppositional pedagogy. This body of theory about teaching and institutional function tries *not* to replicate the values and ideological underpinnings of the paternal romance. It has attempted self-consciously to deploy the strategies of oppositionalism as educational theory and practice without the traditional ties to Western versions of "natural" and supposedly value-free hierarchies in teaching. Drawing as it does from several forms of contemporary radical and oppositional thought, this project may be the least credited and yet potentially the most efficacious attempt to "forget" the father. Since Paulo Freire's *Pedagogy of the Oppressed* (1968), oppositional pedagogy has struggled to release itself in theory and practice from the paternal and hegemonic order associated with Western discourse—from the theory of how teachers teach through ideas about how both common schools and the academy replicate and advance established social commitments and values. This move is part of a self-consciously "oppositional" practice wherein a number of theorists from different disciplines—Michael Apple, Pierre Bourdieu, Henry Giroux, Stanley Aronowitz, Lois Weis, and others—have attempted politically provocative critiques of education in relation to social practices conceived in radical terms.

Oppositional pedagogy is particularly urgent in light of the belief, which Louis Althusser advances, that education occupies the *"dominant* position" as the implementer of state ideology in modern Western societies (152). Those on the right, in contrast, hold education to be a value-free, fundamentally nonpolitical practice; from their perspective, the oppositional pedagogue is frequently viewed as exploiting a privileged position to satisfy vulgar political motives. Oppositional pedagogues inevitably "play a fundamental role in producing the dominant culture," as Henry Giroux and others point out, but are committed nonetheless to offering "students forms of oppositional discourse . . . at odds with the hegemonic role of the university" (480).

The formidable difficulties uncovered by oppositional theorists in education reflect the continuing existence of the paternal romance as a residual discourse. The French pedagogical theorists Pierre

Bourdieu and Jean-Claude Passeron have argued, in *Reproduction in Education, Society, and Culture,* that change in education must overcome ideological barriers that are manifested in psychological ties to symbolic authority, such as the father. This is not an easy task with an encompassing cultural practice as powerful as education, whose prestige and legitimacy derive from its manipulation of powerful symbolic forms quite apart from its announced intent. A case in point for Bourdieu and Passeron is that "anyone who teaches" will "be treated [by students] as a *father*" (19, emphasis added). The school or academy will therein draw to itself a grand version of this symbolic authority and become the institutional "one who is supposed to know," the symbolic "father" postulated by psychoanalysis. This process masks the functional aim in the promotion of state or cultural ideology. Freud and Lacan speak at great length of this process of learning in relation to an idealized father figure.

Oppositional pedagogues have attacked the main tenets of the paternal romance in their revisions of contemporary educational theory. First, they have attacked the fixity of the father, or any representative of authority, as the sole or permanent occupant of the speaking subject's position in discourse. They have also explored specific ways of empowering the subaltern, or subordinated person, moving oppressed students and teachers alike into a different relation to knowledge and power, into positions from which they can voice previously unarticulated concerns. Finally, they have sought ways to transform the ideological discourse that creates the apparent necessity and inevitability of rigidly fixed hierarchical orders.

By now the father as a concept can no longer be assumed to authorize the cultural institutions traditionally associated with it. Yet, paradoxically, none of the attacks on substantialism, all of which end up attacking the father, ever seem to lay him completely to rest. *The Dead Father,* in which Donald Barthelme describes a Rabelaisian, postmodern patriarch, ludicrous and chimerical yet not without impact—"Dead, but still with us, still with us, but dead" (3)— captures the sense of the lost but residually present Father in the late twentieth century—not completely "remembered," and not in a position to be completely forgotten.[1]

The practice of radical pedagogy reaches back to the antipaternalistic Sophists, who were arguably the first Western teachers in the sense of being professionals pursuing "careers" in education. Every version of the paternal romance in this book could be measured by the standard of the Sophists, in that all major theories of the father advance definitions of "truth" and "error" and standards of

legitimation for understanding and judging cultural practices. Any
theory of pedagogy imparts a version of *technē*, standards and procedures—traditionally a "male" technology. Students are trained to
distinguish truth from error according to an official and ideologically
oriented heuristic. All incarnations of the paternal romance implied
in various approaches to pedagogy can be understood in one of two
modes. In a metaphorical mode, the characteristic gesture is the correction of "error" through the absolute substitution of a truth for a
falsehood. This one is "metaphoric" in that it involves substitution
of one figure for another. In the metonymic mode, the main gesture
is the instructive maintaining or correcting of a balance among relationships or parts of a whole. This correction might involve read-
justing the relations of parts, instead of substituting something
"better" for those parts.

In Greek religion, for example, Zeus does not try to substitute
himself for the other gods or destroy polytheism; he does not try to
destroy the natural elements or the gods that represent them. Through
changes among existing relationships in civil society, he merely re-
aligns the strata of the Pantheon and the Kosmos. By contrast, Greek
philosophy in the fifth and fourth centuries B.C. demonstrates deliberate and self-conscious attempts to move away from the metonymic
mode of Greek religion and to situate the operation of culture along
highly rationalized, metaphoric, and non-narrative lines. The pre-
Socratics, as emerging natural scientists, attempt to reduce the sense
of plurality and heterogeneity in Greek poetry by projecting a world
governed by unified natural law. Parmenides' sense of the Kosmos
as a single, rational, and static mechanism is a clear instance of
this thinking. In decisive developments in Greek culture, Plato and
Aristotle actually try to suppress the poetic "vagueness" of epic narratives altogether; in so doing, they put Greek culture on a rational
and critical foundation with philosophy. The logic and the scientific
attitudes they develop move Greek thought dramatically away from
ideas about cultural metonymy and diversity. Particularly Aristotle's
institution of the principle of the *hupokeimenon* defines cultural
"truth" and "error" within a strongly monologic and metaphoric
paradigm. By contrast, the Sophists, as Havelock and Jarratt argue,
resist these reformulations and continue to promote a systematic recognition of the diversity and plurality of culture. The pedagogy of
the Sophists continues, then, in the metonymic mode, as an interpretation of existing relations.

Finally, in Christianity "truth" and "error," grace and sin, are
rational and metaphoric constructions. The doctrine of the Trinity,

for example, is a totalized picture of the relations of the godhead, as well as of the correction of error in the created world. Christ imparts spiritual health to the world when, through the Word, he provides a channel for the divine spirit to "spirate" from God and substitutes it for the evil already at work on Earth. Likewise, through a grand process of metaphoric substitution in the correction of error, God is the principle of perfection and eternity. He promises to replace evil with good in the ultimate metaphoric substitution at the Apocalypse, a moment when the whole of the mutable world will be "corrected" forever with the substitution of the divine and perfect world.

In these several versions of the paternal romance, there is a gradual movement from metonymic to metaphoric models of truth and error. No form that "pedagogy" takes, as Jane Gallop notes, is in any sense innocent of a distinction between truth and error. As a cultural practice pedagogy has *always* carried with it specific ideological freight as is reflected in its etymology as the "teaching of boys." As a cultural practice, pedagogy *is* the teaching of boys in that it has a metaphoric connection, ideological in significance, to male social privilege. In teaching's formative social power, in other words, there is not only the reproduction of the specific conditions of knowledge and power that position men as superior knowers (as is suggested in Aristotle's theory of the *hupokeimenon*), but the advancement—through the social system pedagogical institutions serve—of their superior status as access to social and political privilege. By dismantling pedagogy as a universal and timeless institution, Freire and other oppositional theorists want to unsettle the fixity of pedagogy's implicit maleness, its monologic fixity. Barbara Johnson, for instance, questions the Western repression of "feminism" in teaching—the absence of girls in the boys' school (182)—and points out that the connection often exists between the flight from traditional pedagogy and the advent of a "deviant" or oppositional teaching. Molière's phrase *"L'Ecole des femmes"* (Johnson 165)—the girls' school—makes this connection between a "female" pedagogy and the subversion of ideology in opposition to the traditional male orientation of schooling.

I am introducing feminist critiques of the paternal romance in order to emphasize the contemporary working through of cultural impasses under the sign of the father. For example, in *The Second Sex*, Simone de Beauvoir argues not only that the paternal romance is a Western institution constituted by special cultural practices, but also that it is analyzable as a set of rules, and that those rules are potentially reformulable. Reframed by feminist critique, those "new relations of flesh and sentiment" can be adjusted and re-aligned to be "friendships [between the sexes], rivalries, complicities, comradeships—chaste or sensual—which past centuries could not have conceived" (688). She proposes, in short, to correct the errors of the paternal romance through the metonymic readjustment and reformulation of already existing relations.

I am not suggesting that a monolithic feminist pedagogy exists; yet my focus here is not on the diversity of feminist pedagogies, but on the exemplary cases of Hélène Cixous and Gayatri Chakravorty Spivak. I shall argue that whereas Cixous explicitly advances a body of pedagogic theory based on a critique of the paternal ro-mance, Spivak critiques the foundations for oppositional theory upon which Cixous draws in her formulation of écriture féminine. Both approaches, in any case, are instances of the "new relations of flesh and sentiment." Cixous engages the paternal romance in the explicitly "oppositional" terms I have been discussing, and she encounters the usual difficulties of speaking outside of the dimensions of an encom-passing order. By contrast, in recasting feminist theory in the terms of postcolonial discourse, Spivak focuses explicitly on the proble-matics of complicity with the paternal romance that critiques such as Cixous's raise. Spivak's theoretical "solutions" to these problems of ideological "collaboration" bear directly on the possibilities of an effective critique of the paternal romance, or of any ideology. As de Beauvoir proposes, Cixous and Spivak in these stances both attempt to critique oppositional theory itself, as well as the textual practice it engenders. Their goal is to lessen the effects of, and ultimately to disarm, what remains of the paternal romance in modern culture.

The comparison of Cixous and Spivak that I have in mind can only take place within a range of current feminist critiques of the paternal romance. Peggy Kamuf in "Replacing Feminist Criticism" and Nancy K. Miller in "The Text's Heroine: A Feminist Critic and Her Fiction," for example, play out many issues arising from the comparison of Cixous and Spivak. Kamuf and Miller take sharply opposed positions on the question of effectively transforming the paternal romance, what cultural critique is, and how it works. In a retrospective exchange about their debate, Kamuf asserts, "If one concludes that . . . there is nothing beyond oppositional modes of thought and being, no outside from which something else can inter-vene which is not already programmed by the dialectical machine, then indeed one's oppositional strategy must fully espouse the logic of change (of history) made possible there and in those terms" ("Parisian Letters" 125). Kamuf's own stance is that while "one cannot take up a position against [the idea of ideological] positions" (125), effective "oppositional tactics" must necessarily keep "open a space for possible dislocation . . . giving the traces of the non-opposable other a chance to make their mark before they are too quickly reduced to recognizable positions and thereby made available to dialectical reason and its institutions" (126).

Kamuf's critique of oppositionalism suggests that such modes of rational critique as I have been adopting may only be able, finally, to reiterate the terms of the paternal romance. Judith Butler makes the same point when she says that "the masculine sex" necessarily "*appears* to originate meanings and thereby to signify" those meanings as an effect with ideological ends (45). Within patriarchal discourse, woman will always and only be, and only be presented as, "the masculine sex *encore* (and *en corps*) parading in the mode of otherness" (12). Of course, I have returned to these same impasses of the paternal romance in relation to various texts discussed throughout this book.

Kamuf and Miller demonstrate that this debate over oppositional discourse is not so much an argument to be resolved as itself a mode of feminist discourse. This is so in that feminist discourse operates productively in conflict and continues to change. In short, feminist discourse is grounded on cultural values that, in turn, must continue to be critiqued. Diana Fuss argues for this view of feminist critique as needing to remain dynamic and in "conflict" when she says that "'essentially speaking' . . . we need both to speak and, simultaneously, to deconstruct these spaces [of discourse] to keep them from solidifying" (118). "Such a double gesture," she goes on, "involves once again the responsibility to historicize, to examine each deployment of essence, each appeal to experience, each claim to identity in the complicated contextual frame in which it is made" (118). In the poststructuralist rigor of this double gesture, there is a historical account of the bases of prior and quite different feminist critiques of the paternal romance—"bases," as Susan Jarratt argues, for understanding two dominant models of "the two previous feminisms" that defined women's studies in the Western world (68).

For instance, Jarratt describes an essentialist model of feminist discourse that assumed in its critique a "universal human essence" from which women were being excluded (68). Within this model of feminist critique, the response to the paternal romance consisted of an argument for equal consideration within the definition of a "universal human essence." Within a second essentialist model, feminist critiques worked out of the assumption of an "essential sexual difference" that was supposedly not recognized enough by men (68). Men needed to acknowledge in more ways the essential "difference" of women. The response to the paternal romance here involved struggle for recognition of women's particular nature in a way that could enlarge that sphere for women's benefit. Jarratt argues that one or another of these models served as the basis for many feminist critiques in the past and "historically provided the grounds of political action for women" (68).

By contrast, the poststructuralist model of feminist critique, as described in Fuss's summary, recognizes a double gesture: the inevitability of needing to critique essentialism, albeit while risking essentialism in one's choice of strategies in order to speak at all. The argument here is that critique must inevitably critique itself in order to understand its own material conditions. Increasingly many feminists see the effective critique of gender as necessarily moving toward establishing the critique of theory in relation to the material conditions and historical situation of actual women's lives. Hence the mutuality of feminist and cultural critiques.

Cixous

Cixous enters this discussion about oppositional theory through her formulation of *écriture féminine*. In the United States she is generally known as the avant-garde feminist author of "The Laugh of the Medusa" and *The Newly-Born Woman*, works in which she emerges as the visionary guide to reading and writing like a woman. In her role as "oppositional critic," which is my interest here, she self-consciously chooses a style of confrontation with dominant cultural practices in order to understand and change the culture. Like Edward W. Said, Michel Foucault, Monique Wittig, Jean Baudrillard, and Fredric Jameson, Cixous reads the discourses of contemporary culture to expose crucial oppositions as misrecognitions of truth and error, key binarities—such as father/mother, man/woman, active/passive, nature/culture, superior/inferior—that govern the exercise of power.

Like other such cultural critics, Cixous has tried to maneuver herself into strategic conflicts with oppressive cultural practices. She emerged from the student-worker uprisings of May 1968 in France as a radical academic in a "revolutionary" university (in Vincennes), a feminist theorist writing for the Women's Press, and a "feminist" avant-garde fiction writer. She accomplished all of this in the "oppositional" style of one working from within an institution and its ideological matrix—in this case as teacher, writer, and feminist theorist—to challenge prevailing authority and engineer a new pedagogical practice.

Cixous's primary strategy has been to alter the effect of gender relations in the way people read. She has attempted this in her classroom, criticism, fiction, and drama—at least into the mid-1980s—through her own innovative reading and writing of cultural texts. Her goal has been to expose, and even to begin to dismantle, the paternal romance in the academy and in the institution of cultural criticism and theory. She strives to create for her students and readers a revolutionary cultural frame that legitimizes a feminine dimension of textuality and therein shifts the cultural relations of power between male and female. Her work has been in the avant-garde both in the literary and in the political sense.

Ann Rosalind Jones, Monique Wittig, and other feminist critics describe Cixous's teaching and writing in this way, too, but they worry that the intensity of her "oppositional" reading of culture may have the hidden weakness of, at the same time, imprisoning her work within "the very ideological system feminists want to destroy"—that is, the patriarchy and what I am calling the paternal romance (Jones 369). In the late 1980s Cixous and her strategies for instituting and understanding "feminine discourse"—a theoretical approach to "feminine" reading and writing—became of far less urgency to those thinking and writing about women's issues in literary or cultural studies. Many critics currently committed to *"theories of writing and reading,"* as Alice Jardine reported, actually "posit themselves and their work as hostile to, or 'beyond,' feminism" such as Cixous's (20), as there developed a strong commitment in the late 1980s "to move outside that male-centered, binary logic" (Jones 369) that I have identified with Aristotle but that is here tied to Cixous.

However, given the extent of Cixous's intervention in literary and cultural studies, and the uncommon strength and appeal of her work, she must be considered an enormously strong initiator of cultural change from within an institution. If she can't do it, we must wonder, then who can? Jones's and others' judgment of Cixous's apparent "failure" to inform and influence very recent women's studies raises disturbing questions about the ideological commitments of oppositionalism in contemporary culture—about the potential to subvert and change culture from within. Such was the common goal of Western intellectuals in the late 1960s through the mid-1970s, most prominently Michel Foucault and Noam Chomsky.[2]

The medium of Cixous's "oppositionalism" is "feminine writing."

Since the mid–1970s Cixous, Luce Irigaray, Julia Kristeva, Michele Montrelay, and Catherine Clément, among others, developed a body of thought about reading women's texts in particular contexts of women's experience. The general strategy of this thought reflects Virginia Woolf's notion of a feminine writing that relies not on a biological conception of the sexes—a "given" essence of male and female characteristics—but on culturally determined features, such as "openness" in feminine texts, with "openness" being a lack of repressive patterning in discourse and a tendency to retain a sense of the indeterminant and the random. Such a designation would be as applicable to the reading of Marcel Proust as of Virginia Woolf, the criterion being "openness" in a text and not the gender of the author. These theorists have tried to accomplish three things: to expose the mechanism by which Western texts (literary and otherwise) have been written to advance the prestige of patriarchal culture, to understand how women's writing has been effaced and suppressed by male discourse, and finally to recover, or reinvent, a way of reading feminine writing (including writing *by* women) that does not duplicate and advance the paternal romance. Such theorizing, pursued in the atmosphere of post–May 1968 France and deconstruction, has predictably asked questions about the relations of writing, politics, and gender—what "writing" is, how texts deploy power, how to read a feminine (non-patriarchal) text, and (with even greater urgency) what the "feminine" is.

Common among these critics, whose ideas are otherwise divergent, is that feminine writing (*écriture féminine*)—both escaping and situated within the paternal romance—is best understood in metaphors related to "orgasm" (*jouissance*) or, in Cixous's case, *sortie*, which means "excess" (again suggestive of *jouissance*) and the "way out," "exit," or a "leaving" (see "Sorties" in *The Newly-Born Woman*). Taken together, these metaphors suggest the common aim, through an underlying metaphor, of finding a "beyond" or "way out" from patriarchal discourse and the analytical double binds it fosters. Cixous, for example, calls for "leaving" behind "the signs of sexual opposition" altogether ("Laugh" 311)—that is, simply abandoning the binarity of gender as a way of defeating the Western tendency to elevate men and efface women. Patriarchal (Western) culture, Cixous argues, is generated out of oppositions based ultimately on what she calls "the power relation between a fantasized obligatory virility meant to invade, to colonize, and the consequential phantasm of woman as a 'dark continent' to penetrate and to 'pacify'" ("Laugh" 310; also "Castration" 44). Cixous focuses on oppositions, including

activity/passivity, great/small, nature/history, transformation/iner-
tia, and white/black, which all "come back to the man/woman opposition" in that all require fundamental adjustments in language and
discourse, changes in the linguistic and social context of language
use ("Castration" 44).

"Laugh of the Medusa" and "Castration or Decapitation?" present Cixous's case for the reading of feminine writing. In "Laugh," for
example, she presents writing as structured by a "sexual opposition"
favoring men, one that "has always worked for man's profit to the
point of reducing writing . . . to his laws" (313). Writing is constituted
in a "discourse" of social, political, and linguistic relations that can
be characterized in a masculine or feminine "economy." The masculine, traditionally dominant in the West, is a system of militant
exclusion wherein patterns of linearity (patriarchal "logic") over-
emphasize the hierarchical nature of (sexual) difference in discourse
and give a "grossly exaggerated" view of the "sexual opposition"
actually inherent in language (311). Cixous does not say this merely
to denigrate the idea of "masculine economy," which is, she argues—
if seen outside the exaggerations of patriarchy—naturally a part of
writing and reading. "Castration," the symbolic rule of discourse
conceived on the male model, "is fundamental [to writing], unfor-
tunately" (Conley 156). "Isn't it evident," Cixous asks, "that the penis
gets around in my texts, that I give it a place and appeal?" ("Laugh"
319). The concept of castration is necessary, she goes on (somewhat
at odds with Deleuze and Guattari), because it would be "humanly
impossible to have an absolute economy without a minimum of
[masculine] mastery" (Conley 139). One needs a rule of exclusion
(symbolized by castration) in order to organize the dynamics of
writing. The problem, of course, is that the male economy *has* gone
beyond the functional need for "repression" in writing and has
imposed very restrictive rules on the deployment of power, rules that
always favor a masculine view and men.

Whereas Cixous sees the masculine economy as superimposed
linearity and tyranny, she sees the feminine as the "overflow" of
"luminous torrents" ("Laugh" 309), a margin of "excess" eroticism and
free play not directly attributable to (not fully accounted for by) the
fixed hierarchies of masculinity. In the feminine economy there are
no strict rules of dismissal; rather, the play of writing as an "openness"
contains "that element which never stops resonating," an undecidable
inscription of "white ink" on white paper that writes itself free of
masculine rules of decidable order and (hierarchical) contrast (312).
The "openness" of such writing is evident in Cixous's own style, as

when she writes, "We the precocious, we the repressed of culture, our lovely mouths gagged with pollen, our wind knocked out of us, we the labyrinths, the ladders, the trampled spaces, the bevies—we are black and we are beautiful" (310). In such writing Cixous forces expository sense into the economy of poetic association and controls the "excess" of imagery through repetition and nonlinear (non-male) accretions. Woolf also speaks of such writing in contrast to "male" ("shadowed," or violently imposed) writing. This is Kristeva's conception, too, of *jouissance*, the poetic discourse "beyond" the masculine text of reason and order. All three critics assume that the feminine economy of excess does not need to be made anew, because it has always persisted in the margins and gaps, as the repressed of male-dominated culture. Women, and in theory even men, can find the *"sortie"* from, and the "beyond" of, patriarchal culture precisely by looking for and acknowledging the feminine economy that *already* exists within and around the margins of male discourse. Hence the importance of the *"sortie"* ("excess" and "exit") as Cixous's controlling metaphor.

We can see how Cixous participates in the oppositional tradition by looking at her handling of the man/woman opposition. Using the terms of the classical oppositional square, we find that she couples two propositions that form a "contrary" relationship, as in man/woman. The pairing forms the axis of possible significations running from the possibilities of courtship and marriage to incest and homosexuality. We can posit a second level in her analysis in a supposed square of opposition and find the third term of patriarchalism. The "Father" is the designation of power in the man/woman opposition, the signal that man will be the controlling term. The Father as indicator of ideology, therefore, "understands" the first level of reference, interprets and limits it, by identifying the (patriarchal) hierarchy that organizes it. The fourth term, then, that completes this ideological reading is "Mother"—female sexuality and power. At this furthest reach of the square, "Mother" repeats and alters the category of "woman," stands in opposition to "Father," and gives final expression to (even while it challenges) the patriarchal values from which this discourse is generated. The fourth term marks a new authority emanating from, but at the same time alien to, this discourse. The economy of Cixous's man/woman opposition can be projected as in figure 8.

"Mother" comes into the square as the instance of what was suppressed all along through the insistence in the discourse on various formal oppositions. As a historical phenomenon, the square shows "Mother" to be the core of a specific proposition emerging as a rent

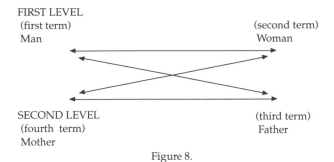

Figure 8.

in the historical fabric, a rupture that has left its trace but cannot yet be represented as a specific textual practice. This is precisely Kristeva's conception of "Motherhood" as being, at this historical moment, within the articulations of the dominant patriarchal discourse, "without a discourse" and, at the same time, on the verge of "reawakening," of being textualized—an emergent but not yet "readable" discourse of women (262). "Mother" is a historical event that the logic of patriarchal ideology inscribes within itself *and* suppresses. Her power persists in patriarchal logic specifically as an effacement; hence the disruptive nature of Motherhood as an agency of power.

Cixous's reading of the man/woman opposition demonstrates the economies of relationship engendered by oppositional binarity. The result for Cixous is a gendered hierarchy of values inscribed by the square's four terms—themselves rising from and thus "escaping" the unintelligibility of "mere" differences, unorganized and non-politicized heterogeneity. Reading the pattern of these values, articulated according to a rule made evident in the square's operation, constitutes an ideological critique of gender. What we are viewing in Cixous's method of reading, as with Aristotle, Jameson, Said, Greimas, and the modern "oppositional" critics generally, is an ideological approach to the problematic of decipherment. The fourth term—equivalent to "female sexuality" or "feminine political power"—is not on the order of a mere logical necessity, ideology being reducible neither to logical entailment (simple rationality) nor to pure contiguity. As a cultural phenomenon, rather, Mother is a manifestation of "history"—the diachronic emergence of the unthought and the initially unreadable.

The issue is not that Cixous follows Aristotelian protocols in any literal fashion. Like Aristotle, Greimas, and Jameson, however, she asserts that the relations of opposition map a logic of resistance within the world text, and that this "logic" is what we call ideology. To the extent that Cixous locates the frame of gender for the oppositions she examines, she is moving around the square's positions and playing out the possibilities of an ideological critique and the "explosion" of something unrepresentable and new. In this specific sense—regarding the potential of ideological analysis—Cixous's reading of the paternal romance as the Man/Woman discourse is oppositional.

Cixous goes on in both "Laugh of the Medusa" and "Castration or Decapitation?" (also in "Sorties" in *The Newly-Born Woman*) to explore the oppositional logic relating the masculine economy to the "overflow" of erotic "excess." In "Castration or Decapitation?" she emphasizes the extent to which the Man/Woman opposition "cuts endlessly across all the oppositions that order culture" (44). "Everything . . . that's spoken," she goes on, "everything that's organized as discourse, art, religion, the family, language, everything that seizes us, everything that acts on us—it is all ordered around hierarchical oppositions that come back to the man/woman opposition" (44). This primary opposition, she concludes, "makes it all work." Therefore, "it's on the [concept of the] couple that we have to work if we are to deconstruct and transform culture" (44). Cixous in this way argues for the primacy of a sexual logic, the "couple" (Man/ Woman) as an orienting polarity of texts. In this concentration, repeated throughout her work—prominent in these essays, but equally so in "Sorties"—she shows the extent to which she assumes a basic oppositional matrix as fundamental to culture. She posits a strategy for reading the feminine and making "opposition"—for good or ill—her primary instrument of analysis.

Cixous, of course, does not celebrate the confinement of her discourse on feminine writing within the bounds of the linear, paternal romance. Rather, Cixous the joyous and sometimes oracular reader of cultural texts chides women and hopes to lure them to follow her to "excess" beyond the patriarchy. In "Laugh of the Medusa," for example, as if composing a feminine "Song of Myself," she challenges women to rise and become more than they have been: "And why don't you write? Write! Writing is for you, you are for you; your body is yours, take it. I know why you haven't written. (And why I didn't write before the age of twenty-seven.) Because writing is at once too high, too great for you, it's reserved for the great—that is for 'great men'; and it's 'silly'" (310). She implores the untutored woman to rise and live fully in the open space of ecstatic discourse and "laughter." Likewise, in "Castration or Decapitation?" she invites women to "laughter that breaks out, overflows, a humour that no one would expect to find in women" (55). Thus intending to transcend narrow male economies, Cixous fashions the "newly-born woman" (as in *La Jeune Née*) as a reader/writer who will be intent on "leaping," who "crosses limits: she is neither outside nor in, whereas the masculine would try to 'bring the outside in, if possible'" ("Castration" 54). The new woman and the female discourse that Cixous calls for will follow the reprise of a female Dionysian experience, the "way out" of the patriarchy and the living of joyful lives at the margins of excess. Finally, just as Cixous calls for reading literature "beyond" the traditional assumptions about realistic (Cartesian) models of character, her new woman will live "beyond" the "character" assigned to her by the patriarchy (see "The Character of 'Character'").

This exuberant discourse has come under relentless attack from other feminists for its inadvertent collaboration with the patriarchy and with what I am calling the paternal romance. Earlier I mentioned that Ann Rosalind Jones had documented a list of objections to Cixous's work (making a special reference to Monique Wittig) in "Writing the Body: Toward an Understanding of *l'écriture féminine*." Jones notes principally Cixous's conception of femininity as "feminine economy," a notion not applicable exclusively to women (as Cixous makes clear), but somehow "natural" and intrinsic to them all the same. Underpinning Cixous's feminine economy, regardless of her sophistication in articulating it, is the assumption of an "essential" femininity in some texts, the identifiable quality that allows feminine discourse to be named as such, the quality of openness that allows a text to resist external control and the imposition of (patriarchal) patterns.

Ironically, though, essentialism—or unproblematic "meaning" as discrete and non-relational—is one of the myths that Cixous's deconstructive project tries to dismantle. In any other context Cixous does not believe in absolute essences and would not recognize their authority. Theoretically, then, Cixous's feminine discourse—based on an essential "femininity"—is problematic. Jones also emphasizes that, in positing such idealized femininity, "French feminists [such as Cixous] make of the female body too unproblematically pleasurable and totalized an entity" (368). The female body, in this view, actually houses the erotic "essence" supposedly distributed throughout a feminine discourse. Jones argues, persuasively and probably decisively, that Cixous's version of *femininity*, based as it is on an essentialist conception of gender, is not viable in theory or practice.

At best, Cixous exemplifies the resistance to male "desire" with her own writing, by opposing the "body" and the materiality (the style) of her own discourse to masculine writing practices. In effect, Cixous wagers the "body" of her eroticized writing against the repressions of masculine textuality. But if we judge from the testimony of other feminists, the overall success of this performance is questionable. Sandra M. Gilbert judges Cixous's "imaginative journeys across the frontier of prohibition" to be pure utopian "voyages out into a no place that must be a no man's and no woman's land" (*Newly-Born Woman* xvi)—a provocative performance, but perhaps not sufficiently connected with other cultural practices to have a significant impact.

Jones's major objection to Cixous, however, is that Cixous's ultimate appeal is to oppositional thinking. Jones argues that any term conceived in binarity necessarily inscribes, and even legitimizes, the oppositional network—the differential system—in which it is articulated. If Cixous strategically advances feminine writing over, in opposition to, masculine discourse, Cixous merely succeeds in reversing "the values assigned to each side of the polarity, but . . . still leaves man as the determining referent, not departing from the male-female opposition, but participating in it" (Jones 369). Jones's point is that the fight with—or opposition to—men could make the paternal romance stronger. This is the predicament of the Foucauldian intellectual, as Jim Merod comments, who "is inscribed within the dominant culture and within the operations of power which he wants to contest. He is, in some undismissible sense, an agent of that power" (158). Cixous's discourse, then, actually serves as an agent of what it opposes. It inadvertently returns to and reinforces the masculine discourse, the structure of the paternal romance, that it was supposed to go beyond and subvert. Cixous-as-oppositional-reader misunderstood the inherent dangers of oppositional criticism and, accordingly, was lured by the appearance of analytical clarity into the trap of accepting an underlying patriarchal ethos. Cixous's oppositional reading, then, is confined and neutralized by the patriarchal frame—the paternal romance—she chose to employ.

This difficulty is yet another version of the impasse often faced by contemporary "engaged" theorists. Intellectuals like Cixous, who wish to think *and* act, or at least to theorize the impact of their reading and writing, have great trouble finding an avenue to action uncompromised by internal contradictions. Worse, they cannot even theorize a mode of action that does not subvert what they set out to achieve. This paradox is particularly disturbing because, especially in Cixous's case, it so vividly challenges the prospect of deliberate and rational intervention, of any political action. In short, the "failure" of Cixous's project does not bode well for the possibility of effective cultural opposition—for change from within. Even without subscribing to oppositionality as a policy, one must see that the impossibility of effective opposition—which is so if opposition automatically cancels itself by restoring legitimacy to the dominant discourse—raises the specter of paralysis and quietism in the face of cultural and political oppression. Since this danger plagues not only the self-identified "oppositional" critic, the radical cultural theorist (like Foucault), or the political strategist of the left (like Baudrillard), the "failure" of Cixous's oppositional project puts the possibility of intervention itself into question. Can a cultural discourse be opposed from within? Or is all such calculated action self-canceling and defeated in advance?

Susan C. Jarratt argues, contrary to my claim here, that the immediate problem in understanding Cixous is not her supposed essentialism. We need to remember, Jarratt warns, that "because [Cixous] envisions a possible future in which difference is not tied ontologically to sex, her practice can be described as strategic rather than essentialist" (71). Jarratt reads Cixous's formulations as localizable, historical interventions, not as universal pronouncements. I think that Cixous *can* be read in this way; but the fact remains that Cixous's discourse does suggest totalized female and male economies, and Cixous founds these notions of gendered discourse on the "fact" of female and male bodies. Also, Cixous's emphasis—often her whole point of cultural intervention—falls on the metaphoric modes of substitution of replacing a closed (male) discourse with an open (female) discourse. In her pedagogical model, the "true" discourse for the dissemination of knowledge is the open one, and the discourse in error is the closed one.

Spivak

Gayatri Chakravorty Spivak addresses these same issues concerning the paternal romance and the possibility of cultural intervention. Spivak does not draw on the same conceptual totalizations, however, nor does she resist the idea of unwitting collaboration between versions of feminist critique and the paternal romance (Jones's charge against Cixous). Spivak freely admits such unavoidable complicity on the part of feminist discourse. She ventures that the ideal of pure and efficacious intervention is impossible, defeated in advance. By contrast, Spivak attempts to theorize the position of the subjugated person generally within postcolonial discourse, and then the woman in history as colonized (divided and compromised) subject. Historically, Spivak views the woman in the West as occupying the position of the "subaltern," or the oppressed. In this she draws on Antonio Gramsci's ideological critique of hegemony as well as (even if unintentionally) the tradition of oppositional thinking in Western thought. Her conclusion is that the person situated in history cannot fail to participate in the interaction of forces that constructs subjectivity.

In Third World discourses such as that of colonized India, for example, "woman" as a cultural position is situated as subaltern, in a position on the periphery of culture and political relations. The inherent strategy of the dominant discourse is not merely to separate women from power, but also to position them against a colonial and hegemonic "center" so as to insure self-limiting and -negating strategies whenever women attempt to act on their own behalf. Spivak's theorizing also reflects a larger critique of the gendered subject in the West, especially of its political relations within postcolonial culture, and certainly in relation to the paternal romance. Spivak's own theoretical countermove against neocolonialism (I think especially of the essay "Can the Subaltern Speak?") is not so much to "oppose" male hegemony, say, as "women" against "male" oppression. As we saw in Cixous's case, doing so may all too predictably replicate the problematic categories and positions of discourse in the paternal romance, offering the scenario of a monolithic collectivity of women poised against an equally monolithic patriarchal system.

Instead, Spivak moves to locate the feminist gesture—say, as exemplified by Hélène Cixous—as part of a critique of the Western subject as it can be reflected in the narratives of the paternal romance. She intends this move fundamentally to redirect the feminist project, in order to address what Alice Jardine and others have discussed as the limited range of Anglo-American feminism, particularly during the 1960s and 1970s. Spivak's recasting of feminism also addresses the frustrations of the feminist project in recent bleak appraisals such as Sandra Gilbert's "Life's Empty Pack: Notes toward a Literary Daughteronomy," and in the writings of many French feminists of the late 1980s and early 1990s who consider themselves part of a movement that is either "post-" or even "anti-feminist."

High on Spivak's agenda is to situate "feminism," or her reconstituted version of it, within a postcolonial critique of imperialism that, in turn, resituates the female subject historically and ideologically. This radical practice constitutes her strategy for Third World feminist discourse within three frames. She begins by situating the social subject within a critique of social contradiction. She then situates Third World feminist discourse in relation to neo-colonial discourse and the West's divided subjectivity. Finally, she suggests how the Third World female subject is constituted within postcolonial discourse.

Spivak's idea of feminism derives from of her conception of the female subject—or any subject—as constituted in contradiction. By "contradiction" here she means largely what Marx and Derrida mean by contradiction in the subject—a "subject" divided in terms of the conflicting value systems that constitute it. To illustrate her point she takes the famous example from *The Eighteenth Brumaire of Louis Bonaparte*, where Marx makes two conflicting observations while discussing a split running through French society. He says that "in so far as millions of families live under economic conditions of existence that separate their mode of life . . . *they form a class*," a kind of totality. He then goes on to say that "in so far as . . . the identity of their interests fails to produce a feeling of community . . . *they do not form a class*" (cited in "Can the Subaltern Speak?" 277). Marx advances these observations to illustrate a structural contradiction of class in the most radical sense. Spivak understands this formulation to suggest the divided constitution of class representation at any one moment. French peasant culture is and is not a class—and this irresolvable contradiction is not the ambiguity of a moment of crisis, although the conditions and exact site of contradiction will change, but the formulation of a structural division inherent to the concept of class and the social subject. The social subject in Marx's example exists simultaneously on opposed sides of an ideological divide, battling its own interests.

The same is true for the subaltern subject (the positions of articulated value found on the "second level" of Aristotle's oppositional square). Spivak considers the case of the Indian woman. Nineteenth-century British attempts to protect women from male violence (ritual suicide, dowry violence, widow suicide) suggest how the Indian woman is supposedly "saved" and then incorporated into colonial culture. However, because she is excluded from active participation in and from access to power in society, she becomes both a victim and an agent of colonial oppression. Insofar as the Indian woman is subject to the culture of the colonizer and necessarily "desires" the ends that constitute her as a colonized subject—in effect, collaborating with the system—she does not join with other oppressed people and does not struggle against the conditions of her situation. She is part of the problem of colonial oppression. Framed in two dimensions at once, the Indian-woman-as-subject manifests the same contradiction of class that Marx identified in the subject of nineteenth-century French peasant society.

An example of the Indian woman as divided, subaltern subject can be seen vividly in the Indian practice of *sati*, the ritual of widow sacrifice in which "the Hindu widow ascends the pyre of the dead husband and immolates herself upon it" (297). Often described in terms of passionate love and great devotion to a man, this rite up through the mid-nineteenth century "was not practiced universally and was not caste- or class-fixed" (297). However, the British outlawed *sati* in 1829 in what must be taken, to a large degree at least, as a humanitarian gesture. But Spivak shows that the specifics of British rule and the interdiction against *sati* expose a contradiction, a vivid but not uncommon replication of the hegemonic regime already in place—in this case, the very hegemonic male practices the new law against *sati* was supposed to be replacing. Within the colonial experience, the outlawing of *sati* was just another instance of "'White men saving brown women from brown men'"—the white colonists, in effect, vying with and defeating brown, Indian men for the sexual allegiance of brown, Indian women (297). In the process, the woman as subaltern subject, to the degree that she accedes to the British, is re-alienated by being re-placed on the periphery of British culture.

Spivak's concern with *sati* as a practice, finally, is a concern with the gendered subject constituted in contradiction and *as* an ideological contradiction—as if, as she says of the subject of *sati*, "knowledge *in a subject* of its own insubstantiality and mere phenomenality is dramatized so that the dead husband becomes the exteriorized example and place of the extinguished subject and the widow becomes the (non)agent [the subaltern] who 'acts . . . out'" the extinction (300). The practice of *sati*, and then its banning, both situate the woman as subaltern, and then reiterate that situation so that the woman is in a position to be subjugated again, and so on. Whether the resulting sexual economy is played out between Indian husband and wife in the *sati* practice or between Indian wife and British governors in colonial practice, it is clear that the "legally programmed symmetry in the status of the subject," wherein the woman is an "object of *one* husband . . . obviously operates in the interest of the legally asymmetrical subject-status of the male." Finally, "the self-immolation of the widow," Spivak concludes, "thereby becomes the extreme case of the general law [of the subaltern] rather than an exception to it" (303). In this way, the contradiction of the subject exposes an ideological aim. Spivak adds that "it is not surprising, then, to read of heavenly rewards for the *sati*"—scenarios in which "ecstatic heavenly dancers, paragons of female beauty and male pleasure[,] . . . sing her praise" (303). In virtually an identical way,

the British offered cultural rewards of legitimacy and British identification for the "good" Indian wife who responded to white admin-
istrators' demands to forego *sati* and, in so doing, rejected their Indian
husbands—that is, rewards for those who rejected Indian for British
culture.

Spivak's rationale for defining Third World feminist discourse
within the critique of colonialism comes out of her understanding of
Western history and the contradiction inherent in the subject. Aligning herself with Marx and Derrida, she reasons that attempts by
Western intellectuals to analyze the Third World subject solely in
terms of power or the operation of economics—as if the investigators
are themselves free of ideology and its representations—actually
reconstitute the same discourse and the same oppressed subject.
Foucault and Deleuze inadvertently posit the existence of a privileged
angle of intellectual observation—a *transparent* and essentialist mode
of investigation—when they attempt to stand back and let the subaltern person "speak for herself"; that is, when the white anthropological investigator chooses merely to listen and record the
supposed self-presentation of oppression. By contrast, Spivak is
intent upon recognizing the intellectual subject's ideological stance at
those moments that involve merely listening. She then argues against
the possibility of purely disinterested inquiry and in favor of avowedly
interested and ideologically committed intellectual participation. She
opposes the interventionist project, as Foucault and Deleuze define
it, precisely because she wishes to take account of and interpret the
constructed colonial subject-as-male-intellectual as it faces the colonized *other* figured in the subaltern female subject.

Spivak here is promoting a theory of neocolonial discourse that
highlights the oppressed person or class not as merely denied a voice,
but precisely as *constructed* in the subaltern position to speak through
ventriloquism. This happens as the oppressed person is given a position and a subaltern voice defined by and standing in a certain relation
to the master discourse. Spivak's own task as a postcolonial intellectual must be to rethink the position from which "opposition" may
emanate. She must retheorize the whole machine of oppositional
analysis that heretofore was thought to function as a counter to the
dominant discourse. But now the oppositional analysis is aimed historically at the very cultural foundations that created the colonial
"contradiction" of an oppressed female subject. Her aim is to situate
the very idea of opposition ideologically, to show that there is no
unmarked position of pure victimage from which opposition may be
initiated in ideal terms. Her own historical and ideological critique

does begin to define a voice other than that of the paternal romance, insofar as she locates strategies for critiquing colonial and neocolonial practice. The nature of Third World domination necessitates that she inquire into "how the third-world subject is represented within Western discourse" (271). The inquiry into the colonial and neocolonial phenomenon must also become an inquiry into the question of the representation of power in Western culture generally, particularly in capitalism, which in turn must be related to the development of the Western subject and its strategies for self-representation.

This complex strategy recognizes that colonialism (and its subtle variations in intellectual colonialism) in effect incorporates the "other" as the "same" of Western culture. In colonial oppression, this means that the subaltern stands in for and marks the place of the other. Foucault and Deleuze see themselves as able to let the "subaltern speak for herself" because they believe the subaltern is an adequate and competent representative, a transparent view, of the "other"— the oppressed person. However, Spivak's disagreement with them suggests rather blatantly that the postcolonial strategy in formulating the subaltern cannot be intended "to represent . . . [the other] but to learn to represent . . . ourselves" (288–89). Spivak's startling admission of a limitation in the postcolonial recognition of the "other"—wherein the "other" by definition cannot be known, cannot be incorporated as the same—is real. While her comment may seem like the admission of weakness, it is intended to create the possibility of ending what Spivak calls "the relentless recognition of the Other by assimilation" (294). Her strategy is to diminish the prestige of colonial, hegemonic discourse, and thereafter to begin to block that discourse from using the subaltern position to mark the place of the other. The subaltern cannot "speak for herself," as Deleuze and Foucault thought was possible, because the subaltern position was literally created by the dominant discourse to say what it wanted to hear.

As regards Spivak's understanding of the gendered subject, she is clearly suggesting a discourse in which the subaltern is not the actual subjugated person. Yet, at the same time, the subaltern cannot be conceived outside specific gender markings based on actual women in real historical settings. The subaltern is a position and a *structural necessity* within the gendered discourse of colonialism, the female subaltern subject being a designation for an "other" constructed precisely to be masterable by the dominant subject of colonial discourse. From a postcolonial perspective, then, female gender is an ideological marker within a complex chain of colonial political/sexual relations.

In Spivak's view, the gendered subject, thoroughly ideological in its implications, is produced out of a base of material relations that, in turn, advance and continually reduplicate a mode of production, a set of relations that distribute and govern power. Colonialism inevitably produces the subaltern, just as Western subjectivity, from Aristotle through the present, inevitably produces the woman-as-the-subaltern.

In these remarks about postcolonialism, I am arguing that the designation of "oppositional critic" fits Spivak, as it does other contemporary theorists who take up positions calculated to disrupt a controlling discourse and dislodge reigning ideologies. Like other such critics, Spivak reads the discourses of contemporary culture to expose crucial oppositions, key binarities that govern the exercise of power. Like Foucault, Chomsky, and Cixous, she tries, in effect, to maneuver herself into strategic conflicts with oppressive cultural practices, in the "oppositional" style of one working from within an institution. Unlike some critics (Foucault, for example), Spivak reconceives of oppositional theory *and* practice in radical terms that allow for no position of intellectual disinterestedness; she envisions no such thing as "pure" theory isolated from the relations of production and practice. Particularly in her most recent work on postcolonial discourse, where she foregrounds her own relation to the subaltern—that is, Gayatri Spivak as postcolonial female intellectual—she asks with great urgency, Can the subaltern speak? The question at first may seem to ask whether the oppressed person can speak about her own struggle. The fact of Gayatri Spivak-as-major-critic would seem to answer Yes to this question. She is herself a Third World woman and a commanding and authoritative voice in contemporary cultural and literary criticism. In these ways, at the very least, Spivak struggles against the oppression of First World cultural hegemony and domination; in this way she has "spoken."

Her answer, though, is decisively No. Such speech must be impossible precisely because the subaltern is equivalent neither to the subjugated person nor the "other" that it is made to stand in for. The "subaltern" is merely the subject position constructed by colonial discourse specifically for its own strategic ends, a mere place holder that cannot be brought to life, liberated, or empowered except through ventriloquism. The subaltern as such cannot be recuperated. Instead, the dominant discourse speaks through the subaltern subject.

So Spivak has arrived at the same point of ideological collaboration that we found in Cixous. Again this paradox is deeply disturbing, because it directly challenges the Western prospect of detached and rational intervention, and threatens Western schemes for systematic liberation and social renewal. Finally, if the subaltern cannot speak, if an oppositional theorist such as Spivak cannot maneuver to allow the speech of the "other," then the itinerary for an oppositional program may be compromised before the fact. There will be no purposeful intervention as such within the cultural matrix.

But as a postcolonial critic and a feminist (in her Marxist, reconstituted version of feminism), Spivak's response is that the apparent impossibility of opposing the dominant discourse from within, virtually of rewriting the paternal romance, is a specter created by neocolonialism. Spivak's argument is in line with that of Nancy Hartsock, who says that "when we look closely at the economic roles of women we see the ways capitalism, patriarchy, and white supremacy reinforce one another and how the ideology of individualism provides a philosophical justification for these structures" (11). Spivak's own three-part itinerary for oppositional discourse begins with a critique of neocolonialism and capitalism and the Western project of disinterested inquiry (as figured in the paternal romance), which supposedly creates a detached and superior observer. She then formulates a strategy for intervention based on the three-part critique I have been discussing. But unlike Foucault (and in this she draws from Marx's and Derrida's critique of the subject, and even Lacan's discourse of the Other), she merges the interested practice of feminism with a philosophical critique of the subject. She thereby opens the possibility of activism, speech directed *to* the other as configured in historically specific settings, rather than made ("disinterestedly") *for* a universalized sense of the other.

Spivak's activist strategy aims to avoid the institution of ideal subject positions, the grand strategy of the paternal romance. As a pedagogical model, her discourse institutes truth and error as functional dimensions built into the divided subject, as phases of function rather than goals of operation. "Truth," for example, is not a commodity or activity awaiting discovery at some moment in history; rather, it is but one construction of the subject-as-a-contradiction at any particular moment. "Error," likewise, is not avoidable for a social subject that can never be in full possession of its own material conditions and interests. In this way the implied pedagogical model of Spivak's discourse avoids the totalizing metaphoric institution of a "true" discourse. Instead, it focuses on such metonymic and error-ridden mechanisms as "collaboration," even in the sense of ideological compromise. This is "pedagogy" in the metonymic mode of preserving yet adjusting the relations of existing elements.

Working through the Paternal Romance

In foregrounding Cixous's and Spivak's major critiques, I am trying to highlight current dilemmas in feminist cultural theory for working through the impasses of the paternal romance, the curved paths and frequent detours, even failures and retreats, of productive critiques. I am suggesting that, in a strategy for altering the paternal romance, the "father" as the speaking subject may be productively superimposed within the context of gender relations historically conceived and then reinserted within the textual conditions that actually produced him to begin with. That act of superimposition, and the process of critique that follows it, will not automatically dismantle the postmodern remnants of the paternal romance. It *will* produce the conditions for further critique. The theory of the father that results runs in two directions—toward an ideological critique of the Western subject, and toward post-semiotic critiques of the gendered subject, principally those influenced by feminist thought. My sequencing of Aristotle/Cixous/Spivak on this issue is meant to highlight the issue of the subject (as what is *known*) and the critique of the gendered subject (as the *knowing subject*). The exercise of oppositional (and substantialist) power that we call the "father" is the power to control the position of speech, as Edward W. Said has said about authority in general and as Cixous and Spivak demonstrate about patriarchal authority specifically. Such power "is formed, irradiated, disseminated" and therefore can be examined and analyzed. In other words, power as a cultural effect—and in this case the "father" as a manifestation of power—is not mystical but "instrumental," and "it must be analyzed" (Said 19). The paternal romance is often persuasive in the effects it reproduces, but it is not God-given. The paternal romance is a social practice with a textual impact, and we can investigate it in terms of its textual function and its cultural value.

Earlier in this book, in "Paternity Suite," I referred to my own intellectual history in coming to discuss culture conceived under the sign of the father. For Western culture, too, the paternal romance constitutes a "history"; at times it almost seems to disappear, and yet never quite vanishes from cultural life. In writing this book, I have been far less interested in avoiding those mystifications, in destroying the paternal romance in one fell swoop, than in *working through* those impasses in various ways and in various texts—through little changes. Kierkegaard's standard for integrity ("purity of heart") as the ability to will one thing is certainly inappropriate, even impossible, for such enterprises. I cannot avoid deep complicity with the strategies belonging to my subject, and I cannot help but write from the very site of compromise—as one still situated within the paternal romance—that constitutes me as an investigator and a knowing subject.

The appearance of absolute distance and rigor must always at some level be a "con," adopting the appearances of academic discourse but accomplishing other (even contradictory) goals at the same time.[3] I attempt to critique the paternal subject as outlined in *The Paternal Romance*; at the same time, this attempt cannot help but be caught in my own compromised strategies of analysis. As Derrida claims, there may be no way to look the father "in the face," and the critique of the paternal romance will be compromised precisely to the degree that it cannot stand back from the old guy and see him clearly.

It is helpful to remember, however, that failed strategy and ideological compromise are not always disastrous. Spivak shows as well as anyone that while the inevitability of "collaboration" in intellectual enterprises is not good news, it may very well be interesting and *useful* news nonetheless. Take *The Hysterical Male: New Feminist Theory*, for example, a text that its editors, Arthur and Marilouise Kroker, describe as exploring the cultural moment of the passing of the paternal romance. This is the moment of postmodern culture in which "post-male power . . . leaves behind male subjectivity as a hysterical photographic negative of itself, and . . . disappropriates women of the privileged ontology of the Other" (ix). These are the alterations of cultural discourse, shifts in the deployment of the signifier, that are my concerns from the *Theogony* through *The Dead Father*. In the Krokers' descriptions of "one last playing-out of old male polyester sex theory, a big zero" (ix), and in many such playfully incisive references to current theory and paternal discourse, they advance cultural critiques in the speech of postmodern "girls" and "guys"—voices that possess cultural savvy but that are also "panicked" about the directions and devolutions of contemporary Western culture. This critical and theoretical voicing, this *performance*—"panic-philosophy," as the Krokers say elsewhere—is largely successful in creating an aura of decadence around the "unitary male subject," paternal authority. They even communicate a radical skepticism toward the otherwise scandalous similarities between the rational economy of critique and the rational economy of the paternal romance.

At the same time, the Krokers' performance criticism ("panic-philosophy") introduces articles by many theorists and critics who are *not* operating in the same postmodern mode. In fact, many of the essays are predominantly "academic" in a more traditional sense than the introduction. Yet, as a whole, *The Hysterical Male* succeeds in combining transgression and intentional irrelevance with the traditional deliberations of critique. That is, the performance of this book juxtaposes incoherence with theoretically compromised rigor and clarity. This postmodern mode of performance as pastiche counsels that, in order to act, we who are caught in the last stages of the paternal romance must abide certain levels of contradiction and collaboration in relation to our traditional modes of understanding and critique—indeed, in relation to paternal authority.

Much as I have argued throughout this book, the Krokers are right about "the fatal breakdown of the symbolic order of the unitary male subject" (xiv). I also spoke earlier of metaphoric and metonymic corrections of "error" and of the importance of understanding historically situated modes of "truth." It could be important not to "solve" the dilemma of the paternal romance in the wrong way, too quickly, somehow to "remove" it prematurely, detour around it, or obscure it—dismiss or "forget" it in the wrong way. I say this because the history of the paternal romance shows that the wrong solution, the wrong "forgetting," simply tends to bring on amnesia about the effects of patriarchal discourse. More useful today is the intellectual working through that Nietzsche describes as "slow reading," an interrogation of what texts *say* rhetorically in relation to the detailed *saying* of those texts. The trauma of cultural suppression and repression operative in all cultural work is an enduring aspect of the history of the paternal romance, one that must be worked through in actual texts.

The very fact of *The Paternal Romance* as an enterprise gives ample evidence of the predicaments and impasses that Spivak discusses. Surely the activity of critique in any guise demonstrates that oppositionalism, and the modern versions of structuralism that embody it, are not "natural" or universal formulations of coherence and authority. Critique as I have deployed it here will necessarily replicate the very tenets of the paternal romance. Still, my wager all through this book is that the form and function of oppositionalism can suggest a useful representation of the paternal authority that characterizes Greek culture. This representation persists in current texts and cultural practices. A critique of paternal discourse, in other words, is necessarily compromised by the mere fact that there is no absolute recourse to a metalanguage, metaculture, or metaself from which to perform an uncompromised critique. As a critic and investigator, I am also a collaborator, in the desirable as well as in the regrettable sense of that term.

In collaborative enterprises such as intellectual and academic work "it particularly often happens that something is 'remembered' which could never have been 'forgotten' because it was never at any time noticed—was never conscious" ("Remembering and Repeating" 149). Freud is here describing what Peggy Kamuf designates as the "non-opposable other" (126), that which cannot be charted or predicted—events that may not register in relation to familiar references and reigning ideologies. Oppositional analysis has its limits, and not all of the effects of complicity will be bad. The fact of "collaboration," even in the negative sense, can be read as a mandate for vigilance—for the necessity of collaborating in the good sense, too, to overcome the blindnesses of restricted and monologic positions. In this book I have attempted to emphasize this productive, critical "remembering," the good sense of collaboration. To deny the paternal romance, or to "forget" it in the wrong way, virtually defines the scenario of a cultural *acting out*, the certain repetition of the paternal romance in ever-changing guises ("Remembering and Repeating" 150). The remedy for "acting out" is *working through*, that is, the successful remembering and understanding of cultural traumas that may never have been "known" (and thus are not "opposable") to begin with. Such working through is a process undertaken through the multiple perspectives of collaboration, in the sense of collective vigilance and knowing in a community of limited and imperfect knowers.

In foregrounding these comments about "working through," I suggest that many current discourses about the paternal romance are productive and deserve to be fostered. The discourses of cultural studies and contemporary feminism are showing that "the first step in overcoming the resistances is made" by a critical "uncovering" of resistances ("Remembering and Repeating" 155). This task of cultural work is not an easy one; if it at times seems "to make the whole situation" simply "more obscure than ever" (155), that is because it is not the whole of our work. A "gloomy foreboding" about this task, and about the work of cultural critique, will have "proved mistaken." The cultural work of critique is an elaborate working through and beyond oppositional analysis, an activity that inevitably entails a "trial of patience." To hold "fast to this conviction" concerning the critique of the paternal romance will spare us "the illusion of having failed when in fact [we are] conducting the treatment on the right lines" (155).

Notes

1. See my "Post-Modern Paternity."
2. See Paul Bové's *Intellectuals in Power*.
3. The conceit of duplicity in a "con" job, unsavory as it may be, is pertinent to critical inquiry, and to my study, in various ways. The *Webster's New Riverside University Dictionary* that happens to sit on my desk lists five different meanings for "con." One is oppositional—that is, literally "in disagreement with or opposition to: AGAINST." In a less familiar meaning, but also one pertinent to a dimension of this book, it means "to peruse, study, or examine carefully," even "to memorize," as in the close attention to texts. In a far less familiar definition, it is nautical and means "to direct the steering or course (of a vessel)"—that is, to move toward a goal. "Con" is also slang, of course, for convict. Last and most dramatic is "con" in the sense of betrayal: "con" job, "to defraud or swindle by soliciting confidence," to fool someone. All of these meanings, even the unsavory ones, suggest aspects, even if inadvertent, of a complex inquiry such as this one. A literary critic or cultural theorist pursues "truth," yet lines of argument either intentionally or inadvertently say less than they should, or even intentionally omit pertinent options. Unflattering as it is to think of one's "serious" work in this way, as a "con," Spivak, Walter Benjamin, Derrida, Milan Kundera, and many others argue persuasively that every critique crosses lines of decorum to collaborate with the commitments inherent to the subject of inquiry.

If I really insist on the multiple meanings of "con" and their direct relevance to *The Paternal Romance*, I eventually expose too much of what makes an academic inquiry possible. There is a certain complicity in all critique, yet critique cannot be unveiled in this way and still retain its apparent force and usefulness, that is, without the dimension of critique itself being destroyed. The paternal romance, in short, is itself a "con" job perpetrated in the Western tradition. It has suppressed and strategically "forgotten" textual dimensions that could not contribute to the model of a unitary and seamless subject and to versions of nonproblematic "truth."

As a confidence game, the "con" job of this book also moves off in other directions. In French, *con* refers frankly to "cunt"—*con*, like other slang, signaling the intrusion of sexual discourse or intent into a context not already marked as explicitly sexual. Here the moment of *con* is the moment of social redirection, disruption, or transgression, the moment of the evident mixing of codes and levels of casual and polite usage, the moment in which genres, intentions, and effects are reordered. This was specifically the case in my analysis of Aristotle's theories of reproduction concerning the intrusion of sexuality into the texts of his abstract and austere logic.

Again, the "con" job refers to the coexistence of multiple and potentially conflicting frames of reference, to the violation of familiar rules and conventions, to the ever-present potential in discourse of dialogism and heteroglossia. "Con" has other, equally diverse and complex meanings in Irish and Spanish, and it also evokes some associations with my own full name, which, by the way, I acquired and was not "naturally" born with.

Works Cited

Adorno, T. W., and Max Horkheimer. *The Dialectic of Enlightenment.* Trans. J. Cumming. New York: Herder and Herder, 1972.

Althusser, Louis. "Ideology and Ideological State Apparatuses." In *Lenin and Philosophy and Other Essays.* Trans. Ben Brewster. New York and London: Monthly Review Press, 1971.

Anderson, Perry. *Passages from Antiquity to Feudalism.* London: Verso Editions, 1978.

Anton, John Peter. *Aristotle's Theory of Contrariety.* London: Routledge and Kegan Paul, 1957.

Apple, Michael W. *Cultural and Economic Reproduction in Education.* London: Routledge and Kegan Paul, 1982.

―――, and Lois Weis, eds. *Ideology and Practice in Schooling.* Philadelphia: Temple University Press, 1983.

Aretaeus. *The Extant Works of Aretaeus, the Cappadocian.* Ed. and trans. Francis Adams. London: Sydenham Society, 1856.

Aristotle. *"Categories" and "De Interpretatione."* Trans. and notes J. L. Ackrill. Oxford: Clarendon Press, 1963.

―――. *Generation of Animals.* Trans. and ed. A. L. Peck. Cambridge: Harvard University Press; London: Heinemann, 1943.

―――. *Historia Animalium.* 3 vols. Trans. and ed. A. L. Peck. Cambridge: Harvard University Press; London: Heinemann, 1965.

―――. *Metaphysics.* 2 vols. Trans. and ed. Hugh Tredennick. London: Heinemann; Cambridge: Harvard University Press, 1956.

―――. *On Interpretation.* Commentary by St. Thomas Aquinas and Cardinal Cajetan. Trans. Jean T. Oesterle. Milwaukee: Marquette University Press, 1962.

―――. *The Organon.* Trans. and ed. Harold P. Cooke and Hugh Tredennick. London: Heinemann; Cambridge: Harvard University Press, 1955.

―――. *Aristotle's Physics.* Trans. and ed. Hippocrates G. Apostle. Grinnell, Iowa: Peripatetic Press, 1969.

―――. *Aristotle's Physics.* Ed. W. D. Ross. Oxford: Clarendon Press, 1955.

―――. *Aristotle's Posterior Analytics.* Trans. and comm. Hippocrates G. Apostle. Grinnell, Iowa: Peripatetic Press, 1981.

————. *Posterior Analytics.* Trans. and ed. Hugh Tredennick. Cambridge: Harvard University Press; London: Heinemann, 1960.

Armstrong, A. H., and R. A. Markus. *Christian Faith and Greek Philosophy.* New York: Sheed and Ward, 1960.

Aronowitz, Stanley, and Henry A. Giroux. *Education under Siege.* South Hadley, Mass.: Bergin and Garvey, 1985.

Augustine. *The Trinity.* Trans. Stephen McKenna. Washington, D.C.: Catholic University of America Press, 1963.

Austin, Norman. *Archery at the Dark of the Moon: Poetic Problems in Homer's "Odyssey."* Berkeley: University of California Press, 1975.

Bakan, David. *Disease, Pain, and Sacrifice.* Chicago: University of Chicago Press, 1968.

Barnes, Jonathan, Jacques Brunschwig, Myles Burnyeat, and Malcolm Schofield, eds. *Science and Speculation: Studies in Hellenistic Theory and Practice.* Cambridge: Cambridge University Press, 1982.

Barthelme, Donald. *The Dead Father.* New York: Farrar, Straus, and Giroux, 1975.

Baudrillard, Jean. *For a Critique of the Political Economy of the Sign.* Trans. and intro. Charles Levin. St. Louis: Telos Press, 1981.

Beauvoir, Simone de. *The Second Sex.* Trans. H. M. Parshley. New York: Bantam Books, 1961 (orig. 1949).

Bernal, Martin. *Black Athena.* New Brunswick: Rutgers University Press, 1987.

Beye, Charles Brown. *The Iliad, the Odyssey, and the Epic Tradition.* Gloucester, Mass.: Peter Smith, 1972.

Bourdieu, Pierre, and Jean-Claude Passeron. *Reproduction in Education, Society, and Culture.* Trans. Richard Nice. London and Beverly Hills: Sage Publications, 1977 (orig. 1970).

Bové, Paul. *Intellectuals in Power: A Genealogy of Critical Humanism.* New York: Columbia University Press, 1986.

Brown, Norman O., trans. and ed. *Hesiod's Theogony.* New York: Liberal Arts Press, 1953.

Burnaby, John. *Augustine: Later Works.* Philadelphia: Westminster Press, 1955.

Butler, Judith. *Gender Trouble: Feminism and the Subversion of Identity.* New York and London: Routledge, 1990.

Cixous, Hélène. "Castration or Decapitation?" Trans. Annette Kuhn. *Signs* 7 (1981): 41–55.

————. "The Character of 'Character.'" Trans. Keith Cohen. *New Literary History* 5 (1974): 384–402.

————. "The Laugh of the Medusa." Trans. Keith Cohen and Paula Cohen. In *Critical Theory since 1965.* Ed. Hazard Adams and Leroy Searle. Tallahassee: Florida State University Press, 1986.

————, and Catherine Clément. *The Newly-Born Woman.* Trans. Betsy Wing. Minneapolis: University of Minnesota Press, 1986.

Clay, Jenny Strauss. *The Wrath of Athena: Gods and Men in "The Odyssey."* Princeton: Princeton University Press, 1983.

Cohen, Morris R., and I. E. Drabkin. *A Source Book in Greek Science.* New York: McGraw-Hill, 1948.

Conley, Verena. *Hélène Cixous: Writing the Feminine.* Lincoln: University of Nebraska Press, 1984.

Cook, Arthur Bernard. *Zeus: A Study in Ancient Religion.* Cambridge: Cambridge University Press, 1914.

Crowley, Sharon. "A Plea for the Revival of Sophistry." *Rhetoric Review* 7 (1989): 318–34.

Davis, Robert Con, ed. *The Fictional Father: Lacanian Readings of the Text.* Amherst: University of Massachusetts Press, 1981.

———. "Post-Modern Paternity: Donald Barthelme's *The Dead Father.*" In *Critical Essays on Donald Barthelme.* Ed. Richard F. Patteson. New York: G. K. Hall, 1992.

———. "Theorizing Opposition: Aristotle, Greimas, Jameson, and Said." *L'Esprit Createur* 27,2 (1987): 5–18.

———, and Ronald Schleifer. *Criticism and Culture: The Role of Critique in Modern Literary Theory.* London and New York: Longman, 1991.

Deleuze, Gilles, and Felix Guattari. *Anti-Oedipus: Capitalism and Schizophrenia.* Trans. Robert Hurley, Mark Seem, and Helen R. Lane. Minneapolis: University of Minnesota Press, 1983. (*L'Anti-Oedipe.* Paris: Les Editions de Minuit, 1972.)

———. *A Thousand Plateaus: Capitalism and Schizophrenia.* Trans. and foreword by Brian Massumi. Minneapolis: University of Minnesota Press, 1987. (*Mille Plateaux.* Paris: Les Editions de Minuit, 1980.)

de Ste. Croix, G. E. M. *The Class Struggle in the Ancient Greek World: From the Archaic Age to the Arab Conquests.* Ithaca: Cornell University Press, 1981.

Derrida, Jacques. *Dissemination.* Trans. Barbara Johnson. Chicago: University of Chicago Press, 1981 (orig. 1972).

———. *Of Grammatology.* Trans. Gayatri C. Spivak. Baltimore: Johns Hopkins University Press, 1976 (orig. 1967).

Dietrich, B. C. *Death, Fate, and the Gods: The Development of a Religious Idea in Greek Popular Belief and in Homer.* London: Athlone Press, 1965.

Dimock, George E. *The Unity of "The Odyssey."* Amherst: University of Massachusetts Press, 1989.

Dodds, E. R. *The Greeks and the Irrational.* Berkeley: University of California Press, 1950.

duBois, Page. *Centaurs and Amazons: Women and the Pre-History of the Great Chain of Being.* Ann Arbor: University of Michigan Press, 1982.

Eckhart, Meister. *Meister Eckhart, the Essential Sermons, Commentaries, Treatises, and Defense.* Trans. and intro. Edmund Colledge and Bernard McGinn. New York: Paulist Press, 1981.

Edelstein, Ludwig. *Ancient Medicine: Selected Papers of Ludwig Edelstein.*
Ed. Owsei and C. Lillian Temkin. Baltimore: Johns Hopkins University
Press, 1967.

Engels, Friedrich. *Dialectics of Nature.* Trans. Clemens Dutt. New York:
International Publishers, 1940.

———. *The Origins of the Family, Private Property, and the State.* New
York: International Publishers, 1942.

Ehnmark, Erland. *The Idea of God in Homer: Inaugural Dissertation.* Upps-
ala: Almquist and Wiksells Boktryckeri, AB, 1935.

Farrington, Benjamin. *Greek Science.* Hammondsworth: Penguin Books,
1944.

Foucault, Michel. *The History of Sexuality: An Introduction.* Vol. 1. Trans.
Robert Hurley. New York: Vintage Books, 1980 (orig. 1976).

———. *The History of Sexuality: The Use of Pleasure.* Vol. 2. Trans. Robert
Hurley. New York: Pantheon Books, 1985 (orig. 1984).

———. *The History of Sexuality: The Care of the Self.* Vol. 3. Trans. Robert
Hurley. New York: Pantheon Books, 1986 (orig. 1984).

———. *The Order of Things: An Archaeology of the Human Sciences.* New
York: Random House, 1970.

Freire, Paulo. *Pedagogy of the Oppressed.* Trans. Myra Berman Ramos.
New York: Continuum, 1982 (orig. 1968).

Freud, Sigmund. "Family Romances." In *Standard Edition of the Works of
Sigmund Freud.* Vol. 9. Ed. James Strachey. London: Hogarth Press,
1953–73. Pp. 237–41.

———. "Remembering, Repeating and Working-Through" (1924). In *Standard Edition.* Vol. 12, pp. 147–56.

———. *Totem and Taboo. Standard Edition.* Vol. 13, pp. 1–162.

Frye, Northrop. *The Anatomy of Criticism: Four Essays.* Princeton: Princeton University Press, 1957.

Fuss, Diana. *Essentially Speaking: Feminism, Nature, and Difference.* New
York and London: Routledge, 1989.

Gallop, Jane. "The Immoral Teachers." *Yale French Studies* 63 (1982):
117–28.

Gernet, Louis. *The Anthropology of Ancient Greece.* Trans. John Hamilton,
S.J., and Blaise Nagy. Baltimore and London: Johns Hopkins University
Press, 1981.

Gilbert, Sandra M. "Life's Empty Pack: Notes toward a Literary Daughteronomy." *Critical Inquiry* 11,3 (1985): 355–84.

Giroux, Henry, David Shumway, Paul Smith, and James Sosnoski. "The
Need for Cultural Studies: Resisting Intellectual and Oppositional Public Spheres." *Dalhousie Review* 64 (1984): 472–86.

Goethe, Johann Wolfgang Von. *Faust, Part II.* Trans. Philip Wayne. Mid-
dlesex: Penguin Books, 1959.

Goldmann, Lucien. *The Human Sciences and Philosophy.* Trans. Hayden V.
White and Robert Anchor. London: Jonathan Cape, 1969.

Goux, Jean-Joseph. *Freud, Marx: economie et symbolique*. Paris: Editions du Seuil, 1973.

Greene, William Chase. *Moira: Fate, Good, and Evil in Greek Thought*. Cambridge: Harvard University Press, 1944.

Griffin, Jasper. *Homer on Life and Death*. Oxford: Clarendon Press, 1980.

———. *Homer: The Odyssey*. Cambridge: Cambridge University Press, 1987.

Guetti, Barbara. "The Old Regime and the Feminist Revolution: Laclos' "De l'Education des Femmes." *Yale French Studies* 63 (1982): 139–62.

Hack, Roy Kenneth. *God in Greek Philosophy to the Time of Socrates*. Princeton: Princeton University Press, for the University of Cincinnati, 1931.

Handelman, Susan A. *The Slayers of Moses: The Emergence of Rabbinic Interpretation in Modern Literary Theory*. Albany: State University of New York Press, 1982.

Hansen, William F. *The Conference Sequence: Patterned Narration and Narrative Inconsistency in "The Odyssey."* Berkeley: University of California Press, 1972.

Harrington, Michael. *The Politics at God's Funeral*. New York: Penguin Books, 1985 (orig. 1983).

Hartsock, Nancy. "Political Change: Two Perspectives on Power." In *Building Feminist Theory: Essays from QUEST*. Intro. Charlotte Bunch. New York and London: Longman, 1981, 3–19.

Hatch, Edwin. *The Influence of Greek Ideas on Christianity*. New York: Harper and Row, 1957.

Havelock, Eric. A. *The Greek Concept of Justice: From Its Shadow in Homer to Its Substance in Plato*. Cambridge: Harvard University Press, 1978.

———. *The Liberal Temper in Greek Politics*. New Haven and London: Yale University Press, 1957.

Heidegger, Martin. *Early Greek Thinking: The Dawn of Western Philosophy*. Trans. David Farrell and Frank A. Capuzzi. San Francisco: Harper and Row, 1984.

Hesiod. *Hesiod*. Trans. Richmond Lattimore. Ann Arbor: University of Michigan Press, 1959.

———. *Hesiod's Theogony*. Trans. and ed. Norman O. Brown. New York: Liberal Arts Press, 1953.

———. *Hesiodi: Theogonia, Opera et Dies, Scutum*. Ed. Friedrich Solmsen. Oxford: Clarendon Press, 1983.

Homer. *Homeri: Opera*. Vols. 3 and 4. Ed. Thomas W. Allen. Oxford: Clarendon Press, 1911.

———. *Iliad*. Trans. Robert Fitzgerald. Garden City, N.Y.: Anchor Press/Doubleday, 1974.

———. *The Iliad of Homer*. 2 vols. Ed. Walter Leaf and M. A. Bayfield. London: Macmillan, 1923.

———. *Odyssey*. Intro. and notes by W. W. Merry, D.D. Oxford: Clarendon Press, 1887.

————. *Odyssey*. Trans. Robert Fitzgerald. Garden City, N.Y.: Anchor Books/Doubleday, 1963 (orig. 1961).

Hubert, Henri, and Marcel Mauss. *Sacrifice*. Trans. W. D. Halls. Chicago: University of Chicago Press, 1964.

James, E. O. *Sacrifice and Sacrament*. London: Thames and Hudson, 1962.

Jameson, Fredric. *The Political Unconscious: Narrative as a Socially Symbolic Act*. Ithaca: Cornell University Press, 1981.

Jardine, Alice. *Gynesis: Configurations of Woman and Modernity*. Ithaca and London: Cornell University Press, 1985.

Jarratt, Susan C. *Rereading the Sophists: Classical Rhetoric Refigured*. Carbondale: Southern Illinois University Press, 1991.

Johnson, Barbara. "Teaching Ignorance: *L'Ecole des Femmes*." *Yale French Studies* 63 (1982): 165–82.

Jones, Ann Rosalind. "Writing the Body: Toward an Understanding of *l'écriture féminine*." In *The New Feminist Criticism: Essays on Women, Literature, and Theory*. Ed. Elaine Showalter. New York: Pantheon, 1985.

Joyce, James. *Ulysses*. New York: Vintage Books, 1961 (orig. 1922).

Jung, Carl. *Psychology and Alchemy*. 2d ed. Trans. R. F. C. Hull. Princeton: Princeton University Press, 1968.

————. *Psychology and Religion: West and East*. Trans. R. F. C. Hull. Princeton: Princeton University Press, 1958.

Kamuf, Peggy. "Replacing Feminist Criticism." In *Conflicts in Feminism*. Ed. Marianne Hirsch and Evelyn Fox Keller. New York and London: Routledge, 1990. Pp. 105–11.

————, and Nancy K. Miller. "Parisian Letters: Between Feminism and Deconstruction." In *Conflicts in Feminism*, 121–33.

Keller, Evelyn Fox. *Reflections on Gender and Science*. New York and London: Yale University Press, 1985.

Kerenyi, C. *Zeus and Hera: Archetypal Image of Father, Husband, and Wife*. Trans. Christopher Holme. Princeton: Princeton University Press, 1975.

Kierkegaard, Sören. *Fear and Trembling*. Trans. Walter Lowrie. Princeton: Princeton University Press, 1974.

Keuls, Eva C. *The Reign of the Phallus: Sexual Politics in Ancient Athens*. New York: Harper and Row, 1985.

Kirk, Geoffrey Stephen. *The Songs of Homer*. Cambridge: Cambridge University Press, 1962.

Knight, W. F. Jackson. *Many-Minded Homer: An Introduction*. Ed. John D. Christie. London: George Allen and Unwin, 1968.

Kristeva, Julia. "Stabat Mater." In *Tales of Love*. Trans. Leon S. Roudiez. New York: Columbia University Press, 1987.

Kroker, Arthur, and Marilouise Kroker, eds. *The Hysterical Male: New Feminist Theory*. New York: St. Martin's Press, 1991.

Lacan, Jacques. "Desire and the Interpretation of Desire in *Hamlet*." *Yale French Studies* 55/56 (1977): 11–52.

————. *The Language of the Self: The Function of Language in Psychoanalysis.* Trans. Anthony Wilden. Baltimore: Johns Hopkins University Press, 1968.

Lamberton, Robert. *Hesiod.* New Haven and London: Yale University Press, 1988.

Laplanche, Jean, and J.-B. Pontalis. *The Language of Psycho-Analysis.* Trans. Donald Nicholson-Smith. New York: W. W. Norton, 1973.

Laqueur, Thomas. *Making Sex: Body and Gender from the Greeks to Freud.* Cambridge: Harvard University Press, 1990.

Lefkowitz, Mary R. *Heroines and Hysterics.* New York: St. Martin's Press, 1981.

————, and Maureen B. Fant, eds. *Women's Life in Greece and Rome.* Baltimore: Johns Hopkins University Press, 1982.

Lerner, Gerda. *The Creation of Patriarchy.* New York, Oxford: Oxford University Press, 1986.

Lévi-Strauss, Claude. *The Scope of Anthropology.* Trans. Sherry Ortner Paul and Robert A. Paul. London: Jonathan Cape, 1967.

Lloyd, G. E. R. *Early Greek Science: Thales to Aristotle.* New York: W. W. Norton, 1970.

————. *Magic, Reason, and Experience: Studies in the Origin and Development of Greek Science.* Cambridge: Cambridge University Press, 1979.

————. *Polarity and Analogy: Two Types of Argumentation in Early Greek Thought.* Cambridge: Cambridge University Press, 1966.

————. *The Revolutions of Wisdom: Studies in the Claims and Practice of Ancient Greek Science.* Berkeley: University of California Press, 1987.

————. *Science and Morality in Greco-Roman Antiquity.* Cambridge: Cambridge University Press, 1985.

Lloyd-Jones, Hugh. *The Justice of Zeus.* Rev. ed. Berkeley, Los Angeles, London: University of California Press, 1983.

Lovejoy, Arthur O. *The Great Chain of Being.* Cambridge: Harvard University Press, 1936.

MacCannell, Juliet Flower. *The Regime of the Brother: After the Patriarchy.* London and New York: Routledge, 1991.

Macrobius, Ambrosius Aurelius Theodosius. *Commentary on the Dream of Scipio.* Trans. William Harris Stahl. New York: Columbia University Press, 1952.

Manuli, Paola. "Fisiologia e patologia del femminile negli scritti ippocratici dell'antica ginecologia greca." *Hippocratica,* Colloque de Paris, CNRS, Paris, 1980.

Merod, Jim. *The Political Responsibility of the Critic.* Ithaca and London: Cornell University Press, 1987.

Miller, Nancy K. "The Text's Heroine: A Feminist Critic and Her Fictions." In *Conflicts in Feminism.* Ed. Marianne Hirsch and Evelyn Fox Keller. New York and London: Routledge, 1990, 112–20.

Moi, Toril. *Sexual/Textual Politics: Feminist Literary Theory.* London and New York: Methuen, 1985.

Murray, Gilbert. *Five Stages of Greek Religion*. Garden City, N.Y.: Doubleday, 1955 (orig. 1912).

Nietzsche, Friedrich. *The Birth of Tragedy, or Hellenism and Pessimism*. Trans. William A. Haussman. New York: Macmillan, 1909.

———. *Thus Spake Zarathustra*. Trans. Thomas Common. New York: Modern Library, 1934.

Ogilby, John. *The Works of P. Virgilius Maro. Translated, Adorned with Sculpture, and Illustrated with Annotations*. London, 1654.

Ohmann, Richard. *English in America: A Radical View of the Profession*. New York: Oxford University Press, 1976.

———. *Politics of Letters*. Middletown, Conn.: Wesleyan University Press, 1987.

Page, Denys Lionel. *The Homeric Odyssey*. Oxford: Clarendon Press, 1955.

Parry, Milman. *The Making of Homeric Verse: The Collected Papers of M. Parry*. Ed. Adam Parry. Oxford: Clarendon Press, 1971.

Pembroke, S. "Women in Charge: The Function of Alternatives in Early Greek Tradition and the Ancient Idea of Matriarchy." *Journal of the Warburg and Courtauld Institutes* 30 (1970): 1–35.

Plato. *The Parmenides of Plato*. Trans. A. E. Taylor. Oxford: Clarendon Press, 1934.

———. *Phaedo*. Trans. R. Hackforth. Cambridge: Cambridge University Press, 1955.

———. *The Republic of Plato*. Trans. John Llewlyn Davies and David James Vaughn. A. L. Burt Company, Publishers, n.d.

———. *Plato's Theaetetus*. Trans. Francis MacDonald Cornford. Indianapolis and New York: Bobbs-Merrill, 1957.

———. *Timaeus*. Trans. Francis M. Cornford. Ed. Oskar Piest. New York: Liberal Arts Press, 1959.

Plotinus. *Ennead V.1: On the Three Hypostases*. Trans. and commentary by Michael Atkinson. New York: Oxford University Press, 1983.

Pomeroy, Sarah B. *Goddesses, Whores, Wives, and Slaves*. New York: Schocken Books, 1975.

Poster, Mark. *Critical Theory of the Family*. London: Pluto Press, 1978.

Pucci, Pietro. *Odysseus Polutropos: Intertextual Readings in "The Odyssey" and "The Iliad."* Ithaca: Cornell University Press, 1987.

Rose, H. J. *A Handbook of Greek Mythology*. London: Methuen, 1965.

Rousselle, Aline. "Observation féminine et ideologie masculine: le corps de la femme d'après les medecins grecs." *Annales: Economies, Societes, Civilisations* (1980): 1089–1115.

———. *Porneia: On Desire and the Body in Antiquity*. Trans. Felicia Pheasant. Oxford: Basil Blackwell, 1988 (orig. 1983).

Said, Edward W. *Orientalism*. New York: Random House, 1979.

Saussure, Ferdinand de. *Course in General Linguistics*. Trans. Wade Baskin. New York: McGraw-Hill, 1966.

Schillebeeckx, Edward. *Jesus: An Experiment in Christology*. New York: Vintage, 1981.

Schlegel, August Wilhelm von. *Lectures on Dramatic Art and Literature.* Trans. John Black. 2nd ed. London G. Bell & Sons, 1902.

Schleifer, Ronald. *A. J. Greimas and the Nature of Meaning.* Lincoln: University of Nebraska Press, 1987.

———, and Alan Velie. "Genre and Structure: Toward an Actantial Typology of Narrative Genres and Modes." *MLN* 102 (1987): 1122–50.

Schleiner, Winfried. "Aeneas' Flight from Troy." *Comparative Literature* 27,2 (1975): 97–112.

Sheehan, Thomas. *The First Coming: How the Kingdom of God Became Christianity.* New York: Random House, 1986.

Shiel, James. *Greek Thought and the Rise of Christianity.* London and Harlow: Longmans, 1968.

Slater, Philip E. *The Glory of Hera.* Boston: Beacon Press, 1968.

Spivak, Gayatri Chakravorty. "Can the Subaltern Speak?" In *Marxism and the Interpretation of Culture.* Ed. Cary Nelson and Lawrence Grossberg. Urbana: University of Illinois Press, 1988, 271–313.

———. "Displacement and the Discourse of Woman." In *Displacement: Derrida and After.* Ed. Mark Krupnick. Bloomington: Indiana University Press, 1983.

Stewart, Douglas J. *The Disguised Guest: Rank, Role, and Identity in "The Odyssey."* Lewisburg, Pa.: Bucknell University Press, 1976.

Vatin, Claude. *Recherches sur le mariage et la condition de la femme mariée à l'epoque hellenistique.* Paris: Editions de Boccard, 1970.

Veith, Ilza. *Hysteria: The History of a Disease.* Chicago: University of Chicago Press, 1965.

Verbeke, G. "The Aristotelian Doctrine of Qualitative Change in *Physics* VII, 3." In *Essays in Ancient Greek Philosophy.* Ed. John P. Anton and George L. Kustas. Albany: State University of New York Press, 1971.

Vernant, Jean-Pierre. *Myth and Society in Ancient Greece.* Trans. Janet Lloyd. Sussex: Harvester Press; New Jersey: Humanities Press, 1980.

———. *The Origins of Greek Thought.* Ithaca: Cornell University Press, 1982.

Virgil. *The Aeneid.* Trans. Robert Fitzgerald. New York: Random House, 1981.

———. *Eclogues.* Ed. Robert Coleman. New York: Cambridge University Press, 1977.

Vivante, Paolo. *Homer.* New Haven and London: Yale University Press, 1985.

———. *The Homeric Imagination: A Study of Homer's Poetic Perception of Reality.* Bloomington and London: Indiana University Press, 1970.

Wehrli, Claude. "Les Gyneconomes." *Museum Helveticum* (1962): 33–38.

West, M. L., ed. *Hesiod: Theogony.* Oxford: Oxford University Press, 1966.

Williams, Raymond. *Keywords.* New York: Oxford University Press, 1985.

———. *Marxism and Literature.* Oxford: Oxford University Press, 1977.

Yaeger, Patricia, and Beth Kowaleski-Wallace, eds. *Refiguring the Father: New Feminist Readings of Patriarchy.* Carbondale: Southern Illinois University Press, 1989.

Index

Adorno, T. W., 56, 132

Aeneid: Aeneas's flight from Troy, 8–11; patriarchal values in, 10–11; "pious Aeneas" in, 12–15

Althusser, Louis, 146

Anaximander: and rise of writing and philosophy, 27, 48, 50–51; theory of life and matter, 109

Anton, John Peter: discussion of oppositional square, 35, 36, 79, 80; and Aristotle's subject of inquiry, 76, 77

Apple, Michael, 146

Aquinas, St. Thomas, 77–78, 83, 93, 112, 116; *Summa Theologica*, 103

Aretaeus of Cappadocia: and Hippocratic gynecology, 87–88

Aristotle, 48, 51, 64, 73–96, 124, 140, 142, 148, 157, 169; assumptions about gender, 6; *Organon*, 15, 17, 27, 73; and Western narrative practices, 16; theory of signs and propositions, 18; *Metaphysics*, 26, 73, 74, 75, 81, 84; *Physics*, 34–35, 73, 75; *Politics*, 43; as pro-paternal, 43–44; and "substantial" inquiry, 53–54, 56, 73; *Acting and Being Acted Upon*, 59, 66; *The Generation of Animals*, 73, 77, 84–85; *Historia Animalium*, 73, 85–86; comparison of Parmenides and Heraclitus, 74–76, 83; *On Interpretation*, 78, 81, 84, 113, 116; discussion of male/female bodies, 84–86, 89; and paternal romance, 93–96, 153; *Posterior Analytics*, 95, 116–17; and subaltern,

167. *See also Hupokeimenon; Oppositional square*

Armstrong, A. H., 109, 112

Arnold, Matthew, 1

Aronowitz, Stanley, 146

Augustine: *De Trinitate*, 15, 103, 108, 114; and Western narrative practices, 16; Father and Son paradox, 98, 108; and Christian love, 101; Trinitarian doctrine, 103–4, 106

Austin, Norman: *Archery at the Dark of the Moon*, 9, 55, 72

Babbitt, Irving, 1

Bakan, David, 100

Bakhtin, Mikhail, 119

Barthelme, Donald: and postmodern paternal authority, 128; *The Dead Father*, 147, 170

Barthes, Roland: and paternal metaphor, 2

Baudrillard, Jean, 152, 161; and "ideology," 5

Beauvoir, Simone de: *The Second Sex*, 149–50

Benjamin, Walter, 173

Bernal, Martin: *Black Athena*, 27, 46

Bourdieu, Pierre: discussion of hidden power relations, 41, 122; and oppositional pedagogy, 146; *Reproduction in Education, Society and Culture*, 147

Bové, Paul, 173

Brown, Norman O., 31

Burnaby, John, 101, 104